Master Books®

WORLD HISTORY Encyclopedia

Creation to the Roman Empire

Nancy I. Sanders

First printing: February 2026

Master Books, P.O. Box 726, Green Forest, AR 72638
Master Books® is a division of the New Leaf Publishing Group, LLC.

ISBN: 978-1-68344-383-4
ISBN: 978-1-61458-901-3 (digital)
Library of Congress Control Number: 2025951363

Managing Editor: Pam Gibbs
Cover & Interior design by Diana Bogardus

Consider requesting that a copy of this volume be purchased by your local library system.

Master Books®
A Division of New Leaf Publishing Group
www.masterbooks.com

Printed in the United States of America

Please visit our website for other great titles:
www.masterbooks.com

For information regarding promotional opportunities, please contact the publicity department at pr@nlpg.com.

To my
wonderful grandchildren,
with love from Grandma Nancy

To Ryan

God is your strength and song.
He will crown you with victory!
See Exodus 15:2.

To Tyler

God delights in you and has great plans for you.
He will fill your life with His blessings!
See Psalm 37:23.

To Caleb

God loves you.
May He fill you with His Spirit of wisdom
as you build great things for His glory!
See Exodus 31:3.

To Annalise

You are favored by God and full of His grace.
He will give you strength!
See Luke 1:28.

...with love from Grandma Nancy

CONTENTS

Introduction....6
Timeline: 4004 B.C. – 1500 B.C....8
The Bible in World History....10
God, the Creator....12
In the Beginning....14
Seven Days of Creation....16
Day One of Creation....18
Day Two of Creation....20
Day Three of Creation....22
Day Four of Creation....24
Day Five of Creation....26
Day Six of Creation....28
Day Seven Of Creation....30
Created in God's Image....32
The Fall....34
Prehistoric or Ancient History?....36
Before the Flood....38
Dinosaurs....40
Therapods....42
Sauropods....44
Ornithopods....46
Marginocephalia....48
Thyreophora . . . and More....50
The Worldwide Flood....52
Noah's Ark....54
Ice Age....56
Tower of Babel....58
Life After Babel....60
Continents and Oceans....62
Life in Sumer....64
Life Along the Nile....66
The Forgotten Indus Civilization....68
Yellow River Valley....70
Pharaohs and Pyramids of Egypt....72
Abraham....74
Joseph in Egypt....76
The Minoans....78
The Mycenaeans....80
Hammurabi's Laws....82
The Hittite Empire....84
Land of Canaan....86
In Egypt....88
Timeline: 1500 B.C. – 600 B.C....90
The Exodus....92
Ten Commandments and the Tabernacle....94
The Promised Land....96
Jericho and Judges....98
Sea Peoples....100
Phoenicians....102
King David of Israel....104
Israel's Golden Age....106
Solomon's Temple....108
Arabian Peninsula....110
Africa's Natural Wonders....112
Ancient Africa....114
Kingdom of Cush....116
Early India....118
The Engineering of Hinges....120
British Isles....122
Celts and Their Customs....124

Forests and Steppes 126
China's Early Emperors 128
Han Dynasty 130
Land of the Rising Sun 132
Tribes of North America 134
Olmecs and Yahgans 136
Ancient Peru 138
Israel's Divided Kingdom 140
Profiles of Prophets and Kings 142
Assyrian Empire 144
Judah Under Attack 146
Timeline: 600 B.C. – 30 B.C. 148
Babylonian Empire 150
Royal Road of Persia 152
Return to Jerusalem 154
Israel's Second Temple 156
Jerusalem's Wall 158
Athens and Sparta 160
Golden Age of Greece 162
Alexander the Great 164
Republic of Rome 166
Building an Empire 168
Roman Empire Rules the World 170
Last Pharaoh of Egypt 172
Timeline: 30 B.C. – A.D. 476 174
Waiting for the Messiah 176
Jesus the Christ 178
Birth of Jesus 180
Early Years of Jesus 182
Herod the Great 184
Herod's Temple Complex 186
Preparation of Jesus 188
Ministry of Jesus 190
Parables of Jesus 192
Miracles of Jesus 194
Divinity of Jesus 196
Last Week of Jesus' Life 198
He Is Risen! 200
Reurrection of Jesus 202
Rome Conquers Jerusalem 204
God's Eternal Plan 206

Index 208
Selected Bibliography 222
About the Author 224

INTRODUCTION

I love looking for buried treasure, don't you? That means I love digging into the past and exploring history. Pyramids. Pirates. Treasure chests filled with diamonds and gold! And the best thing about history is to learn more about how history relates to His Story—God's exciting, marvelous plan for this great big universe—including His big plans for you and me.

This encyclopedia of world history isn't like any other. The *Master Books World History Encyclopedia* looks at history with a Christian, biblical worldview. What does this mean? We believe the Bible is God's holy Word. We use the Bible as the trusted authority on history that began on Day 1 when God spoke the cosmos into existence and all the way to that thrilling day when God will establish a perfect, brand-new heaven and earth where His children will live with Him forever.

You'll discover why we can trust the Bible as our lens to look through as we investigate history. You'll get to know dinosaurs. Travel to faraway islands in the seas. You'll study fascinating facts about places and past events from the ziggurats in ancient Sumer to painted caves in Africa to King Solomon's temple of gold. You'll meet people in ancient civilizations from the Land of the Rising Sun in Japan to the Nazca in ancient Peru to the Romans who built an empire. The Bible is the starting point for our adventures as we travel back through time to find out about people, places, and amazing things that have happened since time began. It's all here—and more!

It's perfect for gathering information you need to complete homework assignments, school projects, and to enjoy for family-time learning and fun. Explore the full-color photographs and illustrations, sidebars, handy charts, important dates, and helpful maps as they bring history to life on this great big globe we call home.

Moses lifted
the wildernes
the Son of Man be
so that whoever
in Him have eterna
16 “For God so loved th
hat He gave His only b
on, that whoever bel
Him shall not perish,
ernal life.
17 “For God did not
into the world
d, but that the

TIMELINE: 4004 B.C. – 1500 B.C.

4000 B.C.

Creation: God Creates the Heavens and the Earth (Genesis 1) 4004 B.C.

4004 B.C. Dinosaurs live on the earth (Gen. 1:24)

God creates Adam and Eve, the parents of all humankind (Gen. 3:20) 4004 B.C.

4004 B.C. God creates the sacred institutions of two genders, marriage between a husband and a wife, the family, and the sanctity of life (Gen. 1:26–31)

The Fall: Adam and Eve and the First Sin (Genesis 3) 4004 B.C.

4004 B.C. God promises a Savior (Gen. 3:15)

Adam, the first farmer (Gen. 3:17–19) 4004 B.C.

c. 3874 B.C. Shepherds and herders (Gen. 4:2)

Living in tents (Gen. 4:20) c. 3874 B.C.

c. 3750 B.C. First cities built (Genesis 4:17)

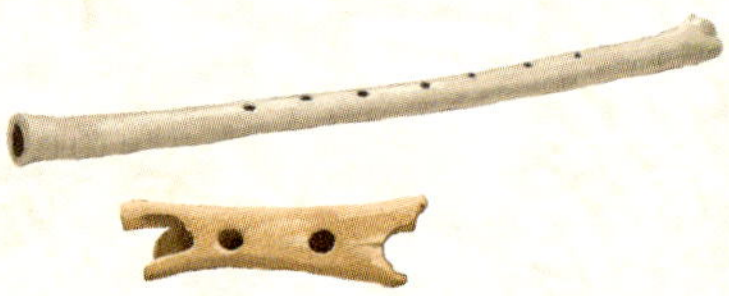

Musical instruments (Gen. 4:21) c. 3475 B.C.

c. 3475 B.C. Bronze and iron tools used (Gen. 4:22)

3000 B.C.

Death of Adam 3074 B.C.

3017 B.C. Enoch taken to heaven

Noah born 2948 B.C.

The Worldwide Flood: Noah and the Ark (Genesis 7) c. 2348 B.C.

2247-2242 B.C. Tower of Babel

Nimrod took Babylon (Mesopotamia) as the first center of his kingdom 2234 B.C.

2188 B.C. Mizraim founds Egypt

Javan founds Greece 2089 B.C.

c. 2070 B.C. Indus River Valley Civilization forms

2000 B.C. — 1000 B.C.

Yellow River Valley civilization forms c. 2070 B.C.

c. 2000 B.C. Horse-drawn chariots with spoked wheels used in Mesopotamia

Death of Noah 1998 B.C.

1996 B.C. Birth of Abraham

Abraham leaves Haran 1921 B.C.

1921 B.C. Abraham arrives in Canaan

First Assyrian Empire 1810 B.C.

c. 1800s B.C. Great Pyramid built

Medical instruments used in Babylon c. 1800 B.C.

c. 1792 B.C. Code of Hammurabi

Babylonian Empire defeats Assyria 1760 B.C.

c. 1728 B.C. Joseph sold into Egypt

Jacob and sons move to Egypt in famine c. 1706 B.C.

c. 1700 B.C. Trading at Poverty Point (Louisiana)

Jacob dies in Egypt 1689 B.C.

1635 B.C. Joseph dies

Emperor Tang founds the Shang Dynasty c. 1600 B.C.

c. 1591 B.C. Hittites attack Babylon; end of the First Babylonian Empire

Moses born 1571 B.C.

c. 1550 B.C. Rhind Papyrus

Aryans invade India c. 1500 B.C.

Chinese weave silk cloth for trade c. 1500 B.C.

c. 1500 B.C. Glass bottles made in Mesopotamia, Egypt, and Greece

c. 1500-1000 B.C. Bantu migration across Africa

Book of Job is written c. 1500-500 B.C.

The Bible is a religious book. Many people believe in it because it is an important part of their faith. Skeptics, critics, and doubters have put the Bible to many tests. What have they discovered? Unlike books of false religions, the Bible is based on historical and scientific facts.

♦ King James Version (KJV) of the Bible, first printing in 1611

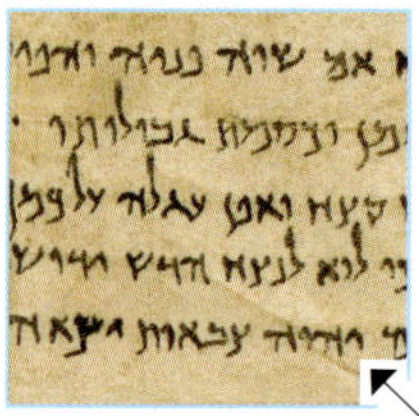

Why Trust the Bible?

The Bible covers the span of world history from the beginning of the very first week of history up through biblical times. It also talks about the end (or last days) of the world. Skeptics often claim that many events in the Bible are just children's bedtime stories, fairy tales, or myths. Yet, exciting historical evidence proves otherwise. This evidence shows the Christian faith is founded on facts, and the Bible is a book with historical accounts people can trust.

Archaeological Finds

Over and over, archaeological discoveries show that the Bible is a trustworthy and accurate book. For instance, the Bible mentions the Hittites over forty times. Yet no evidence had ever been found of their civilization until the 19th century. Skeptics had denied that the Hittites ever existed. To them, the Bible was inaccurate regarding history and thus could not be trusted. This changed, however, in the late 1800s. Since then, writings, artifacts, and entire Hittite cities have been discovered. The Bible was true after all!

Eyewitness Testimonies

In a court of law, eyewitness reports help determine the truth. Both the Old and New Testaments contain many eyewitness accounts. Testimonies from people such as Moses, Samuel, Matthew, and John help show that the Bible is a book of real people and real historic events.

Other Primary Sources

Other ancient written records mention people and events that are included in the Bible. Pharaoh Ramses II of Egypt, Josephus, Pliny the Younger, and others include biblical events and people in their monuments, clay tablets, letters, and manuscripts. Extra-biblical (outside the Bible) writings help confirm the Bible includes actual details of history.

♦ Ancient cuneiform tablet of the Egyptian-Hittite Peace Treaty, also known as the Treaty of Kadesh. It was an agreement between Ramses II of Egypt and Hattusili III of the Hittite Empire. It is recognized as the earliest known peace treaty in history.

Fulfilled Prophecies

Hundreds of predictions (also called prophecies) have come to pass with 100% accuracy! In the Bible, God inspired people called prophets to write about future events. Over 300 of these were fulfilled in Jesus' birth, life, death, and resurrection. The odds against this happening are staggering, once again showing that the Bible can be trusted. Here are just a few of the prophecies that talk about Jesus.

Prophecy	Old Testament Verse	Fulfillment	New Testament Verse
Born of a virgin	Isaiah 7:14	Jesus born of Mary	Matthew 1:22–23
Born in Bethlehem	Micah 5:2	Jesus born in Bethlehem	Matthew 2:1
From the line of Abraham	Genesis 12:3; 22:18	Jesus, descendant of Abraham	Matthew 1:1; Galatians 3:16
Tribe of Judah	Genesis 49:10	Jesus from Judah	Luke 3:33; Hebrews 7:14
Heir to David's throne	2 Samuel 7:12–13	Jesus as King	Luke 1:32–33
Preceded by a forerunner	Isaiah 40:3; Malachi 3:1	John the Baptist prepares way	Matthew 3:1–3; Luke 1:76
Ministry in Galilee	Isaiah 9:1–2	Jesus ministers in Galilee	Matthew 4:13–16
Enters Jerusalem on a donkey	Zechariah 9:9	Triumphal Entry	Matthew 21:4–5
Betrayed by a friend	Psalm 41:9	Judas betrays Jesus	John 13:18, 26–30
Sold for 30 pieces of silver	Zechariah 11:12–13	Judas' payment	Matthew 26:14–16; 27:3–10
Silent before accusers	Isaiah 53:7	Jesus' silence at trial	Matthew 26:62–63; 27:12–14
Hands and feet pierced	Psalm 22:16	Crucifixion	John 19:18; 20:25–27
No bones broken	Psalm 34:20	Jesus' bones unbroken	John 19:33–36
Buried with the rich	Isaiah 53:9	Jesus buried in Joseph's tomb	John 19:38–42

♦ This is a portion of the Great Isaiah Scroll, one of the first seven Dead Sea Scrolls uncovered in a cave in Qumran, Israel. This scroll contains an almost complete version of the Book of Isaiah, and it dates back to roughly 100 B.C. It is important because it is one of the oldest known biblical manuscripts.

♦ Engraving of Isaiah 66:14 carved into the stone of the Western Wall of the Old City of Jerusalem

וראיתם ושש לבכם
ועצמותם כדשא

When you see this, your heart shall rejoice,
And your bones shall flourish like grass;
The hand of the Lord shall be known to His servants,
And His indignation to His enemies.
—Isaiah 66:14

Scientific Discoveries

The authors of the Bible were divinely inspired to write about certain scientific truths thousands of years before scientists discovered them. Laws of physics, biology, and astronomy are confirmed in the Bible. For instance, American oceanographer Matthew Maury discovered ocean currents based on his reading of Psalm 8:8, which talks about "the fish of the sea that pass through the paths of the seas."

Manuscript Reliability

How do we know the Bible we read today is the "real" version? Over the centuries, Bible scholars and translators have carefully studied and compared thousands of ancient biblical writings, like the Dead Sea Scrolls. With such detailed work and manuscript evidence, we can be confident that the Bible we read today is consistent with what the original authors wrote.

The study of world history begins with learning about God and His plan for His creation. We can't really understand events that happened throughout world history until we take a closer look at God, the Creator of the world.

The Trinity

The Bible teaches there is one true God. Yet, God is three persons in one.

He is God the Father. He is God the Son—Jesus Christ who lived, died, and rose again. He is God the Holy Spirit—the Comforter, Counselor, and Teacher who lives inside every believer. The Bible shows us an example of the Trinity at the baptism of Jesus. Jesus was baptized in the Jordan River. When He stood up out of the water, the Holy Spirit came down from heaven upon Him like a dove. God the Father spoke from heaven and said, "This is My beloved Son, in whom I am well pleased" (Matt. 3:17).

God is...

Omnipotent

This means God is all powerful. He can heal someone who is blind, bring a dead person back to life, cause the sun to stop shining, and calm a raging storm. God can create something out of nothing and make the impossible possible. God made the laws of the universe, and He can perform miracles that go beyond those natural laws.

Omnipresent

God is everywhere, all at the same time. He is in heaven, sitting on His throne, yet He is with each person today. He is with you right now as you read this! God has been with all people throughout all of history.

Omniscient

Omniscient means God knows everything. He knows everything that happened in the past. He knows everything that is happening right now. He knows everything that will happen in the future. Unlike people, whose knowledge is very limited, God knows *all* things.

Love

God is love. Love is who He is. Everything God has ever done or will ever do is because of God's unfathomable love for all of us.

And we have known and believed the love that God has for us. God is love, and he who abides in love abides in God, and God in him.
—1 John 4:16

Good

God is good. He does not create confusion, pain, or evil. The Bible says that Satan is the one who seeks to steal, kill, and destroy (see John 10:10). God is a good, loving Father and only wants good things for his children.

Just and Merciful

God is just. The Bible says God will judge evil and give it the punishment it deserves. Yet God is also loving and merciful. God wants everyone to live forever in heaven with Him. That's why Jesus came — to die on the Cross and to rise again. He offers forgiveness and eternal live to those who put their trust in Him.

Perfect

Sometimes we might doubt God or feel angry that He is not doing something the way we think He should. That is because our knowledge of God is limited. Our perspective is limited, too. God is not like Santa Claus. He does not give us everything we want because we ask Him. God is more kind, more loving, and wiser than we can ever understand because He is perfect and His plans are perfect, even if we cannot understand what He is doing.

Eternal

The Bible says God is eternal. He has no beginning and no end. Because He is eternal, He wants each one of us to live forever with Him. How can we have eternal life? We can repent of our sins and tell God we're sorry for the wrong things we've done. We can accept God's forgiveness. We can accept the gift of salvation and trust in the promise of eternal life. We can choose to follow Jesus and allow His Spirit to guide our lives.

Eternal Life

Throughout history, wars and other evil actions have caused pain and suffering. Since God is just (fair and does what is right), He promises to one day give evil the punishment it deserves. For all those who believe in Jesus as their Lord and Savior, God promises eternal life. In eternity with Him, there will be no tears, no sadness, no suffering, and no evil. We will live with our perfect God forever.

God? Or an Idol?

People often make up false ideas about God. They may look at a Scripture describing how God punished sin, and they say, "My God would never do that." They may read a Bible verse that they don't like and declare, "My God isn't like that." That's because their god isn't the true God. They are talking about an idol (a false god) they have created and worship. The Bible teaches that God is bigger, better, and more wonderful than anything we could ever imagine. We can trust God as He is described in the Bible, even when we don't understand everything the Bible says.

The Bible teaches that God created the universe and everything in it. Genesis, the very first book of the Bible, tells the history of how the world got started: In the beginning God created the heavens and the earth (Gen. 1:1).

Author of Genesis

Many Bible scholars agree that Moses wrote the Book of Genesis. How did he know the details of creation if he wasn't there? Most likely he learned it from three sources:

1. Oral traditions handed down over time
2. Ancient accounts of other writers
3. Divine inspiration

After all, the same God who inspired prophets such as Daniel, Isaiah, and the Apostle John to write about future events could also inspire Moses to understand what happened in the past.

Adam lived 930 years. He was alive when Methuselah lived, who was alive when Noah lived. The account of creation was easily passed down.	Son of Adam lived 912 years	Son of Seth lived 905 years	Son of Enos lived 910 years	Son of Cainan lived 895 years	Son of Mahalalel lived 962 years	Son of Jared lived 365 years	Son of Enoch lived 969 years	Son of Methuselah lived 777 years	Son of Lamech lived 950 years

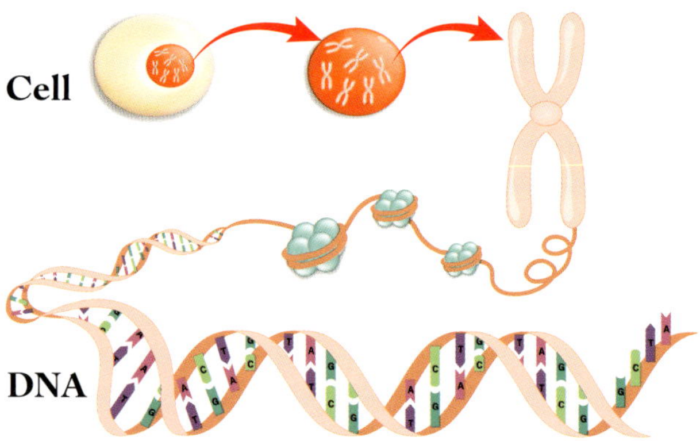

Intelligent Creator

If you went skiing and found an igloo, what would you think? That the igloo appeared by chance from snowflakes randomly forming together? Of course not! Somebody made it. It's the same when we look at the universe. For example, **DNA** is so complex and amazingly perfect that it could not have formed by random chance. Somebody had to create it! The Bible tells us this Creator is God. He made all things in heaven and on earth and He holds the whole world together (Col. 1:15–17).

James Ussher

James Ussher was the archbishop of the Protestant Church of Ireland. He took on the gigantic task of calculating the date of creation based on what was written in the Bible. Using ancient calendars, he compared biblical family trees with the dates of historic events found in ancient documents. After many years of intense research, in 1650, Ussher published his calculations in his book *The Annals of the World.* According to Ussher, God created the universe and everything in it during one week of 24-hour days in 4004 B.C.

King James Bible

Other theologians, mathematicians, and scientists have attempted to use the genealogical records (family histories) in the Bible to calculate the date God created the world. For example, Johannes Kepler calculated creation's date at 3992 B.C. Isaac Newton thought it to be about 4000 B.C. Ussher's calculations for creation and other biblical events became more widely known when the King James Bible published Ussher's dates in the margins of its pages.

The Adams Synchronological Chart

Sebastian C. Adams loved history. In 1871, this pioneer, preacher, and teacher created a monumental work called the *Chronological Chart of Ancient, Modern and Biblical History*. Standing at 27.5 inches high and 22 feet long, this fully illustrated timeline used James Ussher's dates of creation, biblical events, and ancient history. Adams updated Usher's timeline to include United States and modern world history up to the late 1800s.

Creation Scientists

Mistaken ideas about evolution and Charles Darwin's (bottom left) faulty theories traveled around the world. Ussher's calculations of a 6,000-year-old earth (creation at 4004 B.C. + 2,000 years since the birth of Christ) became a topic of ridicule and scorn. However, more and more scientific evidence supports a literal interpretation of the creation account in the Bible. Henry Morris (bottom right), known as the father of modern creationism, was influential in starting the Modern Creation Movement. Organizations like Answers in Genesis and the Institute for Creation Research refer to many dates James Ussher calculated to show that the earth is not millions of years old. Researchers known as creation scientists are continuing to find facts and scientific evidence to support the conclusion that the earth was indeed created about 4,000 years before the birth of Christ, just as the Bible says.

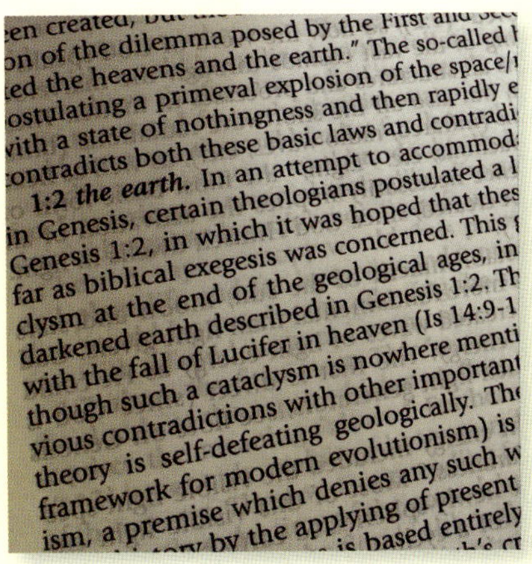

What did God create during the seven days of creation? Read the first chapter of Genesis to see the details.

- **Day 1:** Time, Earth, Space, and Light

- **Day 2:** Sky and Water

- **Day 3:** Seas, Land, and Plants

- **Day 4:** Sun, Moon, and Stars

- **Day 5:** Sea Animals and Birds

- **Day 6:** Land Animals, Man and Woman

Then God blessed the seventh day and sanctified it, because in it He rested from all His work which God had created and made. —Genesis 2:3

- **Day 7:** Day of Rest

Jesus, the Creator

During the week of creation, God spoke and created the universe out of nothing. The Bible also tells us that Jesus is the image of the invisible God (see Col. 1:15) and that all things were created through Jesus. How is this possible? Because Jesus is part of the Trinity, which is defined as God the Father, God the Son, and God the Holy Spirit. Thus, Jesus created the world, sustains it, and holds it all together (Col. 1:16-17).

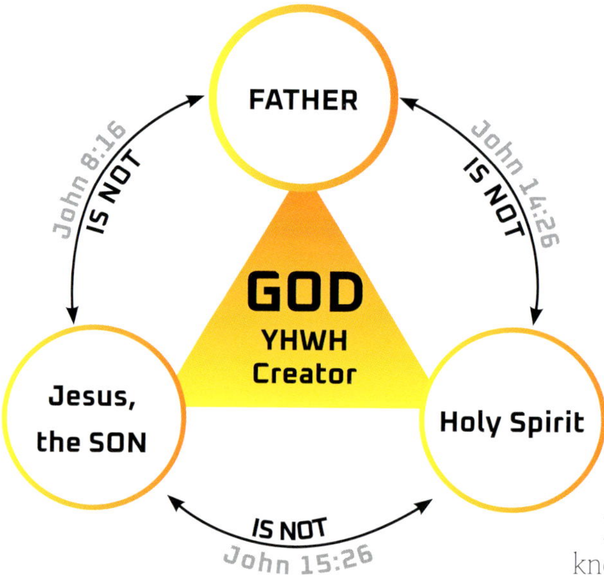

He is the image of the invisible God, the firstborn over all creation. For by Him all things were created that are in heaven and that are on earth, visible and invisible, whether thrones or dominions or principalities or powers. All things were created through Him and for Him. —Colossians 1:15-16

Tough Questions

The Sadducees (religious leaders) tried to trick Jesus by asking Him a tough question about heaven. How did Jesus answer them? He said, "You are mistaken, not knowing the Scriptures nor the power of God" (Matt. 22:23-29). This was a good answer then, and it is a good answer for tricky and tough questions today. For example, many people debate today whether God created the earth in six days or over billions of years. Often, they state their arguments, but they do not know what both the Old and New Testaments say about creation, and they don't acknowledge how powerful God is.

Understanding the Past

Scientific methods dating the universe as billions of years old are being put to the test. New, cutting-edge research with fossils, the ocean, and comets shows evidence to support a young earth. One example is the amount of salt in seawater. According to the proposed evolutionary timeline of a universe billions of years old, oceans should contain much more salt than they do today because the amount of salt increases over time. By measuring the salt levels today, scientists can calculate backward in time to determine that the oceans are much younger than evolutionists claim. These findings (and more) support a 24-hour day account of creation that took place about 6,000 years ago.

24 Hours or Millions of Years?

Hours? Days? Years? Some people debate that each day listed in Genesis 1 could be thousands or millions of years instead of 24 hours. Top scientists in their fields who believe a literal understanding of the Bible say research proves otherwise. One example is the order of creation events. Genesis says light was created on the first day, plants on the third day, and the sun on the fourth day. If God created plants over millions of years, how could the plants grow or survive without the sun? Yes, there was light, but it wasn't from the sun because the sun had not yet been created. Without the sun, photosynthesis could not take place and plants would die. Yet, if God created the plants on the third day and then within 24 hours created the sun (on the fourth day), plants could survive until He created the sun.

Worldview

What Christians believe about creation doesn't change their salvation. Yet, it does affect how they understand the world (called a worldview), what they think about God, and how they live out their faith. It also affects whether they choose to trust the Bible as the starting point and final authority on historical, scientific, and faith issues. Jesus said, "For if you believed Moses, you would believe Me; for he wrote about Me. But if you do not believe his writings, how will you believe My words?" (John 5:46–47).

Scripture Confirms Scripture

Exodus 20:8–10 commands people to work on six days and rest on the seventh. This passage talks about a 24-hour day and a seven-day week. Exodus 20:11a concludes, "For in six days the LORD made the heavens and the earth, the sea, and all that is in them, and rested the seventh day." Many Christian scholars, scientists, and believers agree that this verse verifies that God indeed created the universe and everything in it in six literal 24-hour days. Moses wrote both Genesis and Exodus. Why would he write in Exodus 20:11 that God created the world in six 24-hour days if he meant something different in Genesis 1?

DAY ONE OF CREATION

4004 B.C.

On Day 1 of creation, God created time, earth, space, and light.

In the beginning God created the heavens and the earth. The earth was without form, and void; and darkness was on the face of the deep. And the Spirit of God was hovering over the face of the waters. Then God said, "Let there be light"; and there was light. And God saw the light, that it was good; and God divided the light from the darkness. God called the light Day, and the darkness He called Night. So the evening and the morning were the first day. —Genesis 1:1–5

♦ **Day 1:** Time, Earth, Space, and Light

The First Day

On the first day of creation, God spoke the heavens and the earth into existence. The earth did not yet have the form that we know as our planet today. It was a place with waters, but the atmosphere was not yet separated from the waters below it, and the waters were not yet gathered into seas by the boundaries of land.

Nothing Is Nothing

Atheists are people who don't believe in God or in the Bible. Many, including some scientists, believe that the universe came into existence on its own—without any higher power—and basically came from nothing.

But if you think about it, that doesn't make sense. "Nothing" can't create anything. If something came from "nothing," then it wasn't really nothing at all. There had to be a cause—something (or someone) that started it all. According to the Bible, that someone is God, who created the universe with purpose and design.

Scientifically Speaking

Physicists and other scientists who study the universe identify four basic building blocks of the universe: time, energy, space, and matter. God established these four building blocks on the first day of creation by proclaiming in the very first verse of the Bible:

False Claim

Aristotle was a Greek philosopher. As a pagan (someone who believes in many gods), he did not believe in the one true God of the Bible. Aristotle claimed that matter is eternal. Even though the Bible teaches that only God is eternal, many scientists chose to believe Aristotle instead. The Bible teaches that God created all things, including matter. Aristotle influenced scientists for centuries and helped shape early beliefs in Charles Darwin's theory of evolution.

Expanding Universe

As technology has advanced, scientists have invented bigger and better tools to use, such as powerful telescopes for the sky. They have discovered the universe is expanding. This shows that the universe is *not* eternal. It had a beginning, which means Aristotle was incorrect. Matter is not eternal. The Bible tells us that in the beginning, God created the universe.

Big Bang?

Many scientists, textbooks, and people believe the big bang theory. It says that the entire universe began as an extremely small, incredibly hot and dense point that exploded. Then it organized into the matter, energy, and space that exists today—the galaxies, solar system, and life on planet earth. There are many problems with this idea. For instance, explosions don't organize. Explosions create chaos, destruction, and ruin. The Bible declares God is the creative power who designed, organized, and built the world.

DNA Discovery

Scientists used high-powered microscopes to look inside tiny cells when they discovered DNA, the molecule that contains the genetic code for the traits and characteristics of all living things. The discovery of DNA supports the fact that something (Someone) intelligent designed and programmed the code. The Bible tells us that God is the intelligent, all-knowing, omniscient Creator of the universe.

Let There Be Light

In the very first chapter of the Bible, when God created the heavens and the earth, God created light. This light was not from the sun or moon because those were created on the fourth day. It is interesting to note that in the very last two chapters of the Bible, which describe God creating the new heaven and the new earth, the light of God's glory will shine. This light will not come from the sun or moon because there will be no more need for them (see Rev. 21:23 and 22:5)!

Mystery

The Bible does not give details about the light God created on Day 1. Was it like a sun but not the sun that orbits the earth? Was it shining from Jesus? Was it God's glory made visible? Was it a glowing cloud? The answer will remain a mystery for now. One thing we do know: God created light, and it was good.

It Was Good

When God saw the light, He declared it was good. The Bible establishes a pattern at the end of each day of creation — God saw it was good. Everything He creates is good because He is good. The author of sin, evil, and wickedness is Satan. The devil is first mentioned in Genesis 3, shortly after creation. But God's eternal plan will triumph over evil. There will come a day in God's perfect timing when God will pronounce judgment on Satan and destroy evil forever.

On Day 2 of creation, God created sky and water, separating out the atmosphere from the waters below and above it.

Then God said, "Let there be a firmament in the midst of the waters, and let it divide the waters from the waters." Thus God made the firmament, and divided the waters which were under the firmament from the waters which were above the firmament; and it was so. And God called the firmament Heaven. So the evening and the morning were the second day. —Genesis 1:6–8

♦ **Day 2**: Sky and Water

Firmament

According to Genesis 1:7, God separated the waters so that there was water above and below the firmament. In this context, the firmament refers to the sky. This is supported by Genesis 1:20, where God created birds to "fly above the earth across the face of the firmament of the heavens," suggesting it is the atmosphere that surrounds the earth.

However, the term "firmament" also seems to extend beyond the atmosphere. In Genesis 1:17, God placed the sun, moon, and stars in the firmament, which indicates that it also includes outer space.

Water (H_2O)

Water! We drink it. We wash with it. We swim in it. But what is it? Chemically speaking, water is two hydrogen atoms bonded with one oxygen atom to form the molecule we know as water. It occurs in three states: ice in its solid form; water in its liquid form; and water vapor, or steam, in its form as a gas.

Life

All living things need water to survive. Water is essential for breaking down food so it can be used by cells. It is also an important part of the transportation highway within and between cells in the biological systems of people, animals, and plants.

♦ A living cell is typically 70-90% water.

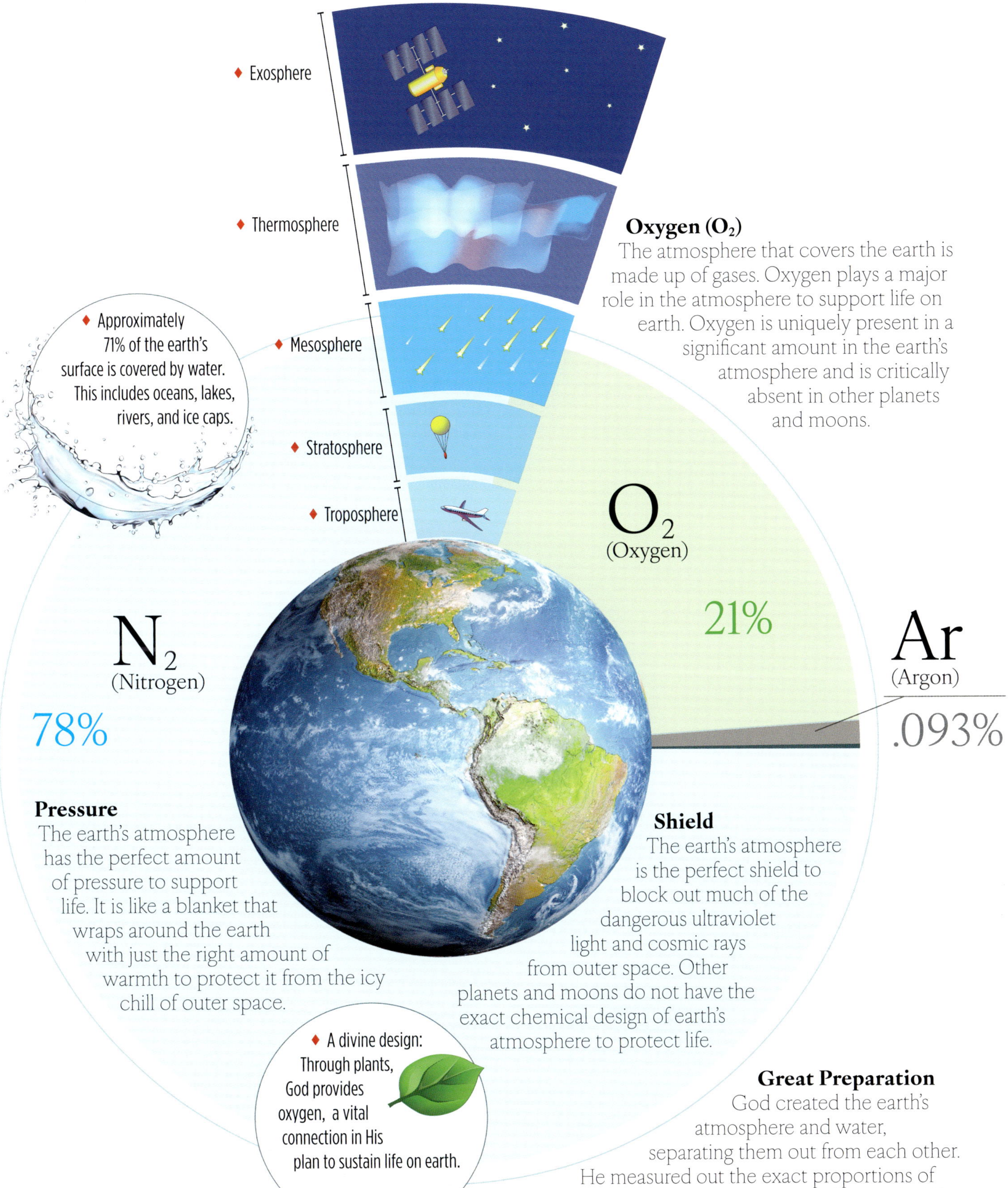

Oxygen (O_2)
The atmosphere that covers the earth is made up of gases. Oxygen plays a major role in the atmosphere to support life on earth. Oxygen is uniquely present in a significant amount in the earth's atmosphere and is critically absent in other planets and moons.

♦ Approximately 71% of the earth's surface is covered by water. This includes oceans, lakes, rivers, and ice caps.

Pressure
The earth's atmosphere has the perfect amount of pressure to support life. It is like a blanket that wraps around the earth with just the right amount of warmth to protect it from the icy chill of outer space.

Shield
The earth's atmosphere is the perfect shield to block out much of the dangerous ultraviolet light and cosmic rays from outer space. Other planets and moons do not have the exact chemical design of earth's atmosphere to protect life.

♦ A divine design: Through plants, God provides oxygen, a vital connection in His plan to sustain life on earth.

Great Preparation
God created the earth's atmosphere and water, separating them out from each other. He measured out the exact proportions of ingredients needed to support life in each. What was He doing on the second day of creation? God was preparing the earth to fill it with life and living things!

On Day 3 of creation, God created the seas, land, and plants.

Then God said, "Let the waters under the heavens be gathered together into one place, and let the dry land appear"; and it was so. And God called the dry land Earth, and the gathering together of the waters He called Seas. And God saw that it was good. Then God said, "Let the earth bring forth grass, the herb that yields seed, and the fruit tree that yields fruit according to its kind, whose seed is in itself, on the earth"; and it was so. And the earth brought forth grass, the herb that yields seed according to its kind, and the tree that yields fruit, whose seed is in itself according to its kind. And God saw that it was good. So the evening and the morning were the third day. —Genesis 1:9–13

♦ **Day 3:** Seas, Land, and Plants

Taking Shape

On day 3, the earth was taking shape into the planet we know today. Outer space was still empty. The solar system did not yet exist. But amazing changes were taking place on planet Earth. God was at work!

Plate Tectonics

God spoke His Word, and dry land appeared. Many scientists today accept the idea of plate tectonics—the theory that there was just one big continent of land and one ginormous ocean in the earth's earliest history. This supports Genesis 1:9 of day 3 of creation. If that is so, how did the seven continents come about? A cataclysmic event could have broken the single continent apart. This supports what the Bible has said all along. The Flood of Noah would have caused cracks in the earth's crust as well as major shifts of land and sea.

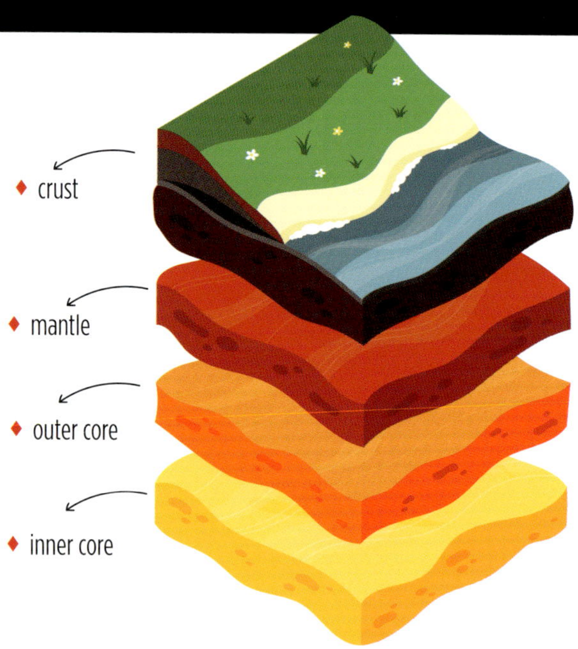

Four Layers

Dry land appeared on the earth's crust, or its top layer. Covered with dirt, soil, and lots of water, the earth's crust is mostly rock. Underneath the crust is the earth's second layer, called the mantle. Most of this layer consists of iron and magnesium rock. Beneath the mantle is the third layer, called the outer core. Intense heat keeps the outer core like fiery, molten lava. It is probably made of iron and nickel. At the center of the earth is the inner core, made mostly of iron. The hottest of all four layers of the earth, the inner core is probably solid because of the intense pressure at the planet's center.

The Order of Creation

Most books on evolution state that the solar system was in place long before plants started to grow. That idea is valid if the earth evolved over millions and millions of years. But the Bible says God created plants *before* the sun. That's a problem for evolutionary theory, because without photosynthesis (process by which plants use sunlight and other elements to make food), plants could not produce food and they would die. But the creation of plants before the sun is possible if God put plants on the earth one day and the sun in the sky the next. Photosynthesis could take place and plants could thrive. The Bible also says God created plants *before* bees and butterflies. If the earth evolved over eons of time, plants would not be able reproduce and would die out. Near the end of the literal 24-hour day and 7-day week, God created bugs. Plants could then reproduce because the world was abundant with pollinators buzzing and fluttering around.

According to Its Kind

On day 3 of creation, God created grass, herbs, and fruit trees that yielded seed "according to its kind" (Gen. 1:12). What does this term mean? When God created plants and trees, the Mastermind of the universe designed unique genetic codes and DNA within every living thing. Each plant has its own genetic codes, which are packed inside its seeds. How can a flat, black seed grow into a round, green watermelon? How can a small acorn grow into a giant oak tree? Because of genetic codes. It seems like a mystery to us, but it's all in God's amazing design!

Another parable He put forth to them, saying: "The kingdom of heaven is like a mustard seed, which a man took and sowed in his field, which indeed is the least of all the seeds; but when it is grown it is greater than the herbs and becomes a tree, so that the birds of the air come and nest in its branches." —Matthew 13:31–32

On Day 4 of creation, God created the sun, moon, and stars.

Then God said, "Let there be lights in the firmament of the heavens to divide the day from the night; and let them be for signs and seasons, and for days and years; and let them be for lights in the firmament of the heavens to give light on the earth"; and it was so. Then God made two great lights: the greater light to rule the day, and the lesser light to rule the night. He made the stars also. God set them in the firmament of the heavens to give light on the earth, and to rule over the day and over the night, and to divide the light from the darkness. And God saw that it was good. So the evening and the morning were the fourth day. —Genesis 1:14–19

♦ **Day 4:** Sun, Moon, and Stars

Outer Space

On the first three days of creation, outer space was empty. On day 4, God created objects that now make up the universe. The sun. The planets. The moons. Asteroids, comets, and black holes. Stars, galaxies, superclusters, and solar systems! In just one day, God designed, arranged, and stretched out the cosmos across 550 sextillion miles (550,000,000,000,000,000,000,000) of outer space. And that's just the *observable* universe—the part that our most powerful telescopes can see!

Solar System

According to Colossians 1:16-17 and Hebrews 1:1–3, Jesus created our solar system and holds each object in its proper place. The sun is a fireball of nuclear power placed at exactly the correct distance from the earth to sustain life. The four planets closest to the sun—Mercury, Venus, Earth, and Mars— have solid surfaces made of rock or metal. The four outer planets—Jupiter, Saturn, Uranus, and Neptune—are made mostly of gases like hydrogen and helium, with no solid surface. However, the earth is the only inhabitable planet. None of the other planets in our solar system can sustain human life.

Age of the Planets & Stars

According to the chronological timetable in the Bible, God created the universe and everything in it during the week of creation roughly 6,000 years ago. Even though He didn't create Adam and Eve until the sixth day of creation, we know He created them as mature humans. God didn't create babies and then expect them to grow. He created adults—but they were just one day old! In the same way, God created mature, fully functioning planets, moons, and galaxies. Even the stars, whose lights take hundreds of years to reach the earth, were already twinkling in the night sky. They didn't evolve over time. Even though every object in space was just one day old, God created a mature and fully functioning universe—the amazing and wonderful home for His children.

Repeating Pattern

Have you ever heard of the Fibonacci sequence? It is a number pattern that shows up in many places in nature. The pattern is made up of numbers where each number is found by adding the two numbers before it. It starts with 0 and 1, and then continues by adding the previous two to get the next one. So, it goes 0, 1, 1, 2, 3, 5, 8, 13, and so on. This series creates a pattern, shape, or ratio.

What's so special about a series of numbers? It's found all over nature! You can see it in spirals of pineapples, sunflower seeds, petals, and seashells (and a lot of other places). The Fibonacci sequence is one of the best pieces of evidence to show God created everything. Explosions (like a big bang) create chaos, disorder, and random placement, not a sequence of order. Galaxies like the Milky Way, which includes our solar system, reflect the Fibonacci sequence. Only an intelligent Designer could organize our world with such precision. The Bible tells us this Creator is God.

When I consider Your heavens, the work of Your fingers,
The moon and the stars, which You have ordained,
What is man that You are mindful of him,
And the son of man that You visit him?
—Psalm 8:3–4

A Day Is a Day

Some people argue that each day in the creation account took place over a thousand years or more, taking 2 Peter 3:8 out of context: "with the Lord one day is as a thousand years, and a thousand years as one day." Genesis 1:14–19 says that God created the sun, moon, and stars to "divide the day from the night." God set them in the sky "to rule over the day and over the night." The Bible repeats the phrase, "so the evening and the morning were the first [or second or third, etc.] day." When we take Genesis 1 in its full context, it is clear that the Bible is describing a 24-hour day on earth with the sun shining during the daytime and the moon and stars shining at night.

Why Create the Sun, Moon, and Stars?

Genesis tells us some of the reasons God created the sun, moon, and stars. First, they establish time as we know it. They define the meaning of the 24-hour day both in Scripture and in life on earth. They also mark the seasons as the earth orbits around the sun. Plus, they point people to God. The marvels of the heavens signal to every person the majesty and glory of God, inviting each one of us to worship our Creator (see Psalm 19:1–4).

Space Detective

Creation scientists examine the evidence of the starry hosts and explain how it supports what the Bible says. Scientists who believe in evolution also publish articles, books, and movies about their ideas concerning outer space. Unfortunately, they often state these ideas as facts, not theories. Comets are one example. Because comets are relatively short-lived on the evolutionary timeline, evolution scientists needed an explanation for where comets are "born." They assert that the Oort Cloud is a birthplace for comets. The Oort Cloud is a theoretical cloud of icy bodies believed to exist far beyond the orbit of Neptune, surrounding our solar system in a spherical shell. However, the Oort Cloud has never been directly observed. It is a *theory*. Creation scientists assert that God crafted comets on day four of creation about 6,000 years ago. Comets still zip around space for us to marvel and enjoy today. When you study outer space, learn to be a space detective! Look for clues that show us that God is the Creator of the entire universe!

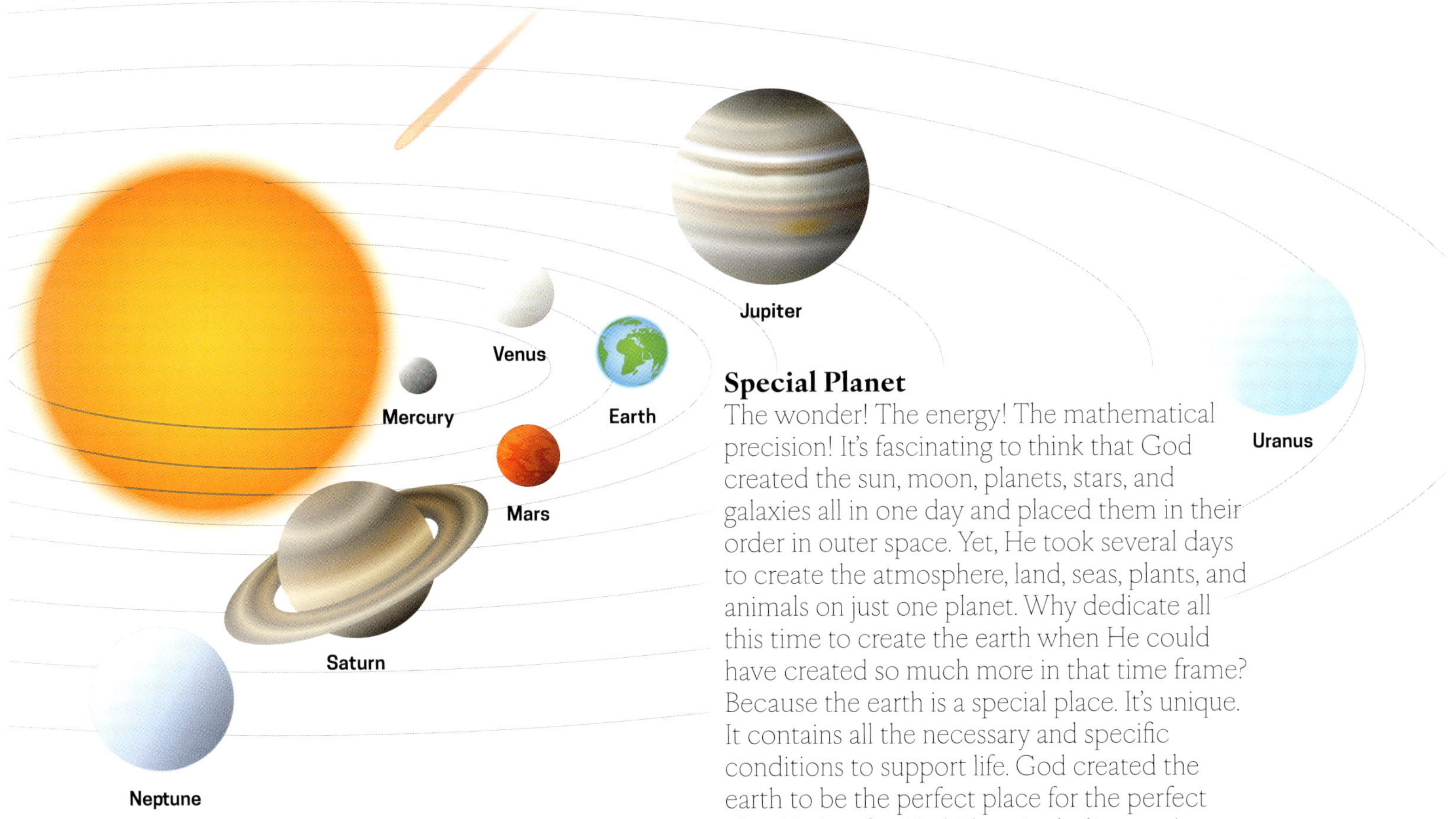

Special Planet

The wonder! The energy! The mathematical precision! It's fascinating to think that God created the sun, moon, planets, stars, and galaxies all in one day and placed them in their order in outer space. Yet, He took several days to create the atmosphere, land, seas, plants, and animals on just one planet. Why dedicate all this time to create the earth when He could have created so much more in that time frame? Because the earth is a special place. It's unique. It contains all the necessary and specific conditions to support life. God created the earth to be the perfect place for the perfect plan He has for His kids . . . including you!

On Day 5 of creation, God created creatures that swim and birds that fly.

Then God said, "Let the waters abound with an abundance of living creatures, and let birds fly above the earth across the face of the firmament of the heavens." So God created great sea creatures and every living thing that moves, with which the waters abounded, according to their kind, and every winged bird according to its kind. And God saw that it was good. And God blessed them, saying, "Be fruitful and multiply, and fill the waters in the seas, and let birds multiply on the earth." So the evening and the morning were the fifth day. —Genesis 1:20–23

◆ **Day 5:** Sea Animals and Birds

Fish

Fish are cold-blooded, which means they cannot regulate their body temperature, so they rely on the warmth of the water for heat. They are vertebrates, which means they have a spine, also called a backbone. Many have fins, scales, and a streamlined design that make them speed through the water like underwater racecars. Some swim alone, but many swim in groups called schools.

Cetaceans

Cetaceans aren't fish. They're mammals! However, they spend all their life in the ocean with fish and other amazing creatures God created on day 5 of creation. Whales, dolphins, and porpoises are examples of cetaceans and have front flippers and a tail with flukes that pump up and down as they zip through the waves.

◆ Dolphins breathe through a hole on top of their head when they surface from the water.

How Do They Breathe?

Animals need oxygen to live. Fish can't breathe air. They have to take in their oxygen out of the water. They suck in water through their mouth where it passes over their gills. Gills are feathery-type, very thin tissues with lots of blood. Oxygen from the water passes through the gills and into their bloodstream

Cetaceans do not have gills. They breathe air through their nostrils. Whales, dolphins and porpoises have to swim up to the top of the water to breathe air. God designed their nostrils (called blowholes) at the top of their head. Before taking in a new breath, they blow out the breath they've been holding. It spouts up, looking like a fountain or a puff of smoke.

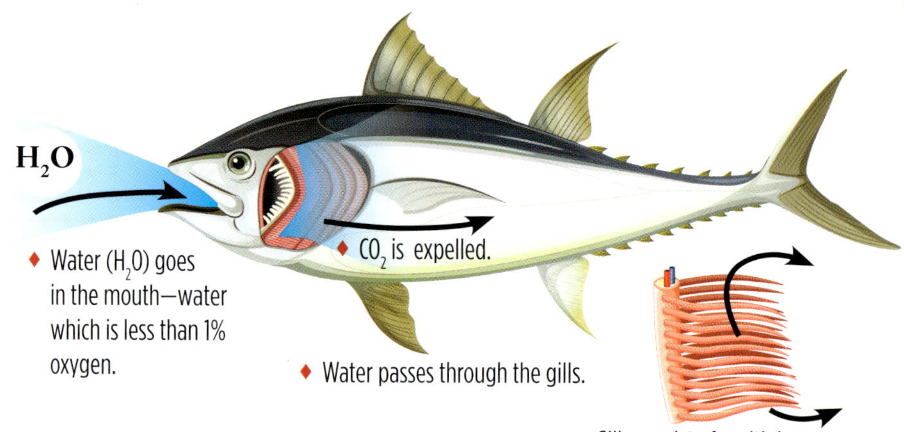

◆ Water (H_2O) goes in the mouth—water which is less than 1% oxygen.

◆ CO_2 is expelled.

◆ Water passes through the gills.

◆ Gills consist of multiple filaments, each containing many tiny lamellae that absorb oxygen from the water and pass it into the blood vessels.

Birds

Birds are warm-blooded vertebrates with wings. Their feathers, beaks, and hollow bones set them apart from other creatures. From the tiniest hummingbird to the giant ostrich, all birds lay eggs. Evolutionists say that dinosaurs evolved into birds, but the Bible says God created birds on day 4 of creation. Dinosaurs were created on day 5 with the other land animals.

♦ The bones in the wings of many birds are hollow.

♦ Emu

Pterodactyls

Is it a plane? A bird? A dinosaur? No! Pterodactyls were giant reptiles with flaps like wings so they could soar through the skies. Some had wingspans of over three feet wide. Interestingly, they are not considered dinosaurs.

♦ Hummingbird eggs

♦ Hummingbirds are the tiniest birds in the world. They average about 3–5 inches long and can weigh the equivalent of one to eight pennies.

Take the Challenge!

The Bible lists a distinct order of events during the creation of the universe and everything in it. Many experts, scientists, and people of faith believe what the Bible says. An atheist does not believe in any gods. They rely on evolutionary theories to explain the world without God. Evolutionists claim that it took billions of years and a different set of events for the solar system, plants, and animals to come into existence. If you have been taught that evolution is scientifically sound, challenge what you've read or heard! Dig deeper to see what renowned creation scientists and creation experts believe about the events recorded in Genesis. Explore the websites of Answers in Genesis, Creation Ministries International, and the Institute for Creation Research.

On Day 6 of creation, God created land animals and the very first man and woman.

♦ **Day 6:** Land Animals, Man and Woman

Then God said, "Let the earth bring forth the living creature according to its kind: cattle and creeping thing and beast of the earth, each according to its kind"; and it was so. And God made the beast of the earth according to its kind, cattle according to its kind, and everything that creeps on the earth according to its kind. And God saw that it was good.

Then God said, "Let Us make man in Our image, according to Our likeness; let them have dominion over the fish of the sea, over the birds of the air, and over the cattle, over all the earth and over every creeping thing that creeps on the earth."

So God created man in His own image; in the image of God He created him; male and female He created them.

Then God blessed them, and God said to them, "Be fruitful and multiply; fill the earth and subdue it; have dominion over the fish of the sea, over the birds of the air, and over every living thing that moves on the earth."

And God said, "See, I have given you every herb that yields seed which is on the face of all the earth, and every tree whose fruit yields seed; to you it shall be for food. Also, to every beast of the earth, to every bird of the air, and to everything that creeps on the earth, in which there is life, I have given every green herb for food"; and it was so. Then God saw everything that He had made, and indeed it was very good. So the evening and the morning were the sixth day. —Genesis 1:24–31

Who, What, When, Where, Why, and How?

In Genesis 1:24-31, the Bible explains when God created each type of creature. It says on day 6 of creation, God created land animals and the first man and woman. In Genesis 2:7-25 and 3:20, the Bible gives more specific details about day 6. It says whom God created, how and why He created them, and where they lived. God created the first man and woman, Adam and Eve, and put them in the Garden of Eden with a specific task: "Be fruitful and multiply; fill the earth and subdue it; have dominion over the fish of the sea, over the birds of the air, and over every living thing that moves on the earth" (Gen. 1:28).

From the Beginning

Evolutionists teach that people evolved into existence hundreds of millions of years after the "big bang." The Book of Genesis in the Bible says that God created Adam and Eve on day 6 of creation. Some people argue that the first chapters of Genesis are mythology, allegory, or pure fiction, while the evolutionary timeline is accurate. But what did Jesus teach? He said, "But from the beginning of the creation, God 'made them male and female'" (Mark 10:6). Jesus believed in the Genesis account of creation, and we can believe it, too! God made people on day 6 during the week of creation, just like the Bible says.

But Did People Evolve?

Many museums, encyclopedias, and student textbooks go to great lengths to show how single cells evolved into complex creatures and how ape-like animals evolved into people. These theories come from an atheist perspective that denies the existence of God. The Bible teaches that God created land animals on day 6 of creation. Then on the exact same day, God created Adam and Eve in His image. People did not evolve from animals. They are not animals with bigger or more advanced brains. People are different than animals—they have a spirit and can worship their Creator.

According to Its Kind

The Bible says God created each land animal and bug "according to its kind" (Gen. 1:21, 24-25). For example, dogs can only give birth to dogs. But there are a lot of varieties of dogs, such as chihuahuas, pugs, and Great Danes. Similarly, cats can only give birth to cats. But God created many kinds of cats, such as Siamese, Manx, and Persian. God designed each kind of animal with its own genetic code to be able to reproduce into many different varieties—all within its own species. The Bible established this scientific truth long before scientists ever studied genetics!

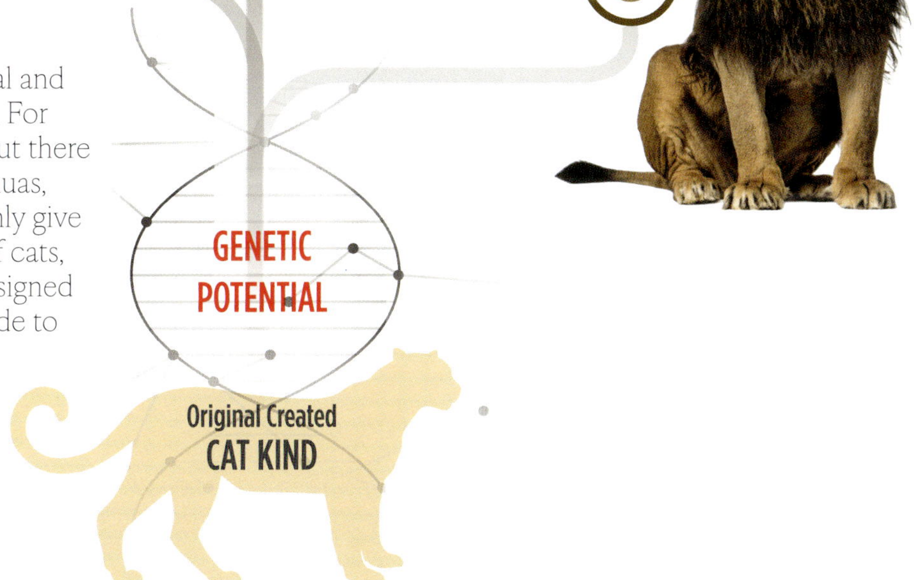

Dinosaurs

The word "dinosaur" is not in the Bible because the word wasn't invented until the 1800s! However, we know that God created all the land animals, including dinosaurs, on day 6.

Dinosaurs in the Bible?

"Look now at the behemoth, which I made along with you; He eats grass like an ox. See now, his strength is in his hips, And his power is in his stomach muscles. He moves his tail like a cedar; The sinews of his thighs are tightly knit. His bones are like beams of bronze, His ribs like bars of iron." — Job 40:15–18

In Job 40:19, this beast (behemoth) is described as ". . . the first of the ways of God." This means it was one of the largest animals God made. Could God be describing a sauropod dinosaur to Job?

On Day 7 of creation, God created a day of rest.

Thus the heavens and the earth, and all the host of them, were finished. And on the seventh day God ended His work which He had done, and He rested on the seventh day from all His work which He had done. Then God blessed the seventh day and sanctified it, because in it He rested from all His work which God had created and made.
—Genesis 2:1–3

The Week

The seven-day week is a pattern God established when He created the world, and it is still used all around the globe today. God worked for six days; on the seventh day He rested. Seasons and calendars are based on calculations of the sun, moon, and orbit of the earth. But not the seven-day week—it was established by God.

Rest

Genesis 2:3 says, "Then God blessed the seventh day and sanctified it, because in it He rested from all His work which God had created and made." God made the seventh day sacred, or set it apart as special. It is a day for people to rest from their work and gather together to worship God. In the Ten Commandments, the Israelites were instructed to take a Sabbath rest each week, which began at sundown on Friday. After Jesus died and rose from the grave on a Sunday, early Christians began to gather on Sunday to worship, which is why most churches gather on that day.

History

Some people say Genesis is a legend, myth, fairy tale, or a beautiful form of poetry. But what does the Bible say? Genesis 2:4 claims, "This is the history of the heavens and the earth when they were created, in the day that the LORD God made the earth and the heavens." The Bible claims Genesis is the true history about how the universe began. We can believe what the Bible says.

A Choice and Decision

Read Genesis 1 to children. They take it literally and believe what it says. The Bible tells us to have the faith of a child. You can choose to believe what God has recorded in Scripture—that God created the whole world during the week of creation, about 6,000 years ago, just as the Bible says. At the same time, our faith is also based on facts. Dig into the chronological history of the world like Isaac Newton, Johannes Kepler, and James Ussher did. Study the science like creationists do today. Examine the discoveries unearthed by archaeologists. You will find plenty of exciting facts on which to build your faith!

♦ Israelite Pottery from the Kingdom of Judah. Impressed with the phrase **lmlk**—meaning "belonging to the king"—royal storage jars were used to collect taxes, hand out military rations, or help the kingdom in times of war. Archaeologists can study this pottery and other evidence to learn how the average person prepared and stored food.

Very Good

During the week of creation, God created the universe, animals, people, and the scientific laws of the universe. During this time, He also created key principles and established sacred institutions (like marriage) that are foundations for human society. Because God established these foundations for human life, we must be very careful to honor and respect His holy ways.

Gender

When God created humans in His image, He created two genders: "male and female He created them" (Gen. 1:27). God blessed them and saw that all that He created was "very good" (Gen. 1:31).

Marriage

God created marriage as a holy covenant (a serious promise intended to last forever) between a man and a woman. God created Adam and Eve and brought them together. With God at the center, marriages can flourish and grow.

Family

On the sixth day of creation, God blessed Adam and Eve and said to them, "Be fruitful and multiply" (Gen. 1:28). Throughout the Bible, many verses declare that children are a blessing from the Lord. The family is the building block of human society.

Sanctity of Life

Genesis 1:26-31 clearly shows how God made humans distinctly different than animals. He made people in His image. This gives great value to every single person—born and unborn, young and old. Every human is precious in the sight of God.

God of Science, God of Miracles

During the week of creation, God created the laws of science. Our all-powerful God also does miracles that work outside these scientific laws. During His ministry, Jesus performed miracles to show that He is God. God still does miracles today—healing broken hearts, providing a way to know Him personally (through Jesus), and giving hope where there was no hope. One day, God will do a great miracle and create a new heaven and a new earth. He wants you to be there to spend forever with Him!

Evolution teaches that people evolved from animals. The Bible, however, teaches that people are made in God's image and with a body, soul, and spirit. In 1 Thessalonians 5:23, Paul wrote, ". . . may your whole spirit, soul, and body be preserved blameless at the coming of our Lord Jesus Christ." Unlike animals, people can choose right from wrong, trust in the Bible, and worship their Creator.

A partial *Australopithecus afarensis* fossil nicknamed Lucy was discovered in Ethiopia in 1974. It is considered by evolutionists to be the "missing link" between primates and human beings. Some scientists mistakenly claim she walked on two feet because of the human-like fossil footprints discovered several years after and 1,000 miles away from Lucy's discovery. However, the bones are mostly small fragments with many pieces missing, including the majority of her skull. The Creation Museum in Kentucky opened a high-tech holographic exhibit that debunked the idea that Lucy was an ancestor of humans. This exhibit gave a conclusive presentation that showed Lucy's bones belonged to an ape-like creature, not a human.

The Value of Life

Does human life have value? If people evolved from ape-like creatures that evolved from ancient organisms, it's easy to not value life. If human life is not sacred, abortion (taking the life of an unborn baby) would be okay because it's just a group of cells.

On the other hand, if people can trace their DNA back to Adam and Eve, who were made in the image of God, then all life holds great value. Each unborn baby is created in God's image in its earliest stage in its mother's womb. Elderly people, people with special needs, and people of every tribe and race and nation all have value because we are all made in the image of God.

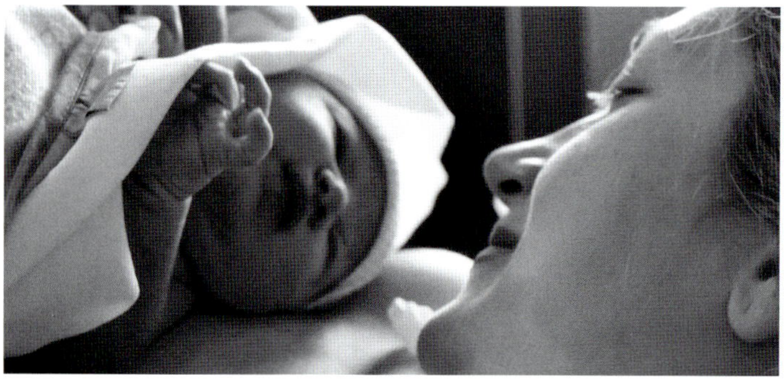

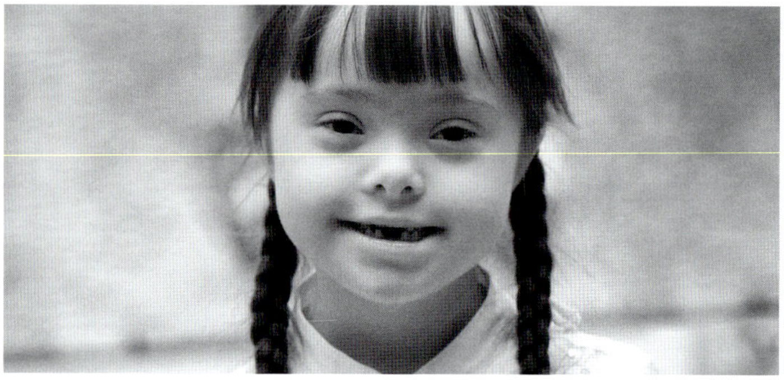

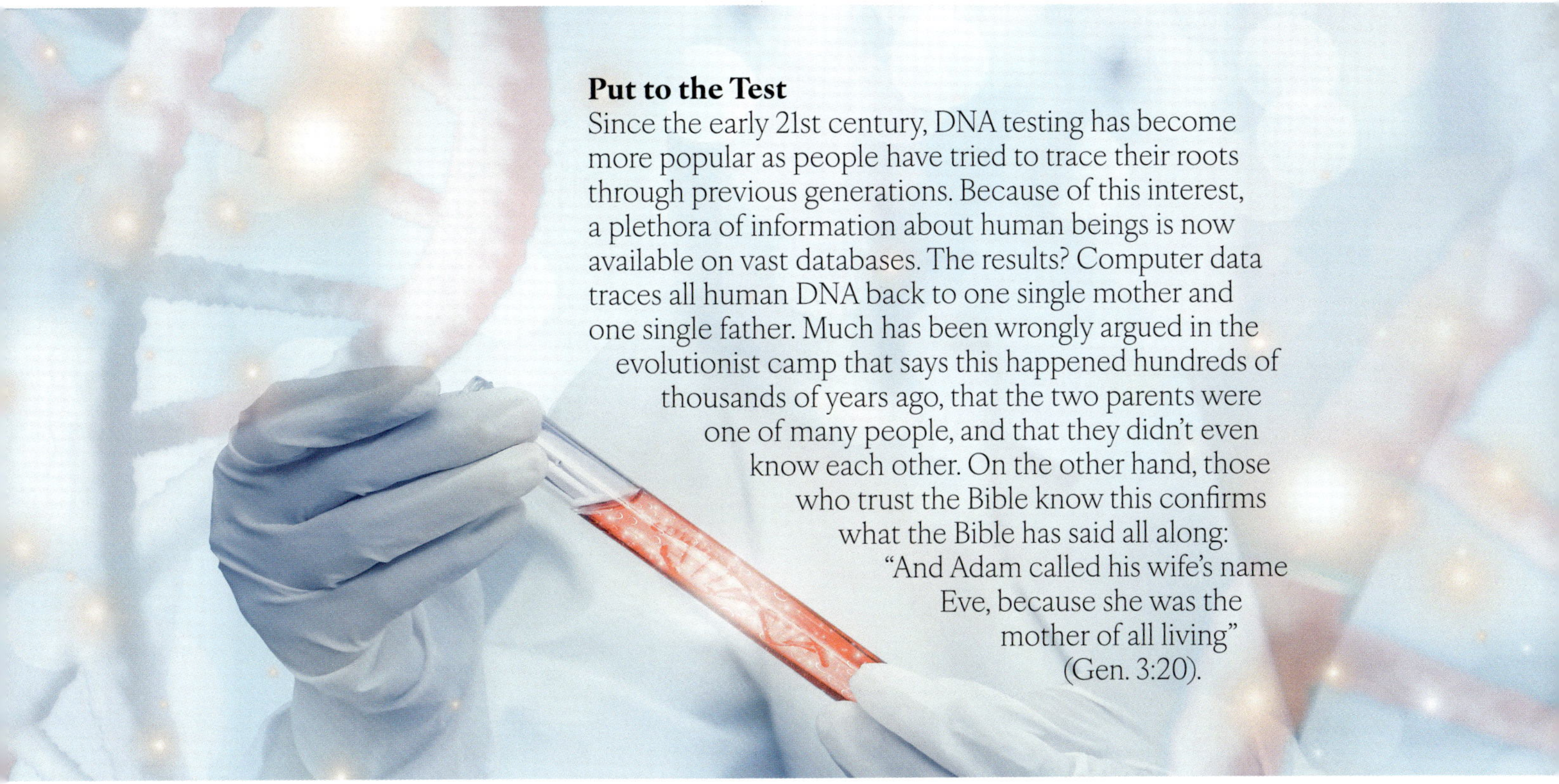

Put to the Test

Since the early 21st century, DNA testing has become more popular as people have tried to trace their roots through previous generations. Because of this interest, a plethora of information about human beings is now available on vast databases. The results? Computer data traces all human DNA back to one single mother and one single father. Much has been wrongly argued in the evolutionist camp that says this happened hundreds of thousands of years ago, that the two parents were one of many people, and that they didn't even know each other. On the other hand, those who trust the Bible know this confirms what the Bible has said all along: "And Adam called his wife's name Eve, because she was the mother of all living" (Gen. 3:20).

The Myth Mistake

Many people, including well-meaning Christians, think the story of Adam and Eve is one of many myths or moral tales in the Bible. If the first humans never actually existed and walked in the Garden of Eden, then their encounter with Satan never took place. Consequently, the Fall would be a make-believe fairy tale with a moral message. If the downfall of humans did not take place, then God's prophecy in Genesis 3:15 regarding a future Savior who would defeat the devil was never fulfilled. If this were true, Jesus did not need offer His life to redeem humanity.

The Truth About Adam and Eve

The Bible says God created Adam and Eve. If this is true (which many Christians believe), then the encounter with Satan in the Garden of Eden really happened. Sin and death entered a perfect world, and God announced the promise of a Savior (Gen. 3:15). Jesus came, died on the Cross to pay the penalty for our sins, and rose again to offer eternal life to everyone who trusts in Him. It matters what people believe about Adam and Eve. It affects what they think about the Bible, sin, salvation, and Jesus Christ.

The Bible tells us heaven is glorious! It is perfect. It is good. It is a wonderful place. There is no sorrow, no suffering, and no sin. The Bible also tells us when God created the earth, it was glorious. At the end of the six days of creation, God saw it was "very good" (Gen. 1:31). There was no sorrow, no suffering, and no sin. It was a perfect world. It was like heaven on earth.

Death Entered the World

God planted the Garden of Eden and put Adam and Eve in it as their home. God was very generous! He said they could eat the fruit of every tree in the Garden, except one: "[B]ut of the tree of the knowledge of good and evil you shall not eat, for in the day that you eat of it you shall surely die" (Gen. 2:17). Satan tempted Eve to question and distrust what God said. She ate the fruit of the forbidden tree and invited Adam to do the same. The result of their sin? Death entered the world. This event is commonly known as "the Fall."

The LORD God planted a garden eastward in Eden, and there He put the man whom He had formed. And out of the ground the LORD God made every tree grow that is pleasant to the sight and good for food. The tree of life was also in the midst of the garden, and the tree of the knowledge of good and evil . . .

Then the LORD God took the man and put him in the garden of Eden to tend and keep it. And the LORD God commanded the man, saying, "Of every tree of the garden you may freely eat; but of the tree of the knowledge of good and evil you shall not eat, for in the day that you eat of it you shall surely die."

—Genesis 2:8–9, 15–17

Robots or Humans

God wanted a relationship with each person who would ever live on the earth, but He wanted people to love Him freely. So, God gave human beings the freedom to choose whether to follow His ways. Otherwise, humans would be like robots that act according to their programming.

Consequences

God meant what He said about eating of the fruit from the forbidden tree. With Adam and Eve's disobedience, death entered the world. As with every act of disobedience, there were consequences for the first couple. God sent Adam and Eve away from the Garden. Eve would experience pain and sorrow, specifically in childbirth. Adam would work much harder for his food and contend with weeds (like thorns). God told Satan that a descendant of Eve (Jesus) would conquer death and evil forever.

Relationship

The Fall isn't just about sin. It's about a broken relationship between people and our Creator. As a fulfillment of the promise God made in Genesis, Jesus came to restore this relationship. Through knowing Jesus as Lord and Savior, each person can know the Creator of the universe as their closest friend. To everyone who turns to Jesus, He promises abundant life now and eternal life to come.

Old or Young Earth?

What does the Fall have to do with evolution? People who believe in an old earth (billions of years old) also believe that fossils show records of death long before people existed. Yet, both the Old and New Testaments explain that death didn't enter the world until Adam and Eve sinned. Romans 5:12 says, "Therefore, just as through one man sin entered the world, and death through sin, and thus death spread to all men, because all sinned."

The Fossil Message

Instead of pointing to millions of years of death and decay before the Fall, a significant number of fossils show records of a catastrophic event that quickly killed animals all around the globe. In other words, many fossils support what the Bible says about a young earth and the Flood, not the scientists' theories regarding evolution.

GOD'S PERFECT PLAN

Despite humanity's sin, God—in His great love, wisdom, and mercy—set into place an exciting plan. God promised to send Jesus, the Savior of the world. When He arrived, He conquered sin and death forever!

Moral Right vs. Moral Wrong

Category	Moral Right	Moral Wrong	Verse(s)
Obedience to God	Seeking to live by God's commands, living a life of faith	Willful rebellion, rejecting truth	Proverbs 1:7
Honesty	Telling the truth, being transparent	Lying, deceiving, hiding the truth	Proverbs 12:22
Respect for Others	Treating others with kindness and dignity	Bullying, discrimination, cruelty	Proverbs 11:17
Making Decisions	Trusting God and relying on His wisdom	Relying on your own knowledge and wisdom	Proverbs 3:5–6
Compassion	Helping those in need, showing empathy	Ignoring suffering, acting selfishly	Proverbs 19:17
Justice	Being fair, seeking what is right	Favoritism, cheating, injustice	Proverbs 29:7
Generosity	Sharing, giving freely	Greed, hoarding, selfishness	Proverbs 11:24–25
Forgiveness	Letting go of anger, offering second chances	Holding grudges, seeking revenge	Proverbs 17:9
Integrity	Doing what's right even when no one is watching	Hypocrisy, compromising values	Proverbs 11:3
Stewardship	Caring for your possessions, honoring God with your money	Wastefulness, neglect	Proverbs 3:9–10

Time and time again, evidence shows that we can trust the Bible. Archaeological finds, scientific research, and other data support what the Bible claims. Yet, trusting the Bible as the foundation for topics such as history, science, and morality is also a choice. It is a both a decision and faith — a faith founded on facts.

Ancient History

The Bible gives details about the history of the earth from the very first day it was created. Nowhere does Scripture speak of "prehistoric man." Evolutionists use this term to refer to the millions of years people supposedly existed before written records. The Bible give details we can trust about people and the world from the very first day of history.

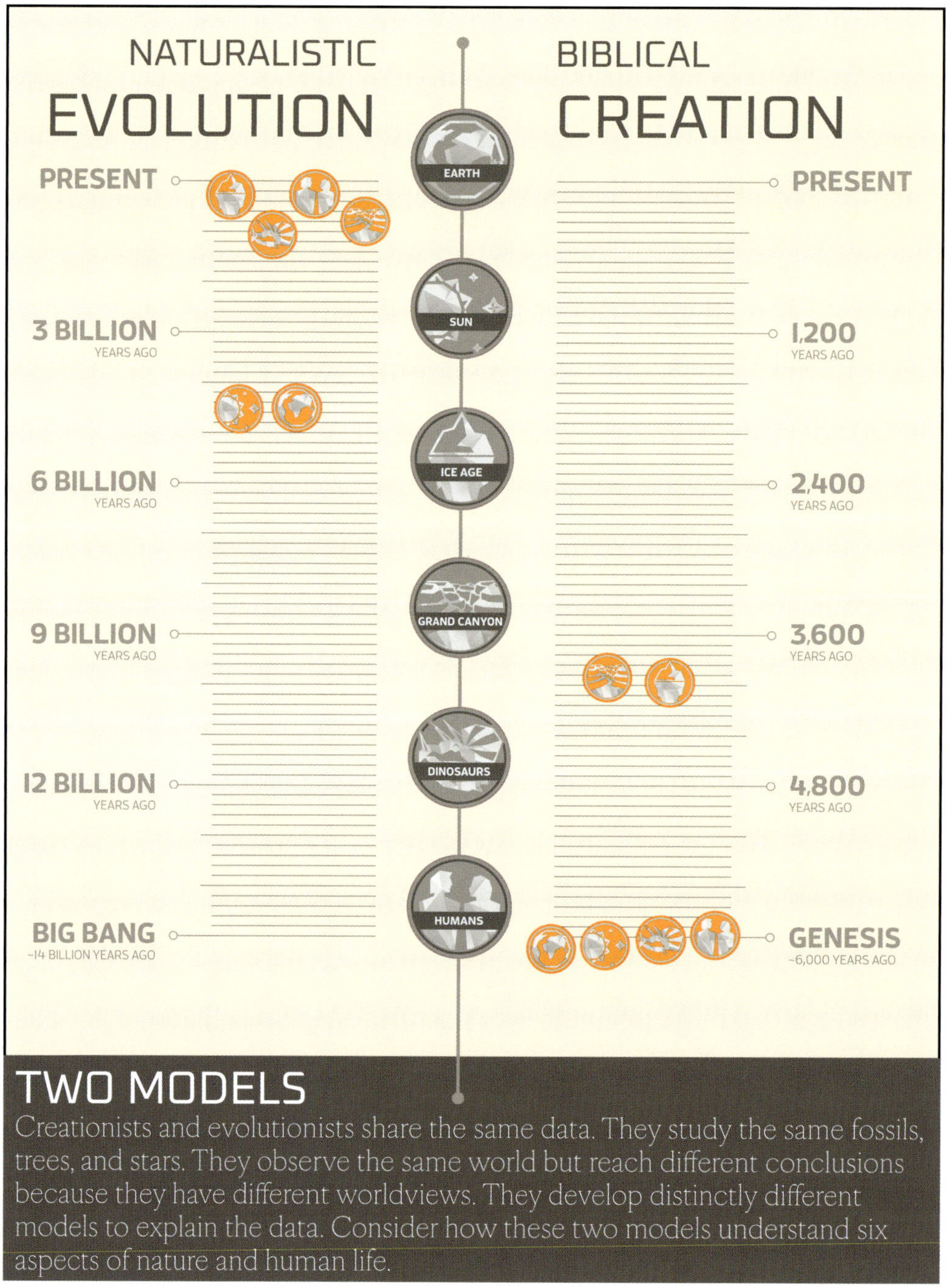

TWO MODELS

Creationists and evolutionists share the same data. They study the same fossils, trees, and stars. They observe the same world but reach different conclusions because they have different worldviews. They develop distinctly different models to explain the data. Consider how these two models understand six aspects of nature and human life.

- EARTH
- SUN
- ICE AGE
- GRAND CANYON
- DINOSAURS
- HUMANS

Effects of Atheism

What will you find in most museums or popular textbooks and encyclopedias? "Prehistoric" displays. Objects "millions of years" old. "Examples" of evolution. Dig deeper, however, and you will discover much of it is based on estimated theories and faulty assumptions. This is one effect of atheism, which denies God's existence and dismisses the Bible as not being trustworthy. Much is done under the name of so-called "science" that causes people to doubt God's Word.

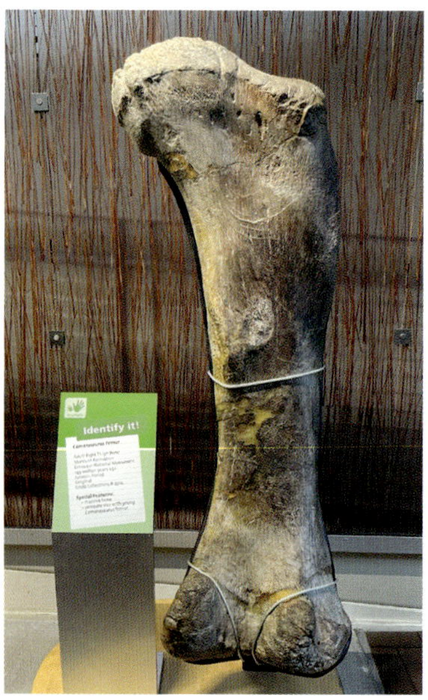

Sign on a *Camarasaurus* femur mistakenly dating the bone's age as 149 million years old.

Doubt and Deception

The Bible says that Satan met Eve in the Garden of Eden and tempted her to doubt God's Word. He asked her, "Has God indeed said . . . ?" (Gen. 3:1) Today, Satan still tempts people to doubt God's Word, especially in reading the Book of Genesis. Satan asks, Did God *really* create the world and everything in it in six days? Did God *really* create people in His image, fully intelligent from the beginning? Does God *really* exist? Yes! God exists, His words are recorded in the Bible, and the Bible can be trusted.

Caveman or Ancient Man?

Throughout history, people have lived in caves. This does not mean they were apes on the evolutionary road to becoming humans.

Many people in Bible times lived in caves: Lot and his daughters, David and his men, Elijah in a cave. They were not ape-like cavemen, but rather people in ancient history. Consider hidden tribes who live deep in the Amazon jungle or the history of Aboriginal people in Australia. Their exposure to culture, technology, and literature has been limited. That doesn't make them ape-like. They are fully human with a body, soul, and spirit.

Scientists Versus Scientists

Scientists who believe in evolution come to different conclusions than scientists who believe in a literal reading of the Bible. There are top scientists in both camps. How can they differ so widely? One group interprets data based on the assumption of evolution. The other looks at information in light of what the Bible says. Which viewpoints will you choose to accept? Those of scientists who are more popular and highly published and who claim their viewpoint as "fact" (not theory)? Or the findings of scientists who believe in the authority of the Bible and claim their research supports what it says?

A Mature Universe

God created a mature universe, meaning He created it fully formed. God made two adults who could have children. He made trees with ripe fruit so they could reproduce. He placed stars at extreme distances in space that could already be seen from the earth. Even though the earth is young, with an age of about 6,000 years, God made it fully developed as we see it today. It did not come together over millions or billions of years.

The Bible provides details about a worldwide flood. It also gives key information about what happened in the time between creation and the Flood. Let's take a closer look at what Scripture says about this important period in history.

The First Farmer

After the Fall, Adam became the first farmer. Genesis 3:17-19 says, "Then to Adam [God] said, 'Because you have heeded the voice of your wife, and have eaten from the tree of which I commanded you, saying, "You shall not eat of it"': Cursed is the ground for your sake; in toil you shall eat of it all the days of your life. Both thorns and thistles it shall bring forth for you, and you shall eat the herb of the field. In the sweat of your face you shall eat bread, till you return to the ground, for out of it you were taken; for dust you are, and to dust you shall return.'"

True or False?

Evolution claims that the earliest people were too primitive to plant seeds, grow crops, or harvest them for food. The Bible, however, says God made people in His image. That means people were intelligent, beginning with Adam and Eve.

♦ Quartzite stones used as weapons and for hunting animals

♦ Ancient tool

♦ Stone kitchen tool

♦ Hand axe

♦ Sumerian harvester's sickle, made of baked clay

♦ Stone axe

Hunters and Gatherers

Clues from the past show that some ancient civilizations lived as hunters and gatherers, and some lived as farmers. Evolutionary theories claim that the earliest form of humans were hunters and gatherers who didn't discover farming until around 10,000 B.C. Yet, according to the chronology of genealogies in the Bible, God created the earth and everything in it around 4004 B.C. The Bible tells us that Adam was a farmer.

Shepherds and Flocks

Genesis 4:2b says, "Now Abel was a keeper of sheep, but Cain was a tiller of the ground." Cain and Abel were Adam and Eve's oldest sons. The first family on earth farmed and raised flocks of sheep. Yet, evolutionists claim that it took thousands and thousands of years for people to evolve enough to keep flocks. People who believe the historic account in the Bible know that the earliest humans were shepherds, just as the Bible says.

Smart from the Start

Evolution teaches that people evolved from cells into organisms, which morphed into creatures with backbones, then later into four-legged creatures, then to mammals and apes, and finally into humans. Evolutionists divide history into different ages such as the Stone Age, Bronze Age, and Iron Age. They claim that humans progressed from using stone tools to working with metals, from living in caves to building cities, and from hunting and gathering to farming. One problem with these "ages" is that they disagree with the Bible. Scripture teaches that God made people in His image, smart from the start.

Villages & cities

And he built a city, and called the name of the city after the name of his son—Enoch. –Genesis 4:17b

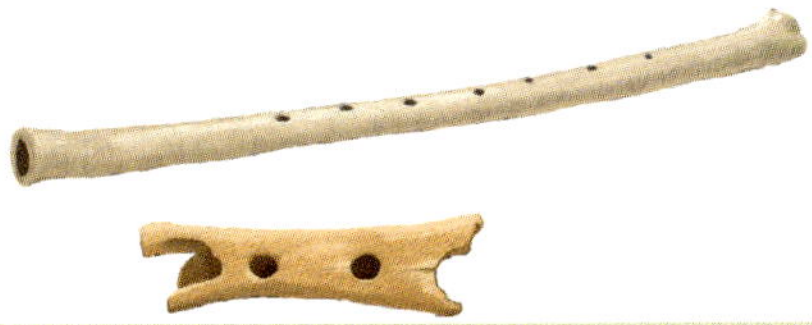

Musical instruments

His brother's name was Jubal. He was the father of all those who play the harp and flute. –Genesis 4:21

Bronze & iron tools

And as for Zillah, she also bore Tubal-Cain, an instructor of every craftsman in bronze and iron.–Genesis 4:22a

Cities

According to the evolutionary timeline, it took humans thousands and thousands of years to discover farming and then start living together in villages or cities. Yet Genesis 4:17 says that Cain (Adam and Eve's son) built the city of Enoch. The earliest people on earth were intelligent enough to build cities.

Creative at Heart

Cain's descendant Jubal was the "father of all those who play the harp and flute" (Gen. 4:21). Music, art, and creativity are other signs of intelligence that reflect the image of God. The Bible indicates that people were creative long before the Flood.

Working with Metal

Ancient people learned how to work with metal before the Flood (Gen. 4:22). The evolutionary timeline places the Bronze Age starting at around 2300 B.C. and the Iron Age around 700 B.C. The Bible says bronze and iron were in use before 2348 B.C., when the Flood occurred.

Questions and Answers

It's normal to have questions about the past. Non-Christian scientists and evolutionists have used archaeological findings to form theories to support their belief in evolution. When creation scientists examine the same evidence, such as artifacts of cave-dwellers, hunting-gathering, and farming, they conclude something different—that these findings could point to families and cultures using the resources and limitations of their living conditions to survive. Each piece of evidence doesn't need to be divided into separate ages spread across hundreds of thousands of years. For example, in recorded history, the vikings of Greenland farmed the land. Yet, when the Inuit arrived later and took over Greenland, they continued their own tradition as hunters and gatherers rather than adapt to planting or harvesting crops. This has happened in other settings around the world as well. This evidence doesn't match evolutionary theories. Yet, it fits the accounts of history described in the Bible.

Dinosaurs are awesome! They're enormous. The ground shook and thundered as they ran. The Bible says that on the sixth day, ". . . God made the beast of the earth according to its kind, cattle according to its kind, and everything that creeps on the earth according to its kind" (Gen. 1:25a). God made every kind of land animal in the world, including dinosaurs!

Mysteries of the Past

Scientists, archaeologists, and paleontologists (people who study fossils) are like detectives. To piece together what happened in the past, they look for clues in rock layers, fossils, and ancient bones dug up from the ground. Creation scientists start their search with clues found in Scripture. What do they find? The Bible says that animals and people were created on the very same day. Dinosaurs, too!

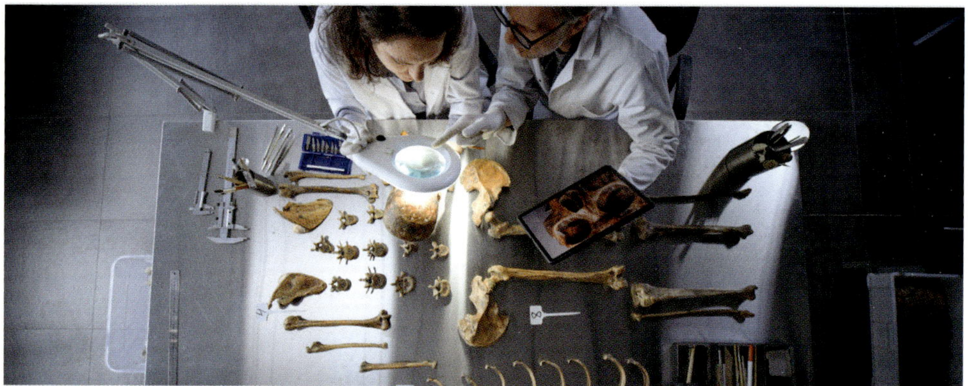

SECULAR WORLDVIEW:

A way of understanding and thinking about the world that focuses on what we can observe and learn through science. It does not include beliefs about God or the Bible as part of its explorations and explanations.

BIBLICAL WORLDVIEW:

Understands and sees the world based on Scripture. Such a person sees the Bible as authoritative, meaning it is the ultimate source of truth. He or she would study science, history, and culture with the Bible as the starting point.

Meet the Dinosaurs!

There are five main groups of dinosaurs.

Therapods were mostly meat eaters and included *T. rex*, the king of the dinosaurs.

Ornithopods such as *Iguanodon* didn't say "quack," even though they had mouths that looked like duckbills and left bird-like footprints.

Models and Theories for the Past

Scientists look at data from the past to build models and theories of how the world began. Evolution scientists interpret fossils based on theories that dinosaurs lived millions of years ago and became extinct long before ape-like creatures evolved into humans. Creation scientists use the evidence found in Scripture to interpret fossils with theories and models that support what the Bible says. Scripture tells us that death entered the world when Adam and Eve sinned. This means that every fossil in the world came after this first sin because fossils are evidence of death.

Where's the Evidence?

Did dinosaurs evolve from birds and reptiles that had evolved from other, less complex creatures? That is what evolution scientists claim. They point to "transitional" fossils as their evidence. "Transitional" fossils, according to evolutionists, show traits of two different groups of animals, such as a fossil that has the body of a fish but leg-like fins to walk on land. There are problems with this theory. First, if these "transitional" fossils are evidence of changes over time, why haven't more of them been uncovered? Second, these "transitional" fossils are fully-formed creatures with variations (such as wide varieties of dogs). The evolutionist theory of "transitional" fossils is often presented as fact in textbooks, encyclopedias, and museums. However, when creation scientists study the same fossils, they can show how they support what the Bible says. The difference isn't in the evidence. The difference is in interpreting the evidence, which is based on a scientist's worldview.

Carbon-14

Secular scientists use a process known as carbon dating to claim that fossils are millions of years old. Every living thing contains carbon, including a specific element—carbon-14 (C-14). When something or someone dies, it no longer takes in that carbon. Carbon dating tries to determine the age of a once-living thing by the amount of C-14 it contains. However, there are limitations and inaccuracies in this process. For example, some dinosaur fossils still contain carbon-14 after thousands of years. Other dinosaur fossils contain soft tissue (fat, muscle, tendons, etc.), which would not exist in an artifact millions of years old. This evidence indicates that these dinosaur fossils are thousands, not millions, of years old (otherwise, the soft tissue would be gone). Discoveries such as these support a young earth of about 6,000 years old. Starting in the first week of creation, dinosaurs rumbled and roared across the land!

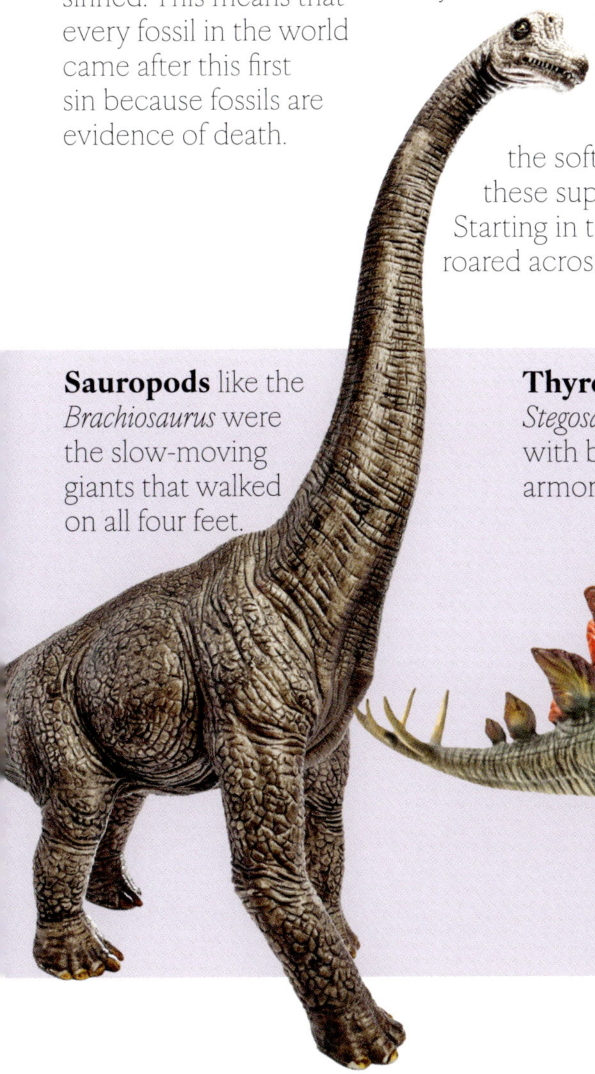

Sauropods like the *Brachiosaurus* were the slow-moving giants that walked on all four feet.

Thyreophora included the *Stegosaurus* and other dinosaurs with bony plates or spikes like armor along their backs.

Marginocephalia like the *Triceratops* had a frill at the back of their heads.

Fast hunters, these dinosaurs were mostly meat eaters. Their name, Therapod, means "beast footed." They walked and ran on their two back feet.

Megalosaurus

A giant fossilized jawbone was dug up from the ground in Oxfordshire, England. Did it belong to an extra-large lizard? An oversized elephant? It was one of the first dinosaur bones ever found and studied, but the word "dinosaur" had not yet been invented. Many people thought it belonged to a dragon! In 1824, it was given the name *Megalosaurus,* which means "great lizard." It was roughly 20-30 feet long and 8-10 feet tall at the hips. It weighed about one ton. Like sharks, the *Megalosaurus* could replace lost or broken teeth throughout its lifetime.

Oviraptor

An American paleontologist was digging around in Mongolia when he unearthed a small dinosaur fossil near a nest of fossilized dinosaur eggs. Roy Chapman Andrews' exciting new find was named *Oviraptor*, or "egg robber." At first, paleontologists thought the small dinosaur, about 6-8 feet long and 3-5 feet tall, was stealing another dinosaur's eggs, but other *Oviraptor* skeletons have been discovered sitting on their own nests.

Velociraptor

Darting in quick to snatch a meal, the *Velociraptor* was about 5-8 feet long and two feet tall at the hips. It could run about 24 miles per hour. Discovered in Mongolia, these predators were famous for the large claw on each of their back feet. Their small, sharp teeth curved backwards to hold their prey, such as small lizards. Its brain was large for an animal that size, so some scientists think the *Velociraptor* was probably one of the smarter dinosaurs. They probably hunted in packs like modern-day wolves or lions.

Allosaurus

Allosaurus

Weighing in at nearly two tons, the *Allosaurus* was 10-12 feet tall at the hips and 28-32 feet long from head to tail. It was smaller than its more famous relative, *Tyrannosaurus rex*. Buried in the Flood, a nearly complete *Allosaurus* skeleton was discovered in Wyoming in 1991. Nicknamed Big Al, it was put on display at the Museum of the Rockies. However, Utah named the *Allosaurus* as its state fossil because more *Allosaurus* bones have been found in Utah than any other place on earth. Paleontologists have also unearthed specimens in Montana, Colorado, Germany, and Tanzania (Africa).

Tyrannosaurus Rex

Tyrannosaurus means "tyrant lizard." Rex means "king." The *Tyrannosaurus rex* is known as the king of the dinosaurs for good reason! *T. rex,* as it is nicknamed, stood about 12-13 feet tall at the hips, over 40 feet long, and weighed 6-9 tons. The most famous *T. rex* fossil was dug up in South Dakota. It was named Sue after Sue Hendrickson, who discovered it. Its skull alone weighed 600 pounds! Evolutionists mistakenly claimed its brain was as small as a bird's, but research shows it was larger. Most likely, it thought and acted like an overgrown alligator. Different than an alligator, though, was the bite of the *T. rex*—it would have been strong enough to crush a car!

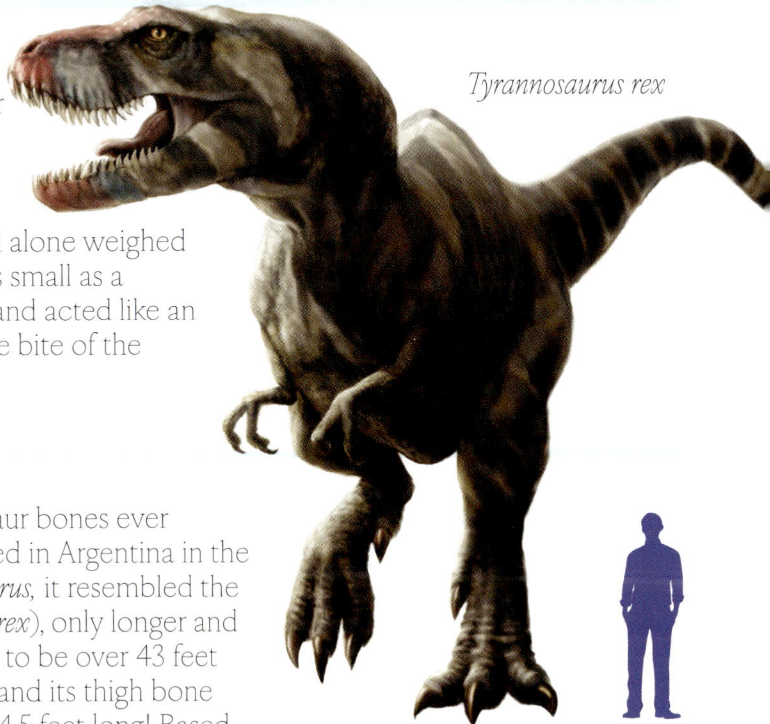

Tyrannosaurus rex

Giganotosaurus

Giganotosaurus

Some of the largest dinosaur bones ever uncovered were discovered in Argentina in the 1990s. Named *Giganotosaurus,* it resembled the king of the dinosaurs (*T. rex*), only longer and lighter. It was estimated to be over 43 feet long from nose to tail, and its thigh bone alone was likely over 4.5 feet long! Based on jaw size, its bite was weaker than that of a *T. rex*..

Spinosaurus

The Largest Theropod?

Until the early 2000s, the *Giganotosaurus* was considered the largest theropod dinosaur. Since then, paleontologists have excavated the remains of the *Spinosaurus*, which was 46-59 feet long. It also sported a six-foot "sail back" along its spine. It is believed that the *Spinosaurus* males took care of their offspring.

SAUROPODS

Sauropods ("lizard-footed") were plant eaters that roamed the entire world. Fossils of these gentle giants have been discovered on all seven continents—even Antarctica! With their long tails and long necks, they looked like some sort of mash-up between an elephant and giraffe, only much bigger!

Diplodocus

Diplodocus

Starting with its big toe, a *Diplodocus* nicknamed Dippy was dug out of the dirt in Wyoming in 1899. This nearly complete skeleton was put on display in what is now Pittsburgh's Carnegie Museum of Natural History. Then, nearly every famous museum at the time wanted their own 84-foot, 16-ton Sauropod. Plaster copies of Dippy were shipped all over the world and assembled for display. Dinosaur fever had begun!

Apatosaurus

One of the biggest of these colossal dinosaurs lived in the western United States. Measuring over 75 feet long from nose to tail, the *Apatosaurus* ate leaves from trees like a giraffe. Some people call it a brontosaurus. With a 20-foot-long neck and a 30-foot-long tail, it stood 15-feet tall at its hips and weighed around 23 tons—that's 3-4 African elephants!

Apatosaurus

Meet Einstein

Found in a Wyoming quarry, the most complete *Apatosaurus* skeleton ever found was named Einstein. Unlike most, it even had its skull attached. Traveling to different parts of the world, Einstein has greeted excited visitors wherever he has been on display.

Cowboys . . . and Dinosaurs?

The American wild, wild West was even wilder than we thought! Of course, no cowboys ever held a shoot-out with a real live dinosaur, but many famous dinosaur skeletons have been dug up in America's western states, like the *Apatosaurus, Triceratops*, and *Tyrannosaurus rex*. When dinosaurs thundered across the land, the West must have been a very wild place indeed!

Stomach Stones

Plant-eating dinosaurs like the Sauropods probably swallowed pebbles and small stones along with their food. Called "gastroliths," these "stomach" stones stayed in their gizzard, or stomach pouch, and helped grind up the rough plants they ate. This process aided their digestion.

Brachiosaurus

Unlike most other Sauropods, the *Brachiosaurus* had longer front legs than its back legs. This helped it reach even higher among the treetops for its food. Its fossils have been found in both North America and Africa. This supports the idea of a single landmass—Pangea—that existed in the past. The Flood described in the Bible caused the rapid burial and fossilization of many creatures, including dinosaurs. The Flood likely triggered catastrophic plate tectonics, rapidly breaking apart the continents and forming the current arrangement of landmasses.

Brachiosaurus

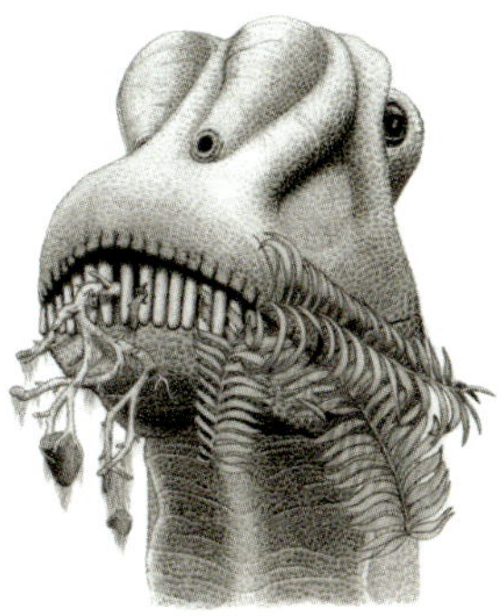

God's Amazing Design

Sauropods are an example of God's amazing design. Some scientists have pointed out that their skeletons were designed in an arch, enabling them to carry tremendous weight between the pillars of their legs. Different dinosaurs with similar characteristics have also been uncovered. These are variations of the same kind of dinosaur, just like there are different breeds of dogs.

Dinosaur hunters discovered gigantic footprints that looked like tracks from a bird. They were actually footprints belonging to plant-eating dinosaurs later named Ornithopods ("bird feet"). Some walked on their two back feet and some walked on all fours. Known as the "cattle of the dinosaurs", they were probably a favorite prey of the meat-eaters because they did not have any armor for protection.

Gryposaurus

Gryposaurus

Duck-billed dinosaurs like the *Gryposaurus* ("hook-nosed lizard") were well-known for their ginormous number of teeth—up to 800 and counting! Three hundred teeth lined their jaw, and 500 extra were ready to replace them (similar to a shark). With chompers like these, some people assumed they were meat-eaters. However, evidence of pine-needles and other tough plants found in the fossilized stomachs of the *Gryposaurus* indicate they were vegetarians.

Iguanodon

Famous for being the second dinosaur ever named, knowledge about *Iguanodon* has increased as more skeletons have been found. One of the larger Ornithopods, it weighed about three tons, stood about 6-feet tall at the hips, and was about 30 feet long. Its thumb on each hand ended in a spike., which could have been used to defend itself or to forage for food.

Iguanodon

Hadrosaurs

Nicknamed the "duck-billed" dinosaurs, these gentle plant-eating giants had a shorter lower jaw and flattened upper mouth that make it look like a duck's bill. They are divided into two groups. The Lambeosaurinae had large hollow crests on top of their heads, while the Hadrosaurinae (also known as Saurolophinae) either had solid crests or no crests at all. They generally ranged from 23-26 feet long and weighed 2-4 tons.

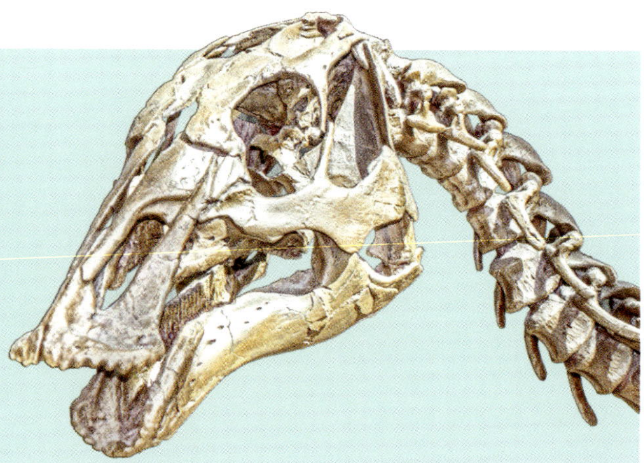

Brachylophosaurus

Brachylophosaurus

A dinosaur mummy? That's right! Paleontologists in Montana uncovered a duck-billed *Brachylophosaurus* nicknamed Leonardo. But unlike most fossils, Leonardo had somehow been preserved with its skin and internal organs (heart, lungs, and stomach). They remained long enough to turn to stone.

Here's more exciting news: A scientist named Mary Schweitzer discovered bone cells in the skeleton of a *Tyrannosaurus rex*. But how could bone cells survive if dinosaurs are millions of years old? Discoveries like these are perplexing for evolutionists, but not for scientists who believe the creation account in the Bible. Bone cells could survive thousands of years, not millions. This supports the chronology of events in the Bible and the Flood that rapidly buried dinosaurs like Leonardo and the *Tyrannosaurus rex*.

Edmontosaurus

The *Edmontosaurus* was one of the largest duck-billed hadrosaurs. They grew to be 42 feet long and stood 10 feet tall at the hips. Trying to crowd two adults of every kind of dinosaur on Noah's ark would have been nearly impossible. But meet Hannah and Eddie! Hannah is on display at the West Virginia Geological and Economic Survey Museum. She stands 8 feet tall and is 16 feet long. Eddie is even smaller, standing 5.5 feet tall and 10 feet long. He lives in the offices at the Institute for Creation Research in Dallas, Texas. He is thought to be only four years old. Juvenile or smaller dinosaurs like Hannah and Eddie could easily have fit onto Noah's ark next to the elephants and giraffes. They would have left the ark to grow up and repopulate like other animals.

Edmontosaurus

Parasaurolophus

Probably the best known of the duck-billed dinosaurs, the *Parasaurolophus* ("lizard crest") sported a long, distinctive head crest. Scientists have come up with different theories about its purpose because it was hollow. The crest might have been used to create sounds (like an elephant trumpeting), to communicate with others, or to control its body temperature. Found in North America, some fossils indicate that the *Parasaurolophus* might have had bumpy, scaly skin.

Parasaurolophus

MARGINOCEPHALIA

Thick skulls. Helmets. Horns and frills. The dinosaurs in this group had bony features on their head or behind their neck. Many even had beaked jaws that made their mouths look like parrot beaks.

Pachycephalosaurus

Skulls of *Pachycephalosaurus* ("thick-headed lizard") have been found up to 10-inches thick, giving these dinosaurs the nickname of "dome heads." Many have bony ridges along the back of the skull. Their diverse set of teeth allowed them to eat both leaves and seeds. First discovered in Montana, a full skeleton has yet to be found.

Pachycephalosaurus

Psittacosaurus

With a name that means "parrot reptile," the *Psittacosaurus* is one of the most famous of the beaked dinosaurs. Hundreds of its fossilized skeletons have been found in Mongolia, China, and Russia. Six inches long when they hatch, these dinosaurs measured 6 ½ feet long and two feet tall as adults. Their few teeth were used for grazing on plants, not for chewing, so they relied on gastroliths, or stomach stones, to help digest their food.

Psittacosaurus

Protoceratops

Protoceratops

Discovered in Mongolia in 1922, *Protoceratops* dinosaurs are known as the sheep of the dinosaur family because of their size. Weighing up to 400 pounds, they were about three feet tall and six feet long—about the same size as a sheep. A large frill (also called a bony shield) rose up at the back of its neck. Its large, parrot-like beak helped chomp off tough plants to eat.

Triceratops

A skull with three horns on its head was dug up in Colorado in 1887. Up to 30 feet long and 10 feet tall at the hip, this elephant-sized dinosaur also had a large frill at the back of its head and a beak to graze on plants. It was nicknamed "three horn face." Because its four legs were almost equal in size, scientists think the *Triceratops* could charge at its enemies to chase them away. Unlike many other dinosaurs, the bones of the *Triceratops* are usually found by themselves. This shows that they may have spent much of their lives alone.

Triceratops

Styracosaurus

Styracosaurus

This dinosaur looked like a big rhinoceros with one long horn on its nose. It also had six to eight long spikes attached to its neck frill. It could reach 30 feet in length and weigh around 12 tons. *Styracosaurus* was first found in 1913 in Alberta, Canada, in an area now known as Dinosaur Park Formation.

Dinosaur Digs

One of the most famous dinosaur graveyards was discovered in Alberta, Canada. Dinosaur hunters found so many skeletons in one spot that it was named Dinosaur Park Formation. It is part of Dinosaur Provincial Park, now designated as a UNESCO Heritage Site. *Styracosaurus, Ankylosaurus, Centrosaurus,* and even *Tyrannosaurus* skeletons have all been dug up there, many in good condition. The catastrophic waters of the Flood during Noah's day would have caused all these diverse fossils to be found together.

These plant-eating giants were the military tanks of the dinosaurs. Sporting armor and plates, they carried their protection around on their backs. Some *Thyreophorans* even had spikes or clubs on their tails, likely used to knock down a predator. These vegetarians had to protect themselves from meat-eaters hungry for a ginormous meal.

Ankylosaurus

Ankylosaurus

Like a turtle that carries its house on its back, the *Ankylosaurus* was covered by bony armor all over its tough-skinned back. The end of its tail looked like a heavy club. Its beak-like mouth was perfect for pulling leaves from bushes and low trees. Short but solid, it stood at only 5-6 feet tall but weighed a whopping five tons. That's the weight of a bulldozer or an ambulance!

Stegosaurus

A full-grown *Stegosaurus* stood 10-12 feet tall, grew up to 30 feet long, and weighed 3-5 tons. It had a double row of upright plates running down the middle of its back. The four spikes on the end of its tail have become known as the "thagomizer," first named in a cartoon. Each spike was about two feet long. When it swung its tail, it was like fighting with four swords at the same time. A *Stegosaurus* fossil was first found in Colorado around 1876. Ta Prohm, an ancient temple in Cambodia, contains carvings on its walls of different animals—including one that looked like a *Stegosaurus*! How did ancient people know what these dinosaurs looked like unless they were living alongside them at that time in that part of the world?

Stegosaurus

Pterodactyl

Pterodactyls can be found in almost any toy dinosaur set, but they are not considered dinosaurs. They are a type of pterosaur, a separate group of reptiles that lived alongside dinosaurs. They were huge reptiles that had wings and could fly. Like bats, a *Pterodactyl's* wings were made of flaps of skin that connected along their system of extra-long finger bones.

Pterodactyl

Dinosaur . . . or Not?

The word dinosaur (meaning "terrible lizard") isn't in the Bible because that word wasn't invented yet. Richard Owen was the first to use the term *Dinosauria* in a report in 1842. He defined dinosaurs as reptiles that walked upright on land like elephants instead of crawling on their bellies like crocodiles. Humongous ancient reptiles that had wings to fly or flippers and fins to swim (see below) are not classified as dinosaurs.

Plesiosaurus

Giants of the Sea

Huge reptiles with flippers or fins swam in the seas during the age of the dinosaurs. The *Plesiosaurus* is not classified as a dinosaur even though it looked like an underwater *Brontosaurus* with flippers. With their long necks, some grew over 40 feet long.

The *Ichthyosaurus,* or "fish lizard," is not considered a dinosaur either. It looked like a dolphin with a sharp, pointed snout. These underwater reptiles had lungs and had to swim to the surface to breathe.

Ichthyosaurus

Disobedience. Rebellion. Evil. It didn't take long after creation and the Fall for people's hearts to turn to wicked things. We don't know all the details, but we can be confident of one thing: As a loving, all-powerful, and wise Father, God always does what's best for His children. God decided to send a flood to wipe out the wickedness on the earth.

Meet Noah!

"But Noah found grace in the eyes of the LORD" (Gen. 6:8). God saw wickedness on the earth, but He also saw Noah. Even though Noah wasn't perfect, he honored God. Genesis 6:9b says, "Noah walked with God." God chose to save Noah and his family from the Flood.

Two by Two

To prepare for the Flood, God gave Noah clear instructions. God told Noah to build a large boat called an ark. God also told Noah to bring two of each kind of animal into the ark. Two by two, male and female, the animals and birds and creeping things entered the ark. For sacrifices after the Flood, God instructed Noah to bring along seven of certain animals and birds. Noah and his wife, and their three sons and their wives, also entered the ark.

A Global Event

How do we know this flood was global? Let's start with the Bible, a trustworthy account of ancient history. Genesis 7:19–21 says, "And the waters prevailed exceedingly on the earth, and all the high hills under the whole heaven were covered . . . and the mountains were covered. And all flesh died that moved on the earth: birds and cattle and beasts

and every creeping thing that creeps on the earth, and every man." After the waters of the Flood dried up, God declared, "Thus I establish My covenant with you: Never again shall all flesh be cut off by the waters of the flood; never again shall there be a flood to destroy the earth" (Gen. 9:11). "All high hills covered" and "all flesh died" means the Flood covered the entire world.

God's Rainbow

God told Noah, "I set My rainbow in the cloud, and it shall be for the sign of the covenant between Me and the earth" (Gen. 9:13). Why was this covenant important? This was God's promise that He would never again send a worldwide flood to punish people for their sins. Why not? Because God had a larger plan. He sent His Son to save us! Jesus took the punishment for sin so that all who repent and trust in Him will be saved. When you see a rainbow, remember God's promise. Sin is real, but so is God's forgiveness. And Jesus Christ is the Savior of the world!

Exciting Evidence

We can choose to believe Noah's ark and the worldwide Flood were actual historic events because the Bible says so. That's called faith. But exciting evidence shows our faith is founded on facts!

Mount St. Helens

First the earthquake. Then the avalanche. Then the blast! On May 18, 1980, Mount St. Helens erupted with the force of more than 20 megatons of TNT. This active volcano, located in the state of Washington, caused cataclysmic damage in a short period of time. A layer of peat quickly began forming. Two hundred geologic layers were deposited in three hours, and entire canyons were carved in months.

Dr. Steve Austin and other geologists studied the aftermath of the eruption. Eyewitness and scientific observations show that rock layers around the world could have formed quickly from a catastrophic event instead of slowly over millions of years. In other words, the evidence seen firsthand at Mount St. Helens supports belief in a young earth that experienced a worldwide flood.

The Grand Canyon

It is commonly accepted in mainstream geology that the Grand Canyon's layers were deposited over thousands and millions of years. However, the "Little Grand Canyon" of the Toutle River is a miniature model of the famous Grand Canyon, but it was only hours in the making. In 1982, another eruption of Mount St. Helens caused a large mudflow. This epic force quickly carved out the Little Grand Canyon . . . within 24 hours! Evidence such as this shows that rock layers in the Grand Canyon could have formed in a short time because of a cataclysmic event. The Bible tells us there was such an event—the Flood described in Genesis 6–9.

The ark Noah built was roughly 510 feet long, 85 feet wide, and 51 feet high. This floating zoo was the same size of a cargo ship today. With three decks, it had plenty of room for all the animals—including dinosaurs!

Starting Small

The biggest fossilized dinosaur eggs ever found were the size of footballs. That means these ancient giants started life relatively small. With eggs as small as footballs and a boat bigger than a football field, they could fit in the ark! Dinosaurs, elephants, giraffes, and other large land animal kinds could have entered the ark at a younger, smaller age to make room for the rest of the animals.

What About Fossils?

Fossils form under cataclysmic (disaster-creating) conditions. Instead of giving clues to the origins of the earth (as evolutionary scientists think), fossils are rock-solid evidence of a colossal flood. Most of the dinosaur and animal fossils found around the globe were animals that didn't board the ark. All those bones could have been trapped very quickly in different layers of rock, just as the eruption of the volcano at Mount St. Helens showed.

♦ A sauropod skull from the Dinosaur National Monument in Utah

Ark Encounter

Popular speaker and creationist Ken Ham is the CEO and founder of the Ark Encounter, which invites visitors to explore the science behind the Scriptures. The Ark Encounter exhibit in Kentucky includes a life-size replica of Noah's ark and an in-depth look at how it survived the Flood.

A New Beginning

The torrential rains stopped. The Flood waters dried up, soaked into the ground, formed rivers and lakes, and drained into oceans and seas. Noah's ark came to rest on the mountains of Ararat, located in ancient Mesopotamia (modern-day Iraq). After a year inside, Noah's family and the animals left the ark. God's instructions were clear: "Be fruitful and multiply, and fill the earth" (Gen. 9:1b).

Ancient Flood Stories

Many ancient cultures have flood stories. This makes sense. As Noah's descendants migrated around the globe, each generation told the next generation stories about the original historic event. Why are the stories so similar yet still so different? Over time, different cultures forgot some details and added others from their own traditions.

♦ Many Native American tribes have flood legends, including the Lakota.

Truth Detectives

With so many ancient flood stories, how do we know the Bible's account is correct? One way is to look for clues. For example, Hawaii's flood story tells of a great canoe with a house on it. It's doubtful if a canoe carrying that much weight would have survived in an epic storm. The Babylonian flood story, *The Epic of Gilgamesh,* describes a boat in the shape of a cube. That's not seaworthy at all! However, when scientists look at the descriptions of Noah's ark, they confirm that a boat of those dimensions could stay afloat on a storm-tossed sea and carry its cargo successfully.

The Flood was a violent and destructive event! Underwater volcanoes boiled the oceans with their scalding blasts. Earthquakes split open cracks and fissures. Landmasses lifted, shifted, and moved. After the Flood, conditions on the earth changed, creating the perfect environment for thick sheets of ice and glaciers to form. The Ice Age had begun.

In the six hundredth year of Noah's life, in the second month, the seventeenth day of the month, on that day all the fountains of the great deep were broken up, and the windows of heaven were opened. And the rain was on the earth forty days and forty nights.
—Genesis 7:11-12

FROZEN BLANKET
Research carried out by creation scientists provides data indicating that a single Ice Age occurred and lasted for hundreds of years after the Flood. Today, ice covers about 10 percent of the earth. During the Ice Age, glaciers and sheets of ice covered about 33 percent (or one third) of the planet.

What Is a Glacier?

How is a glacier different than deep snow? Sometimes snow piles up faster than it can melt. Then it gets compressed and turns into ice. When the compressed ice becomes heavy enough to start s-l-o-w-l-y sliding downhill, that ice is called a glacier.

Crater Glacier

Imagine watching a brand-new glacier grow from the very first snowflake! That's what observers have been doing at Mount St. Helens. When the volcano erupted in 1980, it created a deep horseshoe-shaped crater that faced north (making it shady and cooler). The epic force of the eruption melted the ice and snow. As the mountain settled again, heated rumblings underneath and frigid air above created the perfect conditions for a new glacier to form in the crater. Geologists are monitoring Crater Glacier, this fascinating new phenomenon growing at a surprising rate. It's the youngest glacier in the world!

Glacier Girl

In World War II, eight planes made emergency landings on Greenland. Crew members were rescued and survived. The planes were abandoned for 50 years, until an expedition in 1992 set off to recover one of the planes. To their shock, they found it buried under 250 feet of ice and snow that had accumulated over the years. Nicknamed Glacier Girl, the plane was restored and put to flight.

Same Data, Different Models

Evolutionary scientists and creation scientists often examine the same data, but they come to very different conclusions. Old-earth scientists formulate models that fit into their evolutionary theories. They claim that multiple ice ages took place. They say the first Ice Age started millions of years ago and the last one (called the Pleistocene) ended 11,700 years ago. Creation scientists, however, formulated young-earth models that support the details found in the Bible. They believe the Ice Age began after the Flood. Crater Glacier and Glacier Girl are exciting examples of how quickly glacial ice can form.

♦ Crater Glacier

Deep Ice Cores

Since the second half of the twentieth century, scientists have drilled deep ice cores in frigid areas of Peru, Greenland, and Antarctica. Creation researchers such as Larry Vardiman, Michael J. Oard, and Jake Hebert have examined the data gathered from these cores. Among other things, they evaluated the ratio of oxygen isotopes and the thickness of ice build-up in the different layers of the ice core. Their conclusions? The evidence they found supports the idea of an earth that is 6,000 years old. The evidence also shows a cataclysmic (violent and destructive) Flood and one Ice Age that lasted just hundreds, not thousands, of years.

Circular Reasoning

What do ice cores and seafloors have in common? Secular scientists come to the same conclusion for both research topics: evolution. These scientists have studied deep ice cores and samples from ocean floors. They conclude that the data from deep ice cores supports evolutionary data from the ocean floors. They also conclude that the data from the ocean floors proves the data from deep ice cores. This is an example of circular reasoning, when you try to prove something without outside evidence. Yet scholars who believe in evolution use this method with data from ice cores and cores from seafloors to claim the earth is about 4.5 billion years old.

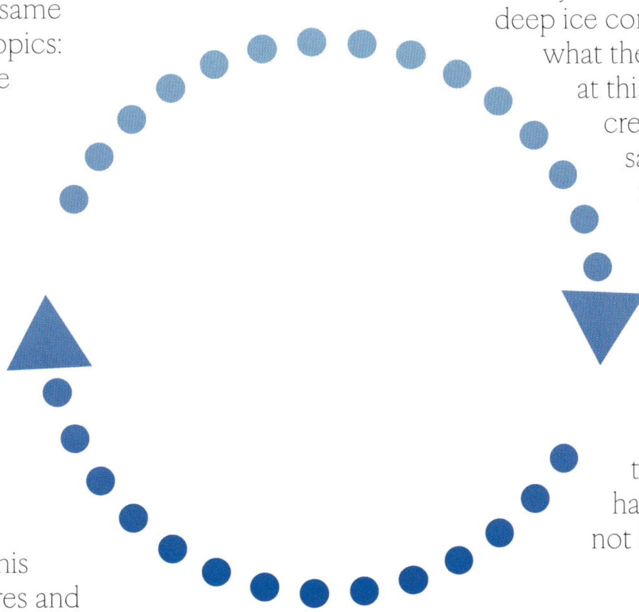

The Uniformitarian Model

Evolutionary scientists and old-earth scientists claim deep ice cores show the earth is older than what the Bible says. How do they arrive at this vastly different conclusion from creation scientists? They believe the same natural processes we observe today have been shaping the earth at similar rates throughout history. Evolutionists call this the Uniformitarian Model. Creation scientists disagree with this framework. They believe the Flood and the Ice Age created most of the fossils found today. They say these two events happened over hundreds of years, not millions, as evolutionists claim.

After Noah and his family left the ark, God gave them a command. Genesis 9:1 says, "So God blessed Noah and his sons, and said to them: 'Be fruitful and multiply, and fill the earth.'" This was the same command God had given Adam and Eve on the sixth day of creation.

♦ Noah's three sons: Shem, Ham, and Japheth

Where Was Shinar?

Noah's descendants quickly multiplied. The ark had settled down on the mountains of Ararat, located somewhere in ancient Mesopotamia. People began to move away from these mountains and scatter to various locations. As they traveled, they discovered a plain in the land of Shinar, around the estuaries of the Tigris and Euphrates Rivers in modern-day Iraq.

Noah's Descendants

Shem lived for about 500 years after the Flood. He was still alive when Isaac married Rebekah. Shem's descendants settled in Mesopotamia and also migrated toward Asia. Shem is the ancestor of the Semites and is listed in the genealogy of Jesus. **Ham** is the ancestor of the Canaanites. Many of his descendants moved farther south to Egypt and Africa. **Japheth's** descendants migrated around the Mediterranean Sea, into Europe, and north toward Russia.

Building a Tower

The Flood was a new beginning for humanity. God gave people a second chance to choose to follow Him, honor Him, and obey His commands. It didn't take long, however, for people to turn to wickedness and evil once again. At that time in history, everyone spoke the same language. The people living in Shinar (southern Iraq) came together and said, "Come, let us build ourselves a city, and a tower whose top is in the heavens; let us make a name for ourselves, lest we be scattered abroad over the face of the whole earth" (Gen. 11:4). God had told the people to multiply and fill the earth, but they decided to do the opposite and stay in one location!

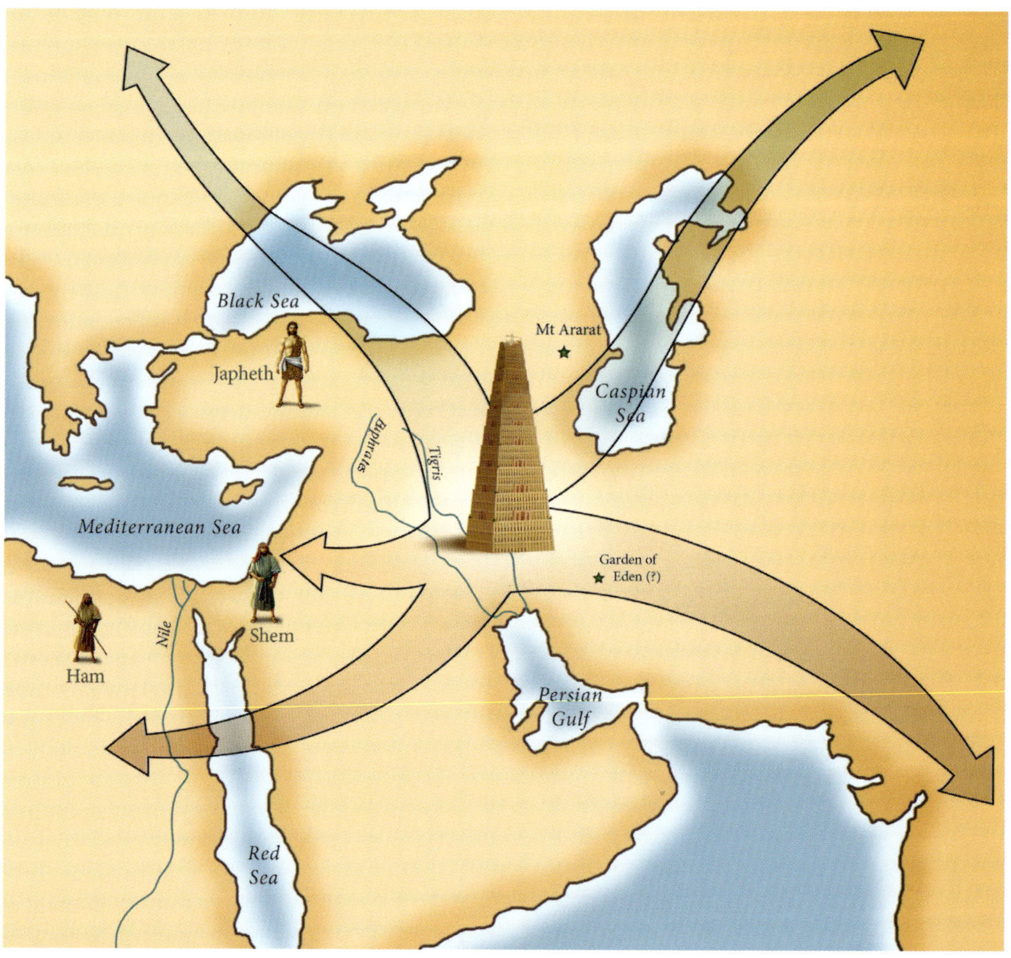

What Went Wrong?

Was constructing the Tower of Babel a sin? Why was God displeased by the people staying together to build a city? We don't know all the exact details, but we do know these descendants of Noah were disobedient and rebellious against God's command. First, God had told the people to fill the earth, which meant spreading out to different locations. Second, the people wanted to make a name for themselves instead of honoring and glorifying God. Third, many pyramids and towers built by ancient people groups were used to worship the sun, moon, and stars. Whatever the reasons, we know that God is a caring and loving Father who wants only the best for His children. His decisions and actions are always perfect and wise even if we don't understand them. In response to their rebellion, God confused the people by giving them many different languages, then scattered them abroad over the earth (Gen. 11:7-9).

♦ Ziggurat of Ur, in Iraq

♦ Giza pyramids in Cairo, Egypt

♦ Chichen Itza, Yucatán State, Mexico

♦ Cahokia Mounds, Illinois

Ancient Civilizations

The Tower of Babel was the first tower ever attempted to be built by a group in ancient history. As Noah's descendants moved away from Babel and spread around the earth, they took the memory of the Tower of Babel with them. Over successive generations, major civilizations settled across the globe and built towers reaching to the sky. People in ancient Mesopotamia (modern-day Iraq) built ziggurats. Egyptians built pyramids. Central and South American cultures built stepped pyramids of stone. The Mississippian culture in North America built earthen mounds.

Historic Event

Many historians believe the Tower of Babel was a true event that occurred around 2247-2242 B.C. They trust the Bible as a historic document, not full of myths or fairy tales. Because of archaeological discoveries, eyewitness reports, and the veracity of the biblical texts, many people accept what the Bible says as fact. Because the Bible is also a book of faith, people can choose to believe the Bible as part of their faith journey even if they don't look for evidence for its validity.

Noah lived for 350 years after the Flood. His family settled in Mesopotamia. After the Tower of Babel event, Noah's family spread out and populated the globe. At roughly the same time, the Ice Age was spreading across parts of the world.

Cavemen

Archaeologists have identified Neanderthals, ancient people who lived as hunters and gatherers. Many lived in caves because it was the best shelter they could find. Evolutionary scientists claim that cavemen and earlier people groups were less intelligent than people today and even label some fossils as "missing links" between apes and humans. However, the Bible says humans were made in the image of God and didn't evolve from apes. People who lived during the Ice Age are similar to people in different cultures of the world today, especially in Arctic regions. Research shows they used tools, kept warm with fire, played musical instruments, and buried their dead. As Noah's descendants multiplied, each new generation used the resources they found in the regions as they migrated to survive.

CAVE DWELLERS TODAY

♦ Triq l-Għerien in Mellieħa, Malta

♦ Inside a cave home

♦ A troglodyte house (built into rock) in La Roque-Gageac in Dordogne, France

Larger than Life

Big. Wooly. Ferocious. The animals left Noah's ark and migrated to the far corners of the planet. These animals quickly developed unique characteristics based on their location and food supplies. A significant number of animals living during the Ice Age were famous for their size. Beavers were eight feet long. Armadillos were as big as small cars. Giant sloths got their name for good reasons! Many Ice Age animals were also hairy, such as wooly mammoths and saber-toothed tigers. These astonishing creatures ruled the frozen lands.

♦ The Giant Beaver was about 8 feet long (snout to tail) and weighed 220 pounds.

Adaptations

Animals don't need thousands of years to adapt to their environment. For example, American bison grow thick, wooly fur on their backs when cold weather sets in. As soon as warm breezes blow in springtime, their coats drop off in great hairy globs. When God created animals, He programmed them with the ability to adapt. As animals left the ark, multiplied, and migrated during the Ice Age, they quickly adapted to the changes in environment they found in different regions of the world.

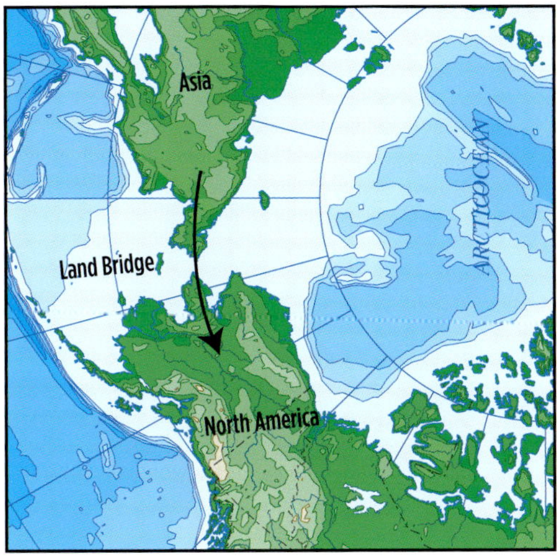

What About the Dinosaurs?

Just like other animals, the dinosaurs left the ark, multiplied, and traveled the globe. With so much ice covering the planet during the Ice Age, the water levels dropped and land bridges appeared instead. Along with wooly mammoths, saber-toothed tigers, and other Ice Age creatures, some dinosaurs crossed the Bering Land Bridge from Asia to the Americas.

North and South America

Hunters and their families followed the animals into North America and eventually into Central and South America. Creation scientist and meteorologist Michael J. Oard estimated that if Noah's descendants only walked two miles a day during the summer months, they could travel from the Tower of Babel to Siberia, across the Bering Land Bridge, and down to the tip of South America in just 60 years!

Mystery

By the end of the Ice Age, the unique animals of that time became extinct. How did this happen? The answer is a mystery. Theories suggest rapidly changing weather patterns or too much hunting, but no one knows for sure.

Questions and Answers

When creation scientists examine archaeological findings of cave-dwellers, hunter-gatherers, and early farmers, they interpret this evidence as proof of Noah's descendants spreading out and filling the earth as God commanded. Generations of people rapidly adapted to different environments and climates after the Flood and Tower of Babel events. These dispersed groups developed tools to survive based on where they lived, the availability of food, and the raw materials in their physical surroundings. Rather seeing the migration of humanity as proof of evolution, creationists believe this evidence reflects a biblical timeline of approximately 6,000 years.

There are seven continents, or huge masses of land, in the world. From smallest to largest, they are: Australia, Europe, Antarctica, South America, North America, Africa, and Asia. The ocean surrounds the continents. It is divided into five main regions. From smallest to largest they are: Arctic Ocean, Southern Ocean, Indian Ocean, Atlantic Ocean, and Pacific Ocean.

North America

North America lies between the **Atlantic** and **Pacific Oceans** with the **Arctic Ocean** on its northern border. Greenland, the world's largest island, is considered part of this continent. It also boasts the world's largest freshwater lake—Lake Superior. The world's largest gulf, the Gulf of America, is in the south. Mount McKinley (in Alaska) is North America's highest point, topping 20,310 feet above sea level. Death Valley in California is its lowest. The Missouri River is North America's longest river, edging out the Mississippi River by 100 miles. Some of the earliest cultures to emerge in North America developed an extensive trade network branching out from Poverty Point, Louisiana.

Asia

Asia is the largest continent in the world and it is the most populated continent, with 60% of the world's population living there. Its nearest islands are considered part of Asia, including Japan, the Philippines, and Indonesia. Israel and the other nations of the Middle East are considered part of Asia. It is bordered by the **Arctic Ocean** in the north, the **Pacific Ocean** in the east, the **Indian Ocean** to the south, and the Mediterranean Sea (part of it) to the west. This continent is home to Mount Everest, the tallest mountain peak in the world (29,032 feet above sea level), and the Dead Sea, the lowest place on earth (1,414 feet below sea level). This vast and varied landscape includes three of the earliest civilizations to emerge after the Tower of Babel: the Tigris-Euphrates Valley (Mesopotamia), the Indus River Valley (northwest India and Pakistan), and the Yellow River Valley (China).

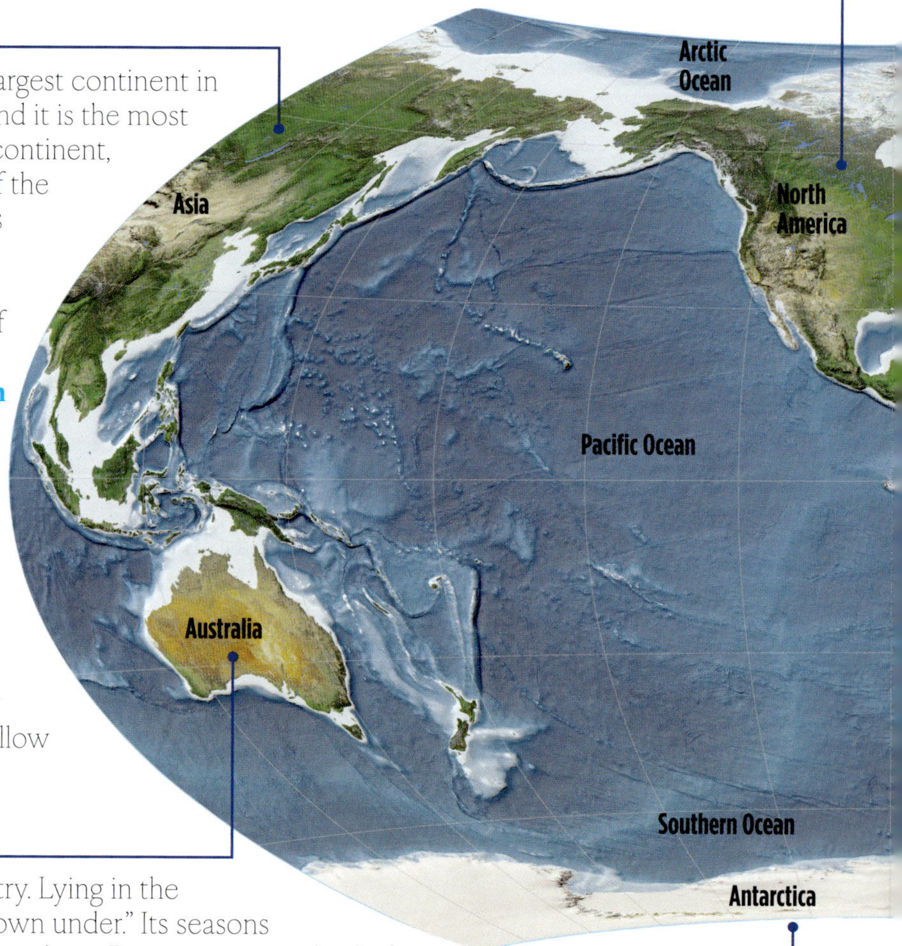

Australia

Australia is the only continent that is also a country. Lying in the Southern Hemisphere, it is known as the "land down under." Its seasons are opposite from countries in the Northern Hemisphere. Deserts cover a third of the continent. Mostly flat, Australia's main mountains are found in the east along the Great Dividing Range. The continent sits between the **Pacific** and **Indian Oceans**. The Great Barrier Reef, the largest group of coral reefs in the world, lies off its Pacific coast. The earliest people who settled Australia probably arrived from Asia by boat or over land bridges that appeared during the Ice Age..

Antarctica

Glaciers. Ice. Snow. Because of its position at the South Pole, Antarctica experiences total darkness for six months of the year. It is home to penguins, seals, terns, and swarms of tiny krill that attract giant whales to its icy waters. Jagged mountains and numerous volcanoes lie hidden under the snow and ice. This frozen continent and its nearby islands are surrounded by the **Southern Ocean**.

Europe

The continent of Europe is a massive peninsula, surrounded on three sides by water. The **Arctic Ocean** sits to its north, the **Atlantic Ocean** lies on its western border, and the Mediterranean Sea borders it to the south. Asia connects to Europe along its eastern border. The majestic Alps are the main mountains in Europe. One of the largest islands in the world, Great Britain, and many smaller islands are considered part of Europe. Known as the birthplace of Western civilization, the earliest civilizations to emerge in Europe include the Minoans and Mycenaeans, early ancestors of Ancient Greece.

Eurasia

The Ural Mountains stretch north to south, forming much of the boundary between Asia and Europe. Together, this large mass of Europe and Asia is also known as Eurasia. Europe and Asia are divided not only because of geological boundaries, but also because of the distinct cultural differences. Each area has its own unique languages, subculture, and history.

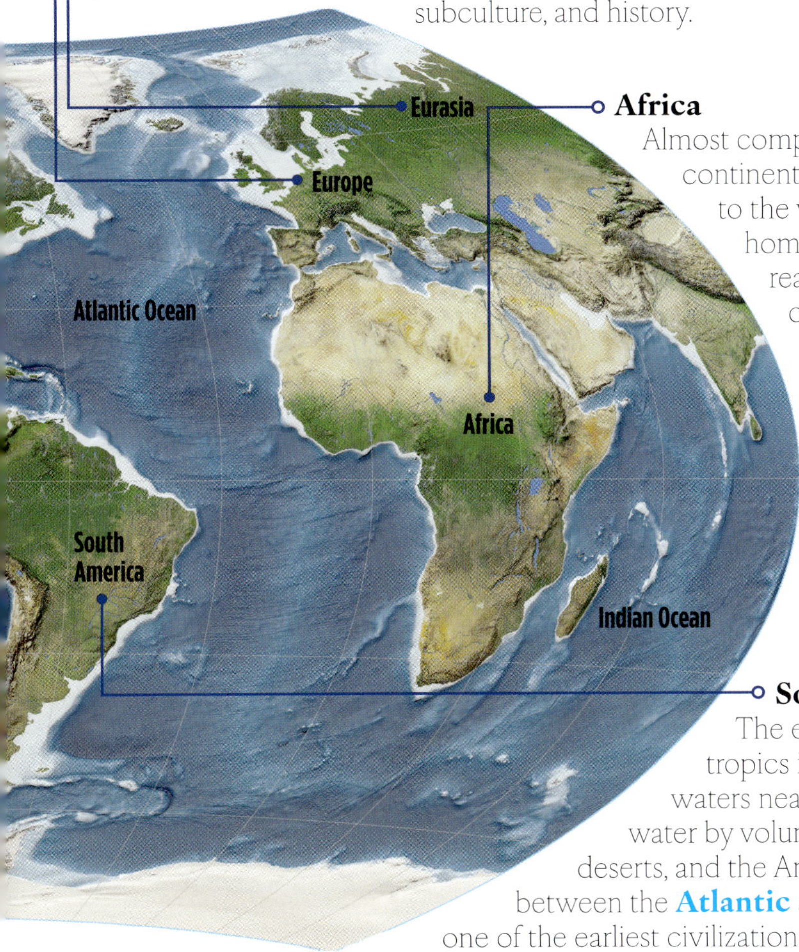

Africa

Almost completely surrounded by oceans and seas, most of the continent of Africa is a plateau, a flat and level land. Africa is home to the world's longest river, the Nile (4,132 miles long). It is also home to the world's largest hot desert, the Sahara, which reaches over 3.5 million square miles. That's about the size of the United States! It is also the second-most populous continent.

Africa contains rain forests, mountain ranges, and miles of beaches along its coasts. Sitting on the equator, the country is famous for its rich resources and grasslands teeming with exotic animals—elephants, lions, giraffes, rhinoceroses, and hippopotamuses. After the Tower of Babel, the earliest civilization was in Egypt along the Nile River.

South America

The equator passes through South America. From the warm tropics in the north, this continent stretches south to the frigid waters near Antarctica. Its major river, the Amazon, carries more water by volume than any other river on the planet. Rainforests, deserts, and the Andes Mountains can be found on this continent that lies between the **Atlantic** and **Pacific Oceans**. The Chavín culture in Peru was one of the earliest civilizations to develop in South America.

Evidence of a Great Flood

Archaeologists were investigating the Nippur library of ancient Mesopotamia (part of Iraq) when they found a large clay prism (four-sided tablet). Known as the Sumerian King List, this tablet registered the names of ancient kings before and after the Flood. Exciting discoveries like these support the Bible's account of a worldwide flood.

LIFE IN SUMER

c. 2300–2000 B.C.

Genesis 9:20a says that after the Flood, "And Noah began to be a farmer." As his descendants scattered out over the earth, some families farmed, some raised flocks and herds, and others lived as hunters and gatherers. Archaeologists have uncovered evidence of these ancient groups, including early civilizations in Mesopotamia, Egypt, India, and China.

Different Dates

The Bible is the trusted authority on ancient history. Genealogical dates given in the Bible start with creation in about 4004 B.C. The evolutionary timeline, however, is based on the belief that the first humans began to evolve millions of years earlier. That is why there are different dates for the same event in ancient history. Which date will you see? It usually depends on whether you are looking at an evolutionary timeline or a timeline based on the Bible's literal account of creation.

Different Names

The Old Testament was written in Hebrew. That's why the names of people and places are often different in the Bible than other books. For example, the Bible says that after the Flood, Noah's descendants settled in the land of Shinar. That is the Hebrew name for Sumer.

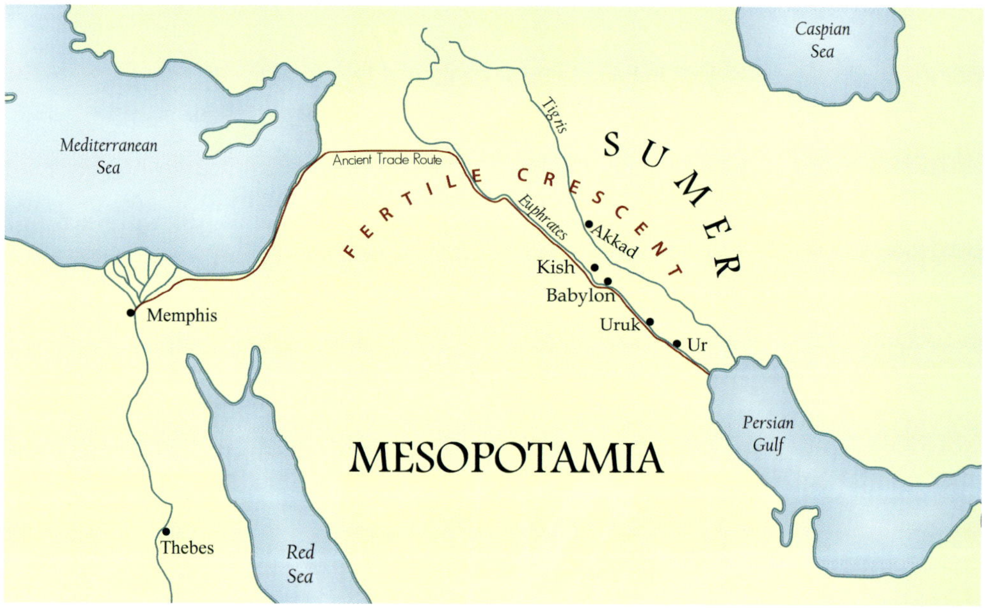

Farming

How could people raise crops in an area with little rain? Workers dug ditches and designed irrigation systems to bring water from the rivers to the fields. With the invention of the plow, Sumerian farmers dug rows in the fertile soil and raised wheat, barley, onions, garlic, and grapes.

Between Rivers

Sumer was in an ancient region of Mesopotamia. This rich farmland included the valley between the Tigris and Euphrates Rivers. Part of a larger curved area known as the Fertile Crescent, the Greek name Mesopotamia means "between rivers."

Nimrod

Mighty hunter. Founder of cities. Empire builder. Nimrod, Noah's great-grandson, was famous in the land of Sumer. Genesis 10:10–11 lists the cities he built, including Babel, Accad, and Nineveh.

History Speaks

Contrary to evolution's theories, the Bible says the first humans had the ability to speak. Adam named all the animals. Adam and Eve spoke with God in the Garden of Eden. People living in ancient Sumer invented a type of writing called cuneiform. A small reed called a stylus was used to make wedge-shaped marks on a wet clay tablet. The tablet then dried hard. Thousands of these clay tablets from Sumer (southern Iraq) have been found.

Calculating Circles

Circles fascinated the Sumerians. They divided a circle into 60, their base unit for counting. That is why we have 60 minutes in an hour and 60 seconds in a minute. It's also why we measure angles in degrees, with a full circle being 360 degrees (60×6). The Sumerians also discovered that if you spin a flat, circular disk horizontally, you can place clay on top of it. As the disk spins, you can shape the clay with your hands to make pots and bowls. This spinning circular platform became known as the potter's wheel, and it is still used today. The Sumerians also turned a flat circle on its side. Surprise! They invented the wheel.

120° 60° 180° 0° 240° 300°

City-States

Magnificent ziggurats dominated the center of the largest Sumerian cities. Young boys attended school there. The king's palace stood nearby. The busy marketplace was crowded with craft makers selling their jewelry, pottery, and fine woolen cloth. Merchants arrived to trade their goods, travelling from the Mediterranean Sea, the Persian Gulf, and as far away as the Indus River Valley. Scribes kept careful records of bills, taxes to be paid, and laws to follow. A tall wall surrounding the city protected brick homes from wild animals and invaders. Farmlands and villages lay outside the wall. These cities in Sumer were so large and powerful that they became known as city-states.

Ziggurats

The Great Ziggurat of Ur is just one of many ziggurats built in Sumer. Shaped like a pyramid, ziggurats had steps that led to the top, where a temple was built to worship false gods.

Ancient Ur

One of the largest city-states was Ur. In the early twentieth century, Leonard Woolley led archaeological digs at Ur, and he uncovered stunning items in the royal cemetery. These amazing artifacts included a queen's golden headdress, a golden lyre, and the royal game of Ur—complete with gameboard and pieces for playing the game. Abraham, a patriarch in the Bible, was born in Ur in 1996 B.C.

c. 2188 B.C.

Noah's son Ham had a son named Mizraim. Mizraim is the Hebrew name for Egypt. After the Tower of Babel, Mizraim migrated south toward Africa, settling with his descendants along the banks of the Nile River. Egypt quickly became one of the most important civilizations in ancient history.

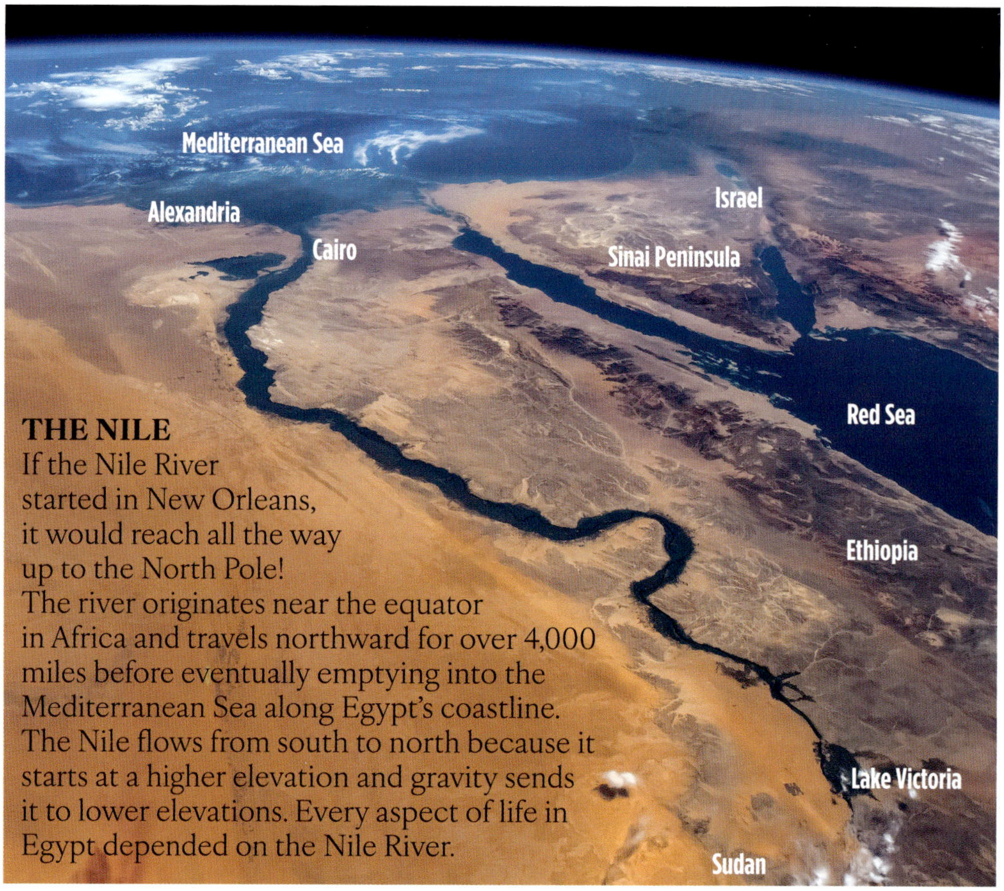

THE NILE

If the Nile River started in New Orleans, it would reach all the way up to the North Pole! The river originates near the equator in Africa and travels northward for over 4,000 miles before eventually emptying into the Mediterranean Sea along Egypt's coastline. The Nile flows from south to north because it starts at a higher elevation and gravity sends it to lower elevations. Every aspect of life in Egypt depended on the Nile River.

Rich Farmland

In Bible times, heavy tropical rains fell into the Nile River during Ethiopia's rainy season. The Nile flooded its banks almost every year. As the floodwaters dried up, they left behind a new layer of dirt, perfect for planting. Farmers grew crops along the banks of the Nile in this rich soil.

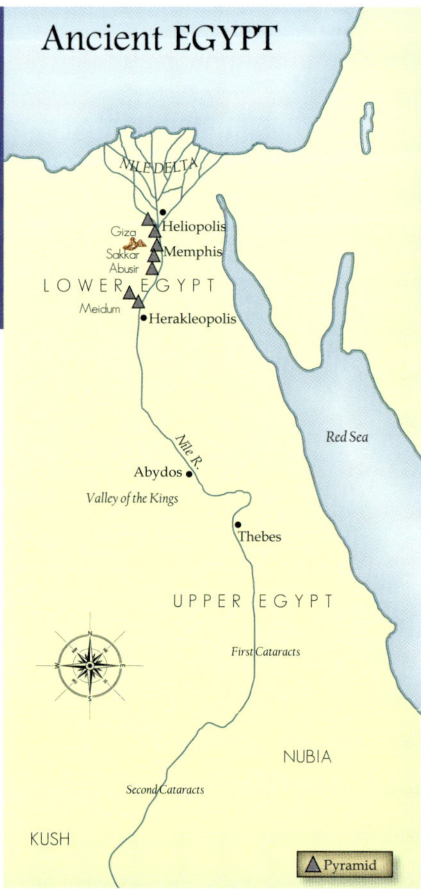

Two Kingdoms

Ancient Egypt was established along the Nile River Valley. It was dominated by the 3.6 million square miles of the Sahara Desert, the largest hot desert in the world. The Nile River gave life to this harsh, dry region, providing rich soil to grow food, as well as transportation for trading between villages and towns. The region was divided between two kingdoms. The swampy lands of the Nile Delta formed Lower Egypt in the north. The rich farmland along the Nile River Valley formed Upper Egypt to the south.

The Practical Papyrus

Lush, green thickets of papyrus plants grew 15 feet tall in the marshes of the Nile Delta. Egyptians invented many clever uses for it. They tied the long reeds together to make small boats. They made it into cloth, sandals, and mats to sit on. They wove it into ropes and baskets. But most importantly, Egyptians used the plant to invent an early form of paper. What did they call that paper? Papyrus, of course!

♦ Papyrus plant

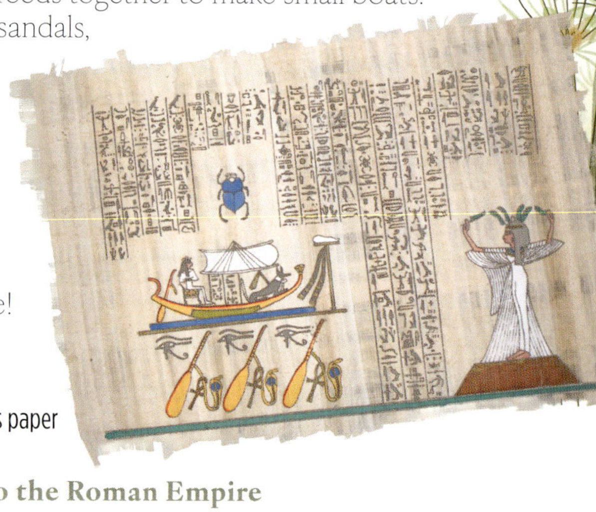

♦ Papyrus paper

The Rosetta Stone

Over the centuries, Egyptian hieroglyphs were eventually replaced by an alphabet borrowed mostly from the Greeks. As a result, new generations couldn't read the ancient writing. Countless Egyptian scrolls, temples, monuments, and pyramids were covered with hieroglyphic writing—but nobody could read it. In 1799, a stone tablet discovered near Rosetta, Egypt, changed that. Known as the Rosetta Stone, it contained the same message written in three different scripts: Greek, Egyptian hieroglyphics, and Egyptian Demotic (a type of cursive hieroglyphic). It took different scholars more than 20 years, but they finally cracked the code and scholars could read Egyptian hieroglyphs. The history of ancient Egypt came to life!

Dating Egypt's Past

Pharaohs. Mummies. Pyramids. Egypt's ancient past fascinates us with its mysteries and golden treasures. Many people have tried to calculate a chronology for events in ancient Egypt, but scholars still debate these dates today. Some assign dates to Egypt's past based on ancient king lists that have been discovered. The problem is that different king lists give different chronologies. Other scholars use ancient Egyptian writing that sometimes assigned events to mythological gods. Evolutionists date Egypt's history beginning before a biblical timeline of creation. And some scholars rely on carbon dating to date treasures dug up from the sands of Egypt. The problem is that the older an artifact is, the less reliable carbon dating has proven to be. As a result, attempts to date Egyptian chronology is confusing at the very least. At its worst, carbon dating can sow seeds of distrust in the authority of the Bible.

Picture Writing

The Sumerians used a form of picture writing called cuneiform, or small but intricate symbols on clay tablets. In contrast, Mayans carved out hieroglyphs on stone temples and palaces. Different pictures, symbols, and elements represented different words, sounds, or ideas. Egyptians invented their own form of hieroglyphic writing as well.

♦ Cuneiform writing on clay

What Does the Bible Say?

Mizraim and his descendants settled along the Nile River. The kingdoms of Egypt and its pyramids were built in the years that followed.

c. 2070 B.C.

The Himalayas are the tallest mountains in the world. When glaciers and snows melt and the rains fall, the waters drain from the northwestern slopes into the Indus River. This river flows through northern India and Pakistan, through the Indus River Valley, and into the Arabian Sea.

Searching for Clues

When is a hill not a hill? When it is a mound of earth that has grown over a forgotten city. Mysterious mounds had been reported in the Indus River Valley. Like detectives searching for clues, archaeologists traveled to the area to dig, and their findings were significant.

Lost and Found

This news made history! In the early 1920s, archaeologists discovered an unknown ancient civilization. They unearthed Harappa and Mohenjo-Daro, two of the most important cities in the Indus River Valley (modern-day Pakistan and northwest India). Since then, archaeologists have uncovered hundreds of lost towns and cities from this area of civilization.

The Great Bath in Mohenjo-Daro

Filling the Valley

As Noah's descendants multiplied and migrated away from the Tower of Babel, some traveled to the east. They discovered a valley next to the Indus River. Like the Nile, its waters flooded yearly, depositing a new layer of rich farmland along its banks. There, Noah's descendants settled down, built cities and towns, and established trade along the Indus River.

♦ Stamp seal impressions with Indus script

♦ Very tall wells built up as flooding and rebuilding raised the elevation

Trade Network

Cities, towns, and farming villages traded with each other along the Indus River. Farmers bartered cotton, grains, and livestock. Craft workers traded tools, pots, jewelry, and toys. Items of bronze, silver, gold, and ivory exchanged hands. In addition, beads, jewelry, and other artifacts indicate the Indus people traded goods with people in Asia, along the Persian Gulf, and as far away as Mesopotamia.

Toys

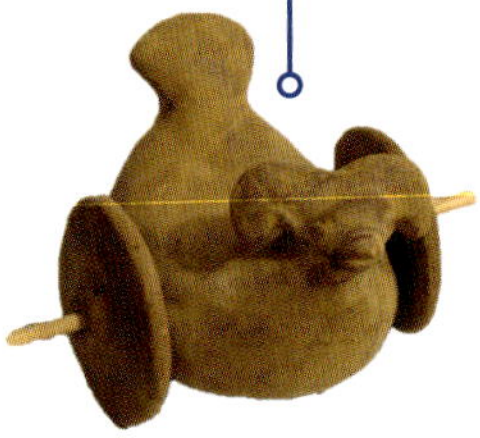

♦ An ancient well and the city drainage canals

City Planners

One of the most startling discoveries of the Indus civilization was the advanced construction of its cities and towns. Streets ran straight and intersected each other in a well-planned grid pattern. Sturdy brick houses lined the streets. Many were two-storied with a central courtyard. The larger cities were surrounded by a protective wall, which was a remarkable feat in those days.

Indoor Plumbing

Pioneers who settled the American West didn't have indoor plumbing, but the cities of the Indus Valley did. These ancient homes had "modern" sewage systems! Many houses had a type of indoor bathroom. Water was often supplied from a well in the central courtyard. Drains led from each house into a city sewage system.

The drainage system at Lothal

Mohenjo-Daro

In 1922, archaeologists discovered the city of Mohenjo-Daro on the banks of the Indus River. A well-planned city, its straight streets crossed each other at right angles. An extensive system of drains emptied into a sewage disposal site. Settlers built a large granary to store the abundant grain that farmers harvested from the fields. Young men attended the city's college to train to become priests. Mohenjo-Daro was one of the earliest and most advanced cities in ancient civilization.

Advanced Civilization

Measurements. Weights. Writings. The Indus civilization developed its own systems for business and trade. Archaeologists have uncovered many objects, including countless square seals engraved with Indus Valley script and pictures of animals. It is like reading secret code, however. No one has been able to decipher the engravings.

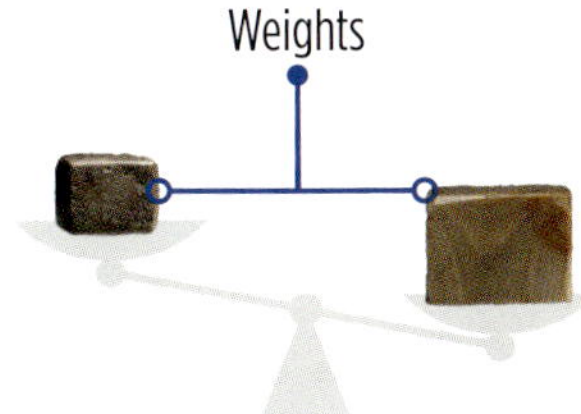

Weights

After the Tower of Babel, Noah's descendants continued to migrate. Some reached a land far to the east where a river shimmered like gold in the sun. The Huang He, or Yellow River, carried along a lot of silt, giving it the color of yellowish brown.

Isolated Culture

Rugged mountains and deserts surround the Yellow River Valley, making travel difficult. With the valley's extreme geological features, people couldn't easily come and go. As a result, people who lived in this area of ancient China developed a culture unique from the rest of the world.

Millet and Rice

Farmers planted a variety of fruits, vegetables, and grains in the yellow soil left after the Yellow River's floodwaters receded. Millet was a primary crop. This grain was used as food for both settlers and livestock. Along the Yangtze River to the south, rice was grown in marshy fields.

Houses and Homes

Early houses in the Yellow River Valley were dug partially into the ground. Along with protecting their homes from earthquakes, the earthen walls kept them cooler in summer and warmer in winter. The houses were covered with a thatched roof.

Hukou Waterfall on the Yellow River in north China's Shanxi province

China's Sorrow

Lightning flashed. Thunder roared. Heavy rains poured down. Flood waters raged down the Yellow River, overflowing its banks. Parents grabbed young children away from the rushing water. Driving their cattle, sheep, and pigs to safer ground, inhabitants of this area watched helplessly as their houses washed away and their crops were destroyed. The Yellow River became known as "China's Sorrow" because of the terrible damage caused by the floods.

Shang Dynasty

Around the 17th century B.C., Emperor Tang founded the Shang Dynasty. His warriors fought to unite feuding tribes along the Yellow River. Armed with bronze spears and weapons, soldiers clattered through the streets in their horse-drawn chariots, enforcing the emperor's rule.

Legend of the Silkworm

One ancient legend says that Empress Xi Ling Ji, wife of the Yellow Emperor, discovered how to make silk. One day, the empress was sitting under a mulberry tree, sipping a cup of tea. Suddenly, a white cocoon dropped into her tea. The hot water made a beautiful silk thread unravel from the cocoon. Legend says the empress began collecting cocoons from the silkworm caterpillars. She taught her maids to spin the threads and weave them into beautiful silk cloth. The Chinese kept the process of making silk a secret for thousands of years.

Oracle Bones

Developed in China during the Shang Dynasty in China, a form of picture writing was engraved on pieces of turtle shells and cattle bones, now called oracle bones. They were used to foretell the future, reveal hidden information, or seek guidance from deities and dead ancestors. The Bible forbids this (Deut. 18:10–12).

Exciting Discoveries

Archaeologists have uncovered many artifacts from the Yellow River Valley cultures. Terracotta pottery, painted clay pots, and massive bronze cauldrons have been found. Other objects were made from stone and animal horns.

Ancient Tradition

According to ancient tradition, Huangdi (the Yellow Emperor) and Emperor Yao were among the earliest Chinese rulers. Emperor Yu, remembered for controlling the great floods, is credited with founding the Xia Dynasty in the Yellow River Valley. Tradition says Yu directed floodwaters into channels and irrigation ditches, protecting nearby agriculture.

Western Xia tombs at the foot of Helan Mountains

The first ruler to unite the Upper and Lower Kingdoms of Egypt was King Menes (or Narmer). He built his capital city at Memphis. King Menes and his descendants who ruled after him are known as the First Dynasty of Egypt.

♦ Ziggurat of Ur

♦ Chogha Zanbil Ziggurat (model)

The Old Kingdom

When were the famous pyramids first built? During the era of Egypt's history known as the Old Kingdom. The first pyramid was copied from the design of ziggurats in Sumer. High priest and architect, Imhotep, had it built for Pharaoh Zoser (Djoser). Called the Step Pyramid, it was built to be the pharaoh's tomb.

♦ The Pyramid of Djoser

The Great Pyramid

Pharaoh Khufu's Great Pyramid of Giza is likely the most famous pyramid of all! It took more than two million stone blocks to build it. Originally standing at about 482 feet tall (it stands about 449 feet now due to erosion), it is still considered the largest pyramid ever built and one of the largest stone structures in the world. The base and three sides each measure 755 feet, and it weighs a whopping 5.74 million tons! This pyramid still stands today near the modern city of Cairo. As if keeping guard over the pyramids, nearby is the Great Sphinx, a giant statue of a lion with the face of a man.

The Middle Kingdom

During the era known as the Middle Kingdom, Egypt grew to achieve great power and riches. Known as the classical age of Egypt, art and literature flourished during this period. Egypt conquered Nubia (also known as Cush or Ethiopia) and developed extensive trade networks via land and sea. Some pyramids were still constructed, but the pharaohs focused more on building irrigation systems and increasing productivity of farmlands. Abraham probably visited Egypt during the Middle Kingdom, when he needed food during times of famine.

Hyksos

Horse-drawn chariots. Improved bows and arrows. Stronger swords and weapons. A group called the Hyksos introduced these to Egypt, eventually conquering the weakening power of the pharaohs to rule over Egypt themselves. Mysteries surround the Hyksos people. They spoke the same language as the Hebrews and seemed to come from the same region Abraham lived in (Canaan). Some ancient writers thought the Hyksos were Hebrews, but modern scholars are still looking for evidence to confirm those claims.

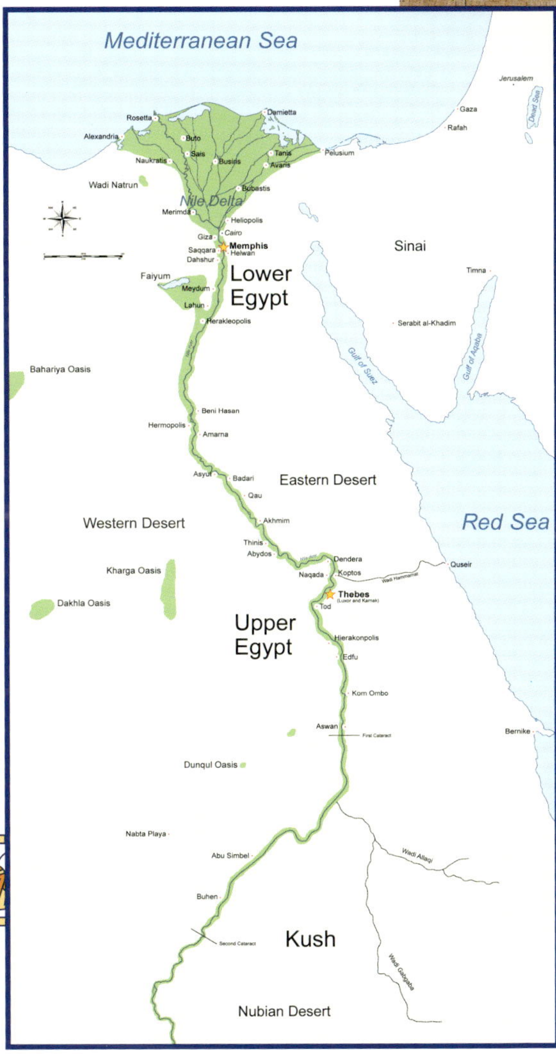

♦ While the Hyksos ruled Lower Egypt, pharaohs ruled Upper Egypt. In c. 1825 B.C., the Hyksos were defeated and Egypt was reunified.

♦ Mortuary temple of Queen Hatshepsut

The New Kingdom

During the New Kingdom, native Egyptians overthrew the Hyksos and ruled their own land once again. Queen Hatshepsut ruled in a time of peace and prosperity. After her death, Pharaoh Thutmose III led Egypt in military campaigns that made Egypt a powerful empire in the ancient world. It was probably during this era that Joseph and his family settled in Egypt and eventually became enslaved. Many workers were needed to build the huge palaces and temples constructed during this time. Egyptians used advanced mathematics to build their massive monuments. To prevent grave robbers stealing their funeral treasures, the pharaohs of the New Kingdom were buried in secret tombs in the "hidden" Valley of the Kings, located near its capital city of Thebes.

Unreliable Dates

Egypt's past is a much studied, much debated topic. Countless artifacts, writings, and monuments have been found in ancient Egypt. The standard dates for these items listed in most books and museums are based on a faulty evolutionary timeline. The Bible doesn't include much information to help confidently date Egypt's past. Also, because the pharaohs' names listed in the Bible were written in Hebrew, scholars have not yet found solid evidence to confirm exactly which Egyptian pharaohs ruled during the days of Abraham, Joseph, and Moses.

A Better Chronology

The Assyrian Empire is much more straightforward and easier to document and date with trustworthy research. The Assyrian Empire eventually conquered Egypt. Chronology and genealogical tables in the Bible support many dates regarding the Assyrian Empire on which most scholars agree. This is why many Bible scholars use references to the Assyrian Empire instead of Egypt's past to calculate and confirm dates for biblical and world events.

Abraham is one of the most important people in history. His name was Abram until God changed it to Abraham, which means the "father of many nations." Three major religions consider Abraham the father of their faith. The Jews claimed Abraham as their ancestor through his son Isaac. Then, with the death and Resurrection of Jesus Christ around 33 A.D., Christians have worshiped Jesus, a descendant of Abraham. And when the "new" religion of Islam began to spread around 632 A.D., Muslims claimed Abraham as their ancestor through his son Ishmael.

♦ "Abraham's House" in Ur

Abraham's Birthplace

In 1996 B.C., Abraham was born in Ur, a city in ancient Sumer. The city was magnificent. An important hub for trade, Ur was also a center for pagan religion and culture. A great ziggurat, temple, and palace dominated the skyline. Citizens of Ur enjoyed an amazing standard of wealth.

♦ Countless gold artifacts have been excavated from Ur.

Now the LORD had said to Abram: "Get out of your country, from your family and from you father's house, to a land that I will show you. I will make you a great nation; I will bless you and make your name great; and you shall be a blessing. I will bless those who bless you, and I will curse him who curses you; and in you all the families of the earth shall be blessed." –Genesis 12:1–3

Answering God's Call

Obedient. Faithful. Righteous. Out of the pagan land of Mesopotamia, God called Abram to follow Him. In 1921 B.C., he (later called Abraham) and his wife Sarai (later called Sarah), along with his father, Terah, and his nephew Lot, migrated together from Ur to Haran (southeastern Turkey). God told Abraham to leave his home, his family, and his country and move to a new land God would give him. God promised to make Abraham's descendants into a great nation in this new land. Abraham put his faith in God, trusted in His promises, and obeyed God's command. He was called righteous because he believed God.

The Land of Promise

What land did God promise to Abraham and his descendants? Canaan included the Jordan River and extended all the way west to the Mediterranean Sea. At that time, the Canaanites (descendants of Noah's son Ham) lived in the region. By King David's reign in c. 1048 B.C., this homeland of the Jews would become known as the nation of Israel.

Eternal Promise

God's covenant with Abraham was more than a promise to inherit land or to bless his family. Through Abraham's descendants, Jesus the Messiah was born. Today, everyone who believes Jesus is Lord is credited with His righteousness. Just as Abraham believed God and was blessed by His eternal promise, all who believe in Jesus as Savior are blessed with God's promise of eternal life.

God's Promise to Abraham

God told Abraham, "I will make you exceedingly fruitful; and I will make nations of you, and kings shall come from you . . . Also I give to you and your descendants after you the land in which you are a stranger, all the land of Canaan, as an everlasting possession" (Gen. 17:6, 8).

God's Promise to Sarah

God told Abraham, "And I will bless [Sarah] and also give you a son by her; then I will bless her, and she shall be a mother of nations; kings of people shall be from her" (Gen. 17:16).

In the Bible, a covenant is a special promise or agreement that God makes with people. God makes covenants to show His love, keep His word, and guide His people. It's not like a regular deal you can break—God always keeps His side of the promise, no matter what.

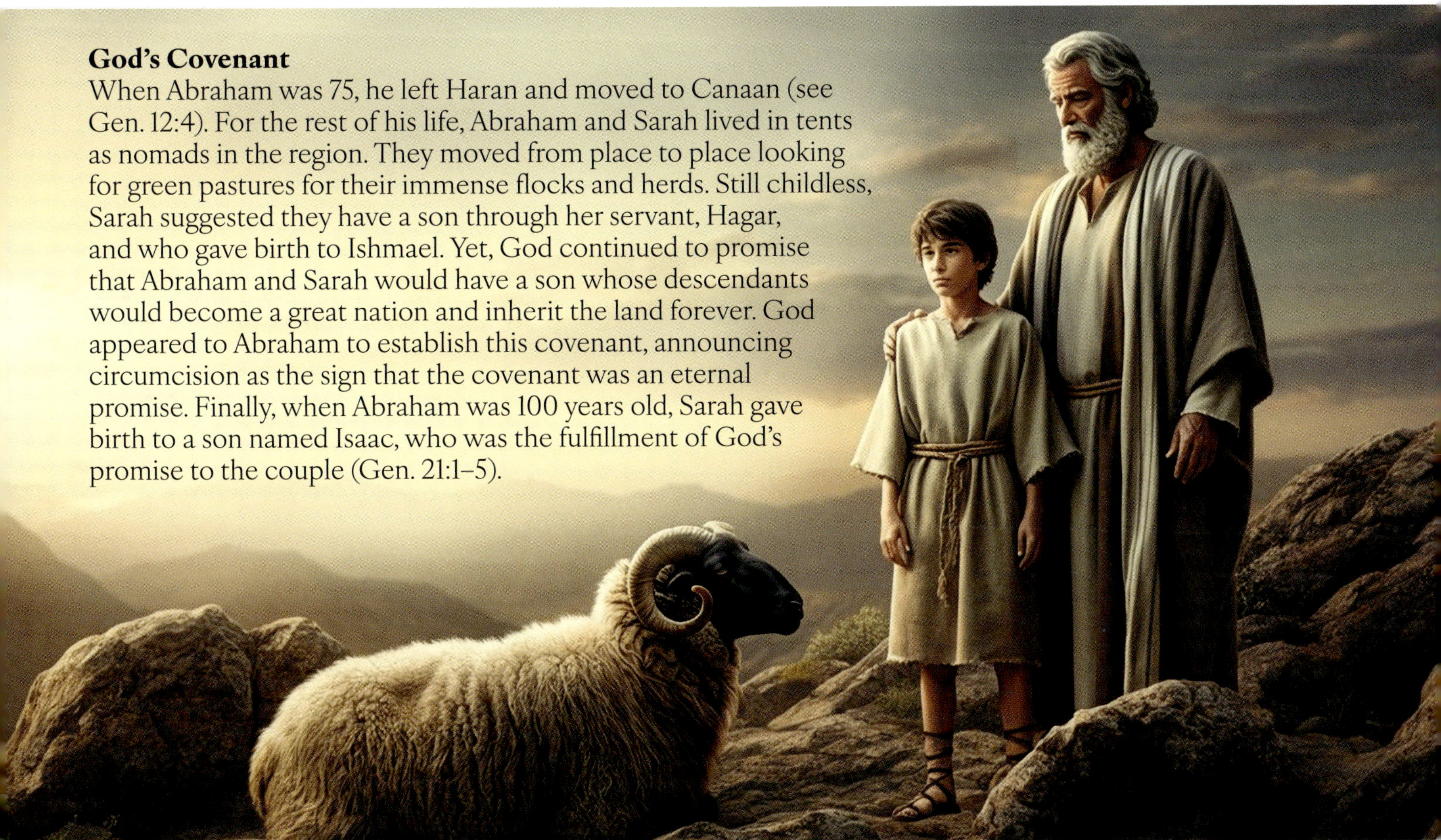

God's Covenant

When Abraham was 75, he left Haran and moved to Canaan (see Gen. 12:4). For the rest of his life, Abraham and Sarah lived in tents as nomads in the region. They moved from place to place looking for green pastures for their immense flocks and herds. Still childless, Sarah suggested they have a son through her servant, Hagar, and who gave birth to Ishmael. Yet, God continued to promise that Abraham and Sarah would have a son whose descendants would become a great nation and inherit the land forever. God appeared to Abraham to establish this covenant, announcing circumcision as the sign that the covenant was an eternal promise. Finally, when Abraham was 100 years old, Sarah gave birth to a son named Isaac, who was the fulfillment of God's promise to the couple (Gen. 21:1–5).

JOSEPH IN EGYPT

1728 B.C.

Together, Abraham and Sarah had Isaac, their promised son. Isaac married Rebekah and had twin sons, Esau and Jacob. After a life-changing experience between God and Jacob, God changed Jacob's name to Israel. Jacob's 12 sons became the 12 tribes of Israel.

Behold, children are a heritage from the LORD,
The fruit of the womb is a reward.
Like arrows in the hand of a warrior,
So are the children of one's youth. –Psalm 127:3–4

Abraham — Sarah

Isaac — Rebekah

Jacob — Esau

Leah (Jacob's first wife)

Bilhah (Rachel's maid)

Zilpah (Leah's maid)

Rachel (Jacob's beloved wife)

Reuben — Jacob's firstborn (Gen. 29:32)

Simeon — second son (Gen. 29:33)

Levi — ancestor of the priestly tribe (Gen. 29:34)

Judah — ancestor of King David and **JESUS** (Gen. 29:35)

Issachar — "wages" or "reward" (Gen. 30:18)

Zebulun — "honor" or "dwelling" (Gen. 30:20)

Dan — "he judged" (Gen. 30:6)

Naphtali — "my struggle" (Gen. 30:8)

Gad — "good fortune" (Gen. 30:11)

Asher — "happy" (Gen. 30:13)

Joseph — "may he add" (Gen. 30:24)

Benjamin — Jacob's youngest son (Gen. 35:18)

12 tribes of Israel

The Dreamer

Joseph was Jacob's favorite son. He had dreams that his family would bow down to him one day. His brothers became so jealous that they sold Joseph to Ishmaelite traders traveling to Egypt to sell their spices. Joseph suddenly found himself torn away from his family and sold into slavery in Egypt. Joseph served Potiphar, a captain of Pharaoh's guard.

From Prison to Pharaoh's Court

Unjustly accused of a crime he didn't commit, Joseph was thrown into prison. Years later, however, Pharaoh had a disturbing dream. Joseph was able to interpret the meaning behind the dream. It was a warning from God! Egypt needed to prepare for seven years of plenty and seven years of famine. Pharaoh appointed Joseph second-in-command over Egypt so he could oversee the preparations to save the nation from ruin.

Famine

When the famine was severe, Joseph's brothers visited Egypt to ask for food. Joseph forgave his brothers and explained that what they had intended for harm, God intended for good—saving many lives during the famine (Gen. 50:20). Joseph invited his father, brothers, and their families to move to Egypt so they could have enough to eat. In Egypt, Joseph's brothers worked for Pharaoh as shepherds to care for his flocks.

Second-in-Command
When Joseph was appointed to his high position, Pharaoh gave him a signet ring, new linen clothes, and a horse-drawn chariot. The signet ring belonged to Pharaoh, and Joseph could use it to stamp Pharaoh's symbol on important documents. Linen clothes (usually white) helped people keep cool in Egypt's hot, dry desert climate. Horse-drawn chariots had been introduced to Egypt by the Hyksos.

Mummies
Egyptians worshiped many false gods and believed pharaohs were gods. Egyptians also believed people needed their bodies after they died to keep on living in an afterlife with these gods. To prepare for that future, Egyptians put a dead body through a special embalming process to preserve it. They removed internal organs and stored them in jars. They treated the body with salts and special spices. Strips of linen cloth were wrapped around the body to mummify it. Mummies were buried with many useful objects and magnificent treasures to use in the afterlife.

Hebrew Burial Customs
The Bible says that when Jacob died in Egypt, his body was embalmed. Even though some of the preparations may have been similar to the Egyptian burial customs, Hebrews worshiped the one true God. Jacob and his family knew dead people did not need their bodies after they died. Joseph led a funeral procession back to his homeland to bury his father in the same tomb as Abraham.

King Tutankhamen
Who was Egypt's most famous mummy? King Tut! Pharaoh Tutankhamen's tomb was discovered in 1922 in the Valley of the Kings, which is located on the west bank of the Nile River near Luxor, Egypt. Other Egyptian tombs had been raided by grave robbers, but King Tut's tomb had remained untouched. Thousands of treasures and large quantities of golden objects were found. One of the most famous was the magnificent funeral mask of the boy-pharaoh.

Then [Jacob] charged them and said to them: "I am to be gathered to my people; bury me with my fathers in the cave . . . which Abraham bought with the field of Ephron the Hittite as a possession for a burial place. There they buried Abraham and Sarah his wife, there they buried Isaac and Rebekah his wife, and there I buried Leah. . . . And when Jacob had finished commanding his sons, he drew his feet up into the bed and breathed his last, and was gathered to his people." –Genesis 49:29–33

The earliest civilization to develop in Europe was the Minoan culture, ancestors of ancient Greeks. After the Tower of Babel, some descendants of Noah's son Japheth migrated to Europe. They settled in regions north of the Mediterranean Sea, including Greece, which lies on the mainland with the Aegean Sea on its eastern coast and the Ionian Sea on its west. Crete, a Greek island in the Aegean Sea, became home to the Minoans.

♦ Reconstruction of the Palace of Knossos

Ancient Legend

Minoans built on the island of Crete. Known as an early form of city-states, each one had a palace. The most famous ruler was based on the legend of King Minos. The Minoan culture was named after him.

Knossos

The city of Knossos became the Minoan capital of Crete, and a magnificent palace was built there. Several stories high, this palace featured grand staircases that climbed to different parts of the structure, along with maze-like halls and corridors that led to many different rooms. The throne, carved from stone, is still standing in the throne room today!

Frescos

Beautiful paintings called frescos (see photo left) covered the walls of many rooms in the palace of Knossos. Minoan artists painted scenes from palace life as well as pictures of plants and animals to decorate the walls.

Indoor Plumbing

Archaeologists have dug up evidence of sophisticated plumbing in Minoan palaces, similar to the findings in the Indus River Valley. Indoor bathrooms with running water and drainage pipes have been found among Minoan ruins.

Seafaring Traders

Ocean waves splashed over the bow of a Minoan trading ship, sending a salty spray into the faces of its experienced sailors. With a cargo full of olive oil and grain grown on the island of Crete, ships like this sailed from port to port around nearby islands and along the eastern coastline of the Mediterranean Sea. In exchange for food, pottery, and jewelry crafted from copper and precious gold, Minoan traders acquired cloth, ivory, and valuable metals.

Early Writing

A vast trade network required a system to track the exchange of goods. Minoans developed their own written language known today as Linear A. Along with other artifacts with writing on them, cylinder seals have been discovered by archaeologists. These cylinders were rolled over soft clay that hardened into tablets that listed important records.

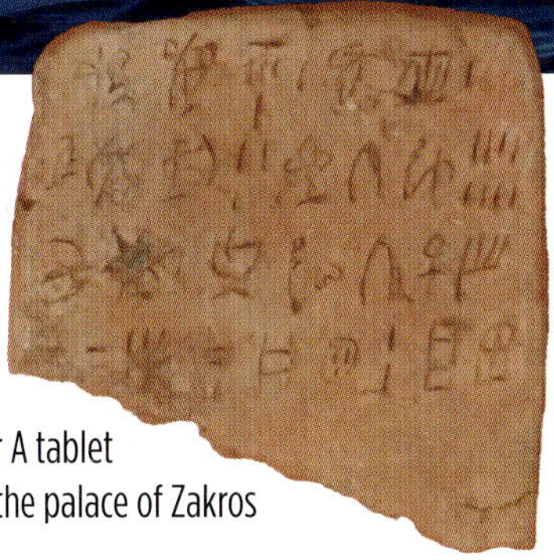

♦ Linear A tablet from the palace of Zakros

Dangerous Sport

Minoan athletes excelled in the strange sport of bull-jumping! Frescos on the walls of palaces show scenes with both young men and women participating in this dangerous activity. Grabbing the bull by the horns (literally!), the athlete did a somersault over the bull's back and landed behind it.

End of the Minoans

The earth shook. A loud blast exploded. Fire, rock, and smoke filled the air. A volcano on the nearby island of Thera spewed ash and destruction over the island of Crete. It's hard to know the extent of the damage, but the eruption likely weakened the Minoan people, and an invasion of the Mycenaeans from Greece probably brought the hobbling civilization to its end.

♦ Akrotiri, an excavation site of a Minoan settlement on the Greek island of Santorini

The Minoans on the island of Crete ruled over the Mycenaeans, people who lived on the peninsula of mainland Greece in the Aegean Sea. Eventually, however, the Mycenaeans grew strong enough to overthrow the Minoans. The war-like Mycenaeans then became the dominant power in ancient Greece.

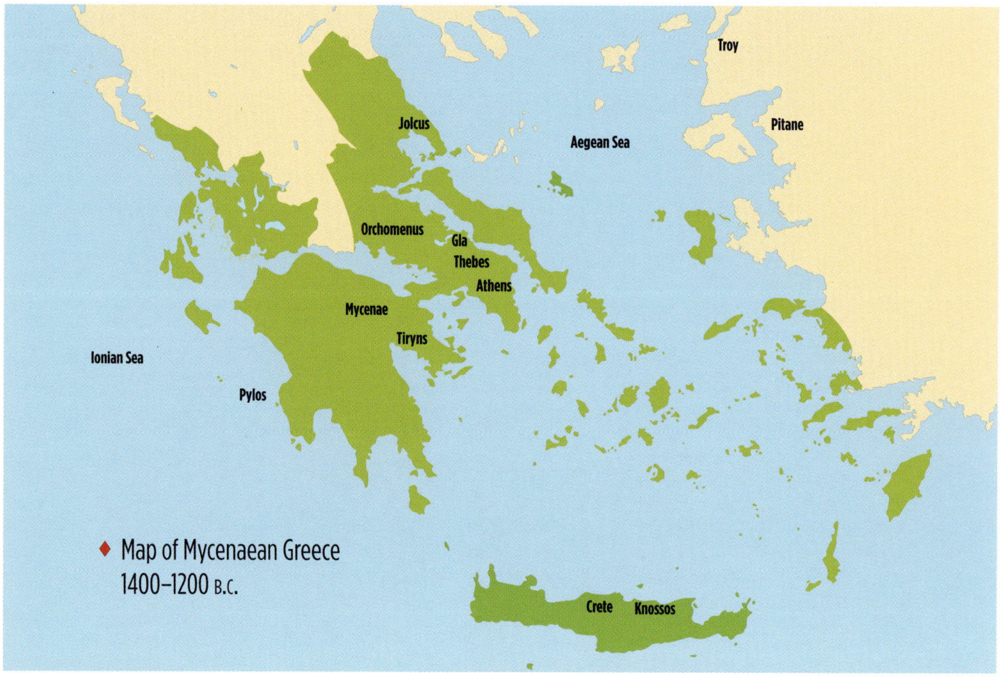

♦ Map of Mycenaean Greece 1400–1200 B.C.

City-States

Rocky. Hilly. Close to the sea. The Mycenaeans built city-states on the southern part of the Greek peninsula, each on top of a different hill. Surrounded by strong walls, each city was like a fort. This type of hilltop city was called an acropolis. The king's palace and a temple were built inside the walls of the city. With the sea so close to each acropolis and farmland limited because of the rocky hillsides, vast trading networks were established around the Mediterranean to bring in the food and supplies they needed.

Trojan Horse

According to an ancient Greek myth, the Mycenaeans sailed across the Aegean Sea and attacked the city of Troy, located in modern-day Turkey. The Trojan War that followed lasted ten years. To end the war, Mycenaean warriors hid inside a large, wooden horse. The Trojan horse was left outside the city gates of Troy and the rest of the Mycenaeans pretended to sail away. Thinking it was a gift from the Mycenaeans as a symbol of their defeat, the citizens of Troy brought the horse inside the city. At night, the soldiers climbed out of the horse and opened the city gate. The ships had returned, and Mycenaean warriors flooded in and conquered the city of Troy. This legend was made famous by the Greek poet Homer, who wrote about it in his famous poem *The Iliad*.

Mycenae

The largest and strongest acropolis was the city of Mycenae. Even though it wasn't as glorious as the Minoan capital city at Knossos, Mycenae adopted much of the culture, architecture, and trade practices of the Minoans. Archaeologists have uncovered extensive remains of this ancient city. They discovered palaces, buildings, and hundreds of graves and tombs. The stones used for building the city wall were so enormous, legends say they were stacked in place by giants.

The Lion's Gate

How many lions does it take to guard a city? Two! Or so the Mycenaeans thought. Carved into the massive gate that leads into the city of Mycenae, two lions stand guard above the entrance.

Deep and High

Early Mycenaeans dug deep, deeper, and still deeper into the ground to bury their dead. These types of pits are known as shaft graves. Later generations built massive tombs, known as beehive tombs, above the ground. Both kinds of tombs have been discovered, and both contained vast arrays of golden and silver treasures, indicating that these early Greeks were wealthy.

Scribes

The Mycenaeans adapted the written language of the Minoans into their own writing, known today as Linear B. Scribes served the king by keeping careful records of property, labor, and traded goods.

End of a Civilization

No one knows for sure how the Mycenaean civilization came to an end. Some scholars think a group of people known as the Dorians attacked from the north. Others think they were conquered by a group known as the Sea Peoples. Still other scholars think natural disasters or poor crops forced residents to abandon their cities and look for a better life elsewhere. After the end of the Mycenaean culture, a new civilization in Greece rose up to make their mark on history.

c. 1792 B.C.

Historic news! A new king sat on the throne. King Hammurabi ruled from the city of Babylon. Under his leadership, he united the cities of Mesopotamia, the land between the Tigris and Euphrates Rivers. In doing so, Hammurabi established the First Babylonian Empire.

The Stele

How should a king rule an empire? With law and order! Hammurabi sent scribes throughout his kingdom to make lists of the laws used in different cities. Then they abolished away laws that didn't apply any more. Organizing the rest, scribes also wrote new laws that were needed. Then they chose a black stone pillar, called a stele, and carved into it 282 laws for the entire empire. Today, this stone is commonly known as the Law Code Stele of King Hammurabi, or the Code of Hammurabi.

Hammurabi's Laws

The Code of Hammurabi was one of the earliest written set of laws in ancient history. It contained laws to protect human rights and to ensure fair business practices. It also outlined laws for farmers, merchants, and doctors. The laws also ensured basic rights for women. Rich or poor, enslaved or free, every person had laws to follow and obey.

Stolen Treasure

In 1901, Egyptologist Gustave Jéquier was working with his team in the ancient site of Susa, now in modern-day Iran. Among the astonishing and magnificent finds was a seven-foot tall, black stele. Writing known as cuneiform was carved into the stone. The Code of Hammurabi had been discovered! But how did it get from Babylon to Iran? Historians say it was likely carried to Susa as a war trophy. Today, the Code of Hammurabi resides in Paris at the Louvre, France's most famous museum.

♦ The engravings of the Code are written in the Akkadian language using cuneiform.

♦ Hammurabi appears next to Moses on the south frieze of the United States Supreme Court Building. The Ten Commandments serve as a spiritual and moral framework meant for all people equally, while Hammurabi's Code was a practical legal system with strict penalties designed to maintain order in a hierarchical society.

	Hammurabi's Laws	The Ten Commandments
Origins	Created by King Hammurabi of Babylon. Written on stone steles and placed publicly for civil governance. Political and societal laws.	Given by God to Moses on Mount Sinai. Religious, covenant laws forming the foundation of Israelite morality and worship.
Purpose	To maintain order, justice, and authority in Babylonian society. Focused on legal punishments, property, and class structure.	To guide people in worshiping God faithfully and living morally with others. Focus on spiritual and ethical conduct.
Content	Covered civil, economic, and criminal law (contracts, trade, marriage, property, wages, slaves, theft, assault, murder). Very detailed: nearly 300 laws with specific consequences depending on social class.	First 4 commands: Relationship with God (no other gods, no idols, honor God's name, keep Sabbath) Last 6 commands: Relationship with others (honor parents; do not murder, commit adultery, steal, lie, or covet)
Style	Case-based law ("If . . . then . . ."). Punishments differed depending on the offender's or victim's status (noble vs. commoner vs. slave).	Short, absolute commands ("You shall not . . ."). Universal moral principles, not tied to social rank.
Justice	Famous for "lex talionis" (law of retaliation): an eye for an eye, a tooth for a tooth. Emphasis on retribution and social order.	Focus on sin against God and moral wrongs against people; consequences are more spiritual and covenantal.
Similarities	Both seek justice and order. Both prohibit murder, stealing, adultery, and false testimony. Both show concern for protecting family and community.	
Differences: Religious vs. Secular	Civil law for society	Religious and covenant-based law
Differences: Equality vs. Class-based	Depended on social class	Applied equally to everyone
Differences: Punishment vs. Morality	Focused on external punishment	Stressed inner morality and loyalty to God

An Eye for an Eye

In ancient times, fair justice meant punishing evil with the same evil that had been done initially. The phrase, "an eye for an eye and a tooth for a tooth," originated from the Code of Hammurabi. When God gave Moses the Ten Commandments and other laws, this principle still held true. Exodus 21:23–24a says, "But if any harm follows, then you shall give life for life, eye for eye, tooth for tooth."

Love Your Enemies

When Jesus taught, He spoke about the practice of an eye for an eye. He said, "You have heard that it was said, 'An eye for an eye and a tooth for a tooth.' But I tell you not to resist an evil person. But whoever slaps you on your right cheek, turn the other to him also . . . You have heard that it was said, 'You shall love your neighbor and hate your enemy.' But I say to you, love your enemies, bless those who curse you, do good to those who hate you, and pray for those who spitefully use you and persecute you" (Matt. 5:38–39, 43–44).

End of an Empire

After the death of Hammurabi, the Babylonian kingdom grew weak. Around 1595 B.C., another group, the Hittites, attacked the capital city of Babylon, leaving it in ruins. This marked the end of the First Babylonian Empire.

When Jacob died in Egypt, Joseph and his brothers carried him to Canaan and buried him in the cave Abraham had bought from Ephron the Hittite (Gen. 50:12–13). The Hittites are mentioned nearly 50 times in the Bible.

Myth or Fact?

There was a problem. The Bible mentioned the Hittites, but for a long time, no archaeological evidence existed anywhere to indicate that the Hittites ever existed. None. Some Bible skeptics claimed the Hittites were an ancient myth like other myths and legends they thought the Bible contained. Bible scholars disagreed because much evidence had been found to support the Bible as an accurate historic document, even if Hittite artifacts had yet to be found. These scholars believed that if the Bible said the Hittites were part of ancient history, it was true.

Lost and Found

Archaeologists followed clues that led them to a mysterious site. In 1906, digging through the earth and sands of time, Hugo Winckler from Berlin and Theodore Makridi Bey of Istanbul conducted excavations in a remote region of modern-day Turkey. What did they find? Hattusha, the ancient capital city of the lost Hittite Empire. This was another proof of the accuracy of the Bible's historical record.

♦ The Lion Gate in Hattusha

♦ Sphinx Gate entrance to the city of Hattusha

Who Were the Hittites?

Much has been learned about the Hittites since archaeologists unearthed their ancient cities and translated their hieroglyphic script. Even though iron had been used before the Flood, the Hittites are recognized for developing the process of smelting iron from its ore, which made it more available and usable. Hittite weapons and chariots were stronger than those of other armies. Trading with neighbors (when not engaged in battle), the Hittites adopted architecture, culture, and art from other kingdoms. From scenes carved into the rock fortress at Hattusha, scholars have learned much about the everyday livelihood of its citizens. Hittite men were easy to recognize in their tall, pointed hats and pointed boots that turned up at the toes. They adopted music as part of their culture. Farmers, metal workers, merchants, and soldiers worked to build this powerful empire.

Battle of Kadesh
Egyptian Pharaoh Ramses II strapped on his armor, grabbed his weapons, and stepped into his war chariot led by a magnificent pair of horses brought from the royal stables. Soldiers in the Hittite Empire gathered to ride their chariots in the army of King Muwatalli II. Spreading out like grasshoppers, the Hittites covered the mountains and valleys surrounding the city of Kadesh. After a fierce battle, both armies withdrew, and neither side achieved a decisive victory.

World's First Peace Treaty

The battle of Kadesh raged back and forth. Who won? Nobody knows for sure. Ramses II was so proud of his own bravery that he had the Poem of Pentaur engraved on temple walls throughout Egypt. It describes his honor and valor during the battle. The Hittites' record of the battle differs significantly, naming them as the victors. Eventually, the two empires crafted a peace treaty, which was inscribed in Egypt's records. A copy of the treaty was also discovered in the city of Hattusha on a clay tablet in the Hittite royal library.

♦ The Hittite version of the treaty found in the royal library

Royal Library

As different archaeologists have conducted excavations in the Hittite capital of Hattusha, they have unearthed some fascinating finds. Portions of a massive wall, numerous towers, the King's Gate, and the Sphinx Gate have been found. Buildings such as the Great Temple have also been discovered, along with portions of an Upper City and a Lower City. One of the most exciting discoveries of all was the royal library! Thousands of baked clay tablets found in a large storage room include information about daily life, letters between kings, and a copy of the world's earliest peace treaty between the Hittites and Egyptians.

Names can be confusing! First, Canaan was a person. He was Ham's son and one of Noah's grandsons. As Canaan's descendants spread out after the incident at the Tower of Babel, some of them settled east of the Mediterranean Sea. This area between the Jordan River and the Mediterranean Sea became known as the land of Canaan. And the people who lived in this region were known as Canaanites.

Canaanite Cities

The land of Canaan was named after Noah's grandson Canaan, and his descendants occupied the land. Other people groups also lived there: Amorites, Hittites, Perizzites, Jebusites, Girgashites, and Hivites. Each group was ruled by its own king. Each small kingdom built a fortified city with walls around it to protect its people from attack. Farms and villages grew up around each city, which included Shechem, Bethel, Hebron, and Jericho. These cities, all found in the Old Testament, were all a part of the ancient land of Canaan.

Religion

The Canaanites worshiped many false gods. One of their most important gods was Baal. The Bible points out many horrendous things the Canaanites did out of devotion to their false gods.

Land of Promise

When God called Abraham to leave his homeland, where did God lead him to go? Canaan! The Canaanites were already living there at that time. Abraham and his family arrived in Canaan and stopped near a terebinth tree in a place called Shechem. There, God affirmed His promise to Abraham: "Then the LORD appeared to Abram [Abraham] and said, 'To your descendants I will give this land' " (Gen. 12:7a). And God kept His promise.

Sodom and Gomorrah

Two of the worst Canaanite cities in the ancient world were Sodom and Gomorrah. The sins committed in these two cities were equal to the days of Noah, when God wiped out everyone on the earth except Noah and his family. In ancient history, many cultures worshiped false gods, which led people to act in sinful and destructive ways. None were as wicked as what took place in Sodom and Gomorrah. These cities were so evil that God sent fire down from heaven to destroy them.

Abraham and Lot

When Abraham and his nephew Lot settled in Canaan, the land could not provide enough grass or water for their huge herds, so they needed to separate. Abraham allowed Lot to choose where he wanted to live. Despite its wickedness, Lot chose to live in Sodom because of its lush, green pastures. Scripture tells us, "Lot dwelt in the cities of the plain and pitched his tent even as far as Sodom. But the men of Sodom were exceedingly wicked and sinful against the LORD" (Gen. 13:12b–13).

Abraham Prays for Sodom

One day, God appeared to Abraham and said, "Because the outcry against Sodom and Gomorrah is great, and because their sin is very grave, I will go down now and see whether they have done altogether according to the outcry against it that has come to Me; and if not, I will know" (Gen. 18:20–21). God planned to destroy the city, but Abraham pleaded for God to spare the town of Sodom if He could find even ten righteous people living in it. God agreed (see Gen. 18:22–33).

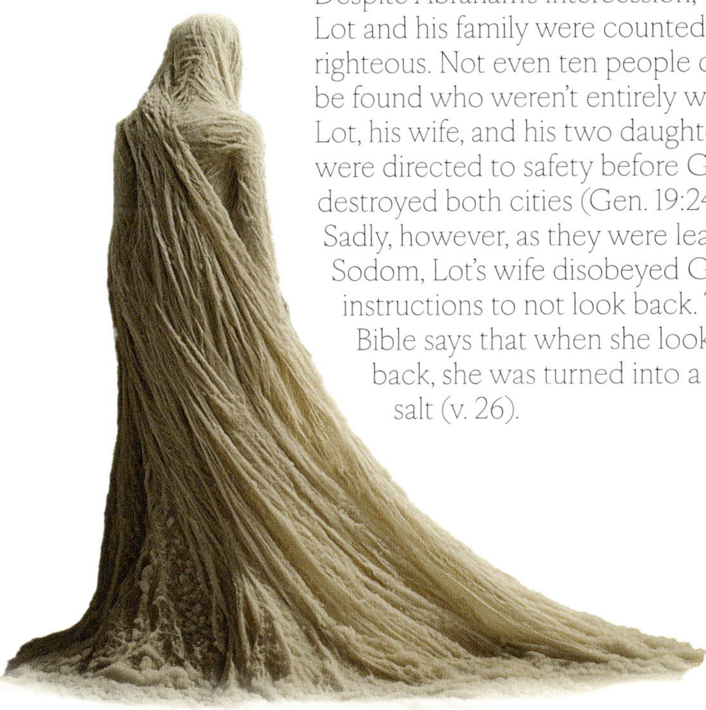

Lot Escapes from Sodom

Despite Abraham's intercession, only Lot and his family were counted as righteous. Not even ten people could be found who weren't entirely wicked! Lot, his wife, and his two daughters were directed to safety before God destroyed both cities (Gen. 19:24). Sadly, however, as they were leaving Sodom, Lot's wife disobeyed God's instructions to not look back. The Bible says that when she looked back, she was turned into a pillar of salt (v. 26).

Jacob's Promise

God eventually spoke to Abraham's grandson Jacob, reassuring him that he would receive the same promise that God had given to Abraham. God changed Jacob's name to Israel and promised to grant the land of Canaan to Jacob and his descendants as their inheritance. Jacob's 12 sons were the ancestors of the 12 tribes of Israel. God had kept his promise to Abraham and allowed His blessings to flow to subsequent generations.

One night, God spoke to Abraham in Canaan and called him outside to look up at the night sky. God told Abraham, "'Look now toward heaven, and count the stars if you are able to number them . . . Then He said to him, 'I am the LORD, who brought you out of Ur of the Chaldeans, to give you this land [Canaan] to inherit it'" (Gen. 15:5b–7). Abraham's descendants would become recipients of this promise, but not immediately.

Strangers in Egypt

God gave Abraham an important message: "Know certainly that your descendants will be strangers in a land that is not theirs, and will serve them, and they will afflict them four hundred years. . . . But in the fourth generation they shall return here, for the iniquity of the Amorites is not yet complete" (Gen. 15:13, 16).

God's Promise to Jacob

When Jacob was an old man, there was a famine in Canaan and Egypt. His son Joseph invited him (Jacob) to leave Canaan and come live in Egypt where he could find food. One night, God spoke to Jacob and said, "I am God, the God of your father; do not fear to go down to Egypt . . . I will go down with you to Egypt, and I will also surely bring you up again" (Gen. 46:3–4a).

From Canaan to Egypt

With the promise they would one day return to the Promised Land, Jacob, his sons, their wives, and their children left Canaan and arrived in Egypt. There were seventy members in his family, not counting his sons' wives. They all moved to Egypt to find food during the famine and lived together in a region of Egypt known as Goshen.

Growing a Nation

Eventually, Joseph died, along with his entire generation. Their descendants "were fruitful and increased abundantly, multiplied and grew exceedingly mighty; and the land was filled with them" (Exod. 1:6–7b). A new pharaoh came to power, and he did not remember Joseph's work or his role in saving Egypt from famine. This pharaoh forced the Israelites into slavery because he feared they would fight against him in war. The Egyptians made the descendants of Jacob live in Goshen and work as slaves, but the more the pharaoh oppressed them, the more the people multiplied and grew. What the Egyptians intended for evil, God worked into something good. Over several hundred years, the number of Israelites grew and grew until there were more than two million people! The family of Jacob was now big enough to become its own nation.

Life in Egypt

What was life like for the slaves living in Egypt? The Hebrew people became the workforce of ancient Egypt. They were trained in metalwork to craft gold, silver, and brass into jewelry and exquisite treasures for the important members of Pharaoh's palace. They learned how to mix exotic spices to create expensive oils and incense. "And they built for Pharaoh supply cities, Pithom and Raamses" (Exod. 1:11b). The Israelites made many of the glories and riches of Egypt during these years.

Moses

When he saw that the people of God continued to thrive even in slavery, Pharaoh announced a new law: throw every Hebrew baby boy into the Nile River as soon as he was born (Exod. 1:15–16). One mother, however, decided to save her infant son. She made a little boat from a basket covered with tar. Placing her baby in the basket, she floated it down the Nile River. When Pharaoh's daughter came down to the river, she saw the basket and looked inside. She took the baby and raised him as her own son. She called him Moses.

Education in Pharaoh's Court

Reading. Writing. Arithmetic. Growing up as a son of Pharaoh's daughter, Moses received a solid Egyptian education. He had access to clay tablets from antiquity and papyrus with eyewitness accounts of historic events since the creation of the world. Young princes in Pharaoh's court studied astronomy, architecture, and agriculture. They learned how to govern, run a profitable trade network, and oversee an army.

TIMELINE: 1500 B.C. – 600 B.C.

1500 B.C.

The Exodus
1491 B.C.

Joshua leads the Israelites into the Promised Land
1452 B.C.

Settlement of Grimspound (England)
c. 1450 B.C.

Vedas written in Sanskrit
c. 1400 B.C.

Gideon judges Israel
c. 1251 B.C.

Troy destroyed (Turkey)
c. 1200 B.C.

Phoenician alphabet created
c. 1100 B.C.

David becomes king
c. 1048 B.C.

First temple constructed by King Solomon in Jerusalem
c. 1012–1004 B.C.

Sparta built
c. 1000 B.C.

Israel splits into two kingdoms, Israel and Judah
975 B.C.

1000 B.C.

1491 B.C.
God gives Moses the Ten Commandments

1451 B.C.
Jericho falls

1430 B.C.
Hittite Empire formed

c. 1278 B.C.
Deliverance by Deborah and Barak

c. 1200 B.C.
Olmec culture begins (Mexico)

c. 1200 B.C.
China casts large bronze bells

c. 1095 B.C.
Samuel anoints Saul king of Israel

c. 1048 B.C.
King David makes Jerusalem his capital

c. 1000 B.C.
Kites & dictionaries in use in China

c. 1000 B.C.
India manufactures sugar from sugar cane

929 B.C.
Omri, king of Israel, moves capital to Samaria

Chavín fashion gold objects (South America) c. 900 B.C.

836 B.C. Civil War in Egypt

Carthage founded 814 B.C.

808 B.C. Jonah swallowed by a great fish

800 B.C.

Α Ω

Greeks use an alphabet c. 800 B.C.

776 B.C. First Olympics held in ancient Greece

Homer wrote *Iliad* c. 760 B.C.

759–698 B.C. Isaiah prophesies

Cush conquers Egypt c. 750 B.C.

748 B.C. Founding of Rome

Assyria destroys Northern Kingdom of Israel 721 B.C.

713 B.C. As a miraculous sign to Hezekiah, the shadow goes backward on the sundial of Ahaz

Celts grow strong in Hallstatt (Austria) c. 700 B.C.

c. 700 B.C. Scythians dominate steppes north of the Black Sea

Assyrians build Jerwan Aqueduct to carry water to Nineveh c. 690 B.C.

629–588 B.C Jeremiah prophesies

Daniel prophesies 607–534 B.C.

604 B.C. Disappearance of Philistines after Babylonian conquest

Hanging Gardens of Babylon c. 600 B.C.

600 B.C.

c. 600 B.C. Celts migrate to Britain

Ezekiel's ministry begins c. 593 B.C.

588 B.C. Judah captured and temple destroyed by Nebuchadnezzar (Babylonians)

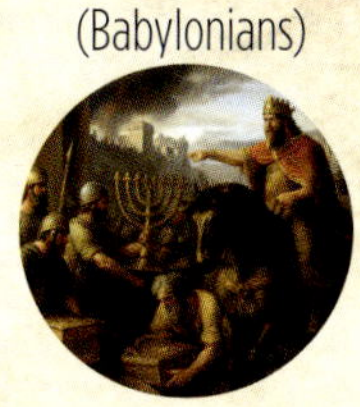

Moses was in trouble. He had seen an Egyptian beating a Hebrew slave. To protect his fellow Israelite, Moses killed the Egyptian. When Pharaoh found out, Moses ran for his life (Exod. 2:15). He fled to the land of Midian and started a brand-new life.

The Burning Bush

When Moses fled Egypt, he became a shepherd for a man named Jethro, who gave his daughter Zipporah to be Moses' wife. One day, as Moses was leading flocks of sheep near Mount Horeb (Mt. Sinai), he saw a bush burning with fire, yet the bush did not burn up. God spoke to Moses out of that bush.

The Promised Land

On that holy ground (Exod. 3:5), God told Moses His plans to rescue the Israelites out of slavery. He called Moses to be their leader and take them back to Canaan, the land God had promised to Abraham and his descendants.

The Great I AM

Moses asked God what His name was. God answered, "I AM WHO I AM" (Exod. 3:14b). Many biblical scholars see this as a declaration of God's self-existence as the ultimate, uncreated, independent, eternal God. Even today, one name people use for God is the Great I AM.

♦ Sunrise over Mt. Sinai in Egypt

Ten Plagues

Moses and his brother Aaron gave God's message to Pharaoh: "Let my people go..." (Exod. 5:1b). Pharaoh refused, so God sent ten plagues against the Egyptians. These miracles gave the Israelites hope, grew their confidence in Moses, and built their trust in God. Even some of the Egyptians began to believe. Yet, Pharaoh became more and more stubborn and refused to release the Israelites from captivity.

TEN PLAGUES OF EGYPT

Plague 1		God instructed Moses to touch the Nile River with his rod, and the water turned to blood.	Boils and sores afflicted all the people and animals in Egypt.		Plague 6
Plague 2		Frogs came up and covered the land of Egypt.	Hail came from the sky and destroyed the land and killed people and animals in Egypt.		Plague 7
Plague 3		The dust became gnats (or another insect) throughout Egypt.	Locusts covered the land until it was black, devouring every tree, plant, and fruit.		Plague 8
Plague 4		Swarms of flies tormented people and livestock in Egypt, but not in Goshen, where God's people lived.	Darkness that could be felt spread over Egypt for three days, but the Israelites had light where they lived.		Plague 9
Plague 5		All the livestock and cattle in Egypt died, but not in Goshen.	Every firstborn son in Egypt died, including cattle. Even Pharaoh's firstborn son was killed.	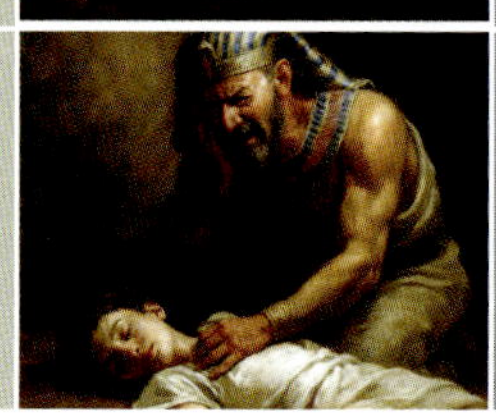	Plague 10

Passover

God protected the Israelites from the ten plagues. To protect their firstborn son from the last and final plague, God gave them very specific instructions to follow. They were to sacrifice a lamb, then use some of its blood to place a mark around the top of their doorways (Exod. 12:3–7). Then they prepared a special meal. As they ate, they were to be dressed and ready to leave their homes. This special feast became known as Passover.

Pharaoh's Change of Heart

The night of the tenth plague, the angel of the Lord passed through the land of Egypt. When he saw the blood on the doorways of the Israelites, he passed over their homes. But when the angel came to the homes of those without blood over the doorframe, the firstborn of every family and of their flocks died. Finally, after his own son died, Pharaoh called Moses and told him the Israelites could leave.

Exodus

The Israelites were ready to go as God had instructed. Earlier, the people had asked the Egyptians for clothing, precious gold, and silver, and the Egyptians complied. The Israelites carried away the treasures along with livestock. Around 600,000 men left with their wives and children, totaling about two million people in all.

Crossing the Red Sea

The Israelites traveled together across the desert. They soon arrived at the shore of the Red Sea. Suddenly bad news reached them. Pharaoh had changed his mind and the mighty army of Egypt was chasing after them! Everyone panicked. Where could they go? What happened next is one of the greatest miracles in the history of Israel. God parted the waters of the Red Sea. Dry land appeared. The Israelites walked safely across. As Pharaoh's chariots rode across in pursuit, God let the waters flow once more. Pharaoh and his army were destroyed (see Exod. 14).

Worship and Praise

The Israelites witnessed an amazing miracle that day. Safe on the other side of the Red Sea, Moses and the Israelites sang in worship and praise to God. Then, Miriam, the sister of Moses, led the women in worship, playing timbrels in their hands and dancing in thanksgiving to God (see Exod. 15:1–21).

The Israelites wandered in the harsh desert-like wilderness. No water. No bread. No meat. How could anyone survive? God provided for their needs. He made water gush out of a rock. He sent quail, enough meat to feed two million people! And each morning, God gave them manna, bread from heaven. It settled on the ground like dew.

Mount Sinai

In the third month after they left Egypt, the Israelites reached Mount Sinai and set up camp at the foot of the mountain. God called Moses to meet with Him on the mountain. He told Moses to tell the Israelites, "You have seen what I did to the Egyptians, and how I bore you on eagles' wings and brought you to Myself. Now therefore, if you will indeed obey My voice and keep My covenant, then you shall be a special treasure to Me above all people; for all the earth is Mine. And you shall be to Me a kingdom of priests and a holy nation" (Exod. 19:4–6a).

Ten Commandments

A new nation needed laws to govern its people. God gave Moses the Ten Commandments on two "tablets of stone, written by the finger of God" (Exod. 20:1–17; 31:18).

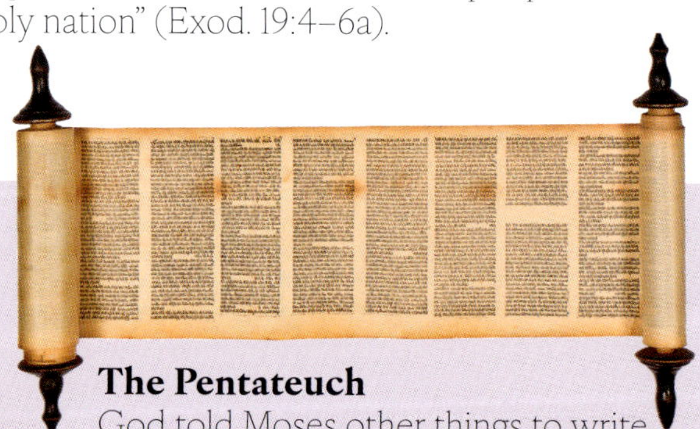

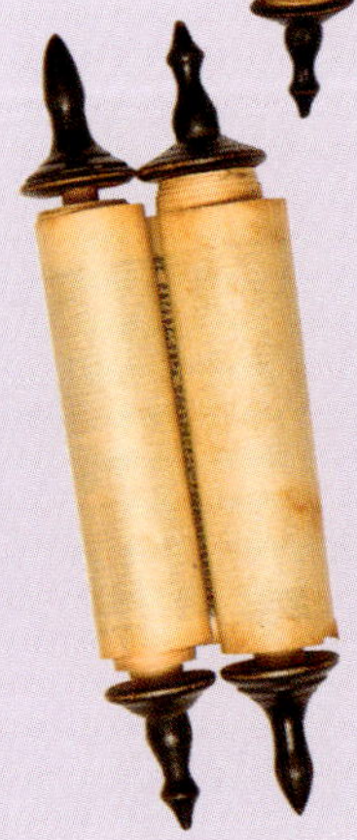

The Pentateuch

God told Moses other things to write down. Exodus 24:4 calls them "all the words of the Lord." Moses wrote the first five books of the Bible, also known as the Pentateuch (literally, "five scrolls"). Genesis tells about the history of the Hebrew people before Moses' birth. Exodus, Leviticus, Numbers, and Deuteronomy contain mostly eyewitness reports Moses experienced as well as laws God gave to the Israelites to follow.

Writing Genesis

How did Moses write Genesis? Having been educated in Pharaoh's courts, Moses had access to ancient documents made of stone, clay, and papyrus. He also heard oral accounts, passed down through generations by word of mouth. Moses knew about key events in the history of the world and of his own people. In the first chapters of Genesis, Moses wrote specific details about the creation of the world. How did he know what happened if he wasn't there? The same God who inspired prophets to write about future events also inspired Moses to write about past events.

The Tabernacle

God instructed the Israelites to build a special place of worship called the tabernacle. God promised to meet with them there. It was a large tent, easy to pack and unpack along their journey to the Promised Land.

And let them make me a sanctuary, that I may dwell among them.
–Exodus 25:8

Holy of Holies
A second, small room was located in the back of the tabernacle, behind a veil. Inside was the golden ark of the covenant. The ark was like a box. It contained the **Ten Commandments, a jar of manna,** and **Aaron's rod** (or staff). Two gold angels called cherubim spread their golden wings over the top of the ark. This was known as the mercy seat, the place God promised to meet with His people.

- Tribe of Levi chosen to serve as priests (Num. 3:5–10)
- Priestly garments (Exod. 28)

Priests
God chose the tribe of Levi to be set apart from the other tribes of Israel. These descendants of Aaron became the priests who burned the sacrifices and served in the tabernacle. The Levites took care of the tabernacle and helped carry it as the Israelite people moved from place to place.

- Golden altar of incense (Exod. 30:1–10)

- Golden candlestick (Exod. 25:31–40)

- Ark of the covenant (Exod. 25:10–22)
- Table of showbread (Exod. 25:23–30)

- Curtain (Exod. 26:1–14)

Furniture
God gave the Israelites specific instructions to make special furniture for the tabernacle. Outside the tent was a bronze laver, a large basin for the priests to wash. The bronze altar of burnt offerings was made so the Israelites could bring their offerings and sacrifices to the priests. Inside the tent stood a golden candlestick. To worship God, incense was burned on the golden altar of incense. Twelve loaves of bread were placed on the table of showbread.

- Bronze altar (Exod. 27:1–8)

- Bronze laver (Exod. 30:17–21)

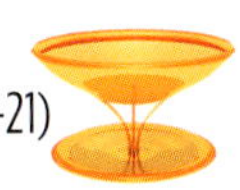

Measurements

- Overall 150 ft. long (100 cubits) by 75 ft. wide (50 cubits)
- Holy of Holies 15 ft. square (10 cubits square)
- Curtain 17 ft. long (28 cubits) by 2.5 ft. wide (4 cubits)
- Holy Place 30 ft. long (20 cubits) by 15 ft. wide (10 cubits)
- Entrance 30 ft. wide (20 cubits)

The reports were in! Moses had sent 12 men into the Promised Land to spy out the land, one from each of the 12 tribes of Israel (See Num. 13). When the men got back, what did they say? There were strong cities with tall walls around them. The kings were powerful and the people were like giants!

Go In or Stay Out?

Ten spies told the people they'd never be able to live in that land. Two spies—Joshua and Caleb—gave a different report. They said the land was full of God's blessings. They said God would lead them into the Promised Land and give them success against their foes.

The King's Highway

The Wilderness of Sinai formed a giant peninsula that looked like an upside-down triangle. The Red Sea was its western side. The Gulf of Aqaba was to the east. An ancient road called the King's Highway led north from the Gulf of Aqaba all the way to Damascus. The road was a key trade route in the days of Moses. It was used in the days of King Solomon as well. Now it is a modern highway in the country of Jordan that people still travel on today.

Forty Years

God told the Israelites not to fear what was in the Promised Land because He would fight for them (Deut. 1:29–30). Yet, the people refused to believe Him, so God judged them. Instead of going directly into the Promised Land, the Israelites would wander in the wilderness for 40 years! After the current generation died (except Joshua and Caleb), God would lead the next generation into the land He promised to give to Abraham, Isaac, and Jacob. A trip of days or months turned into 40 years!

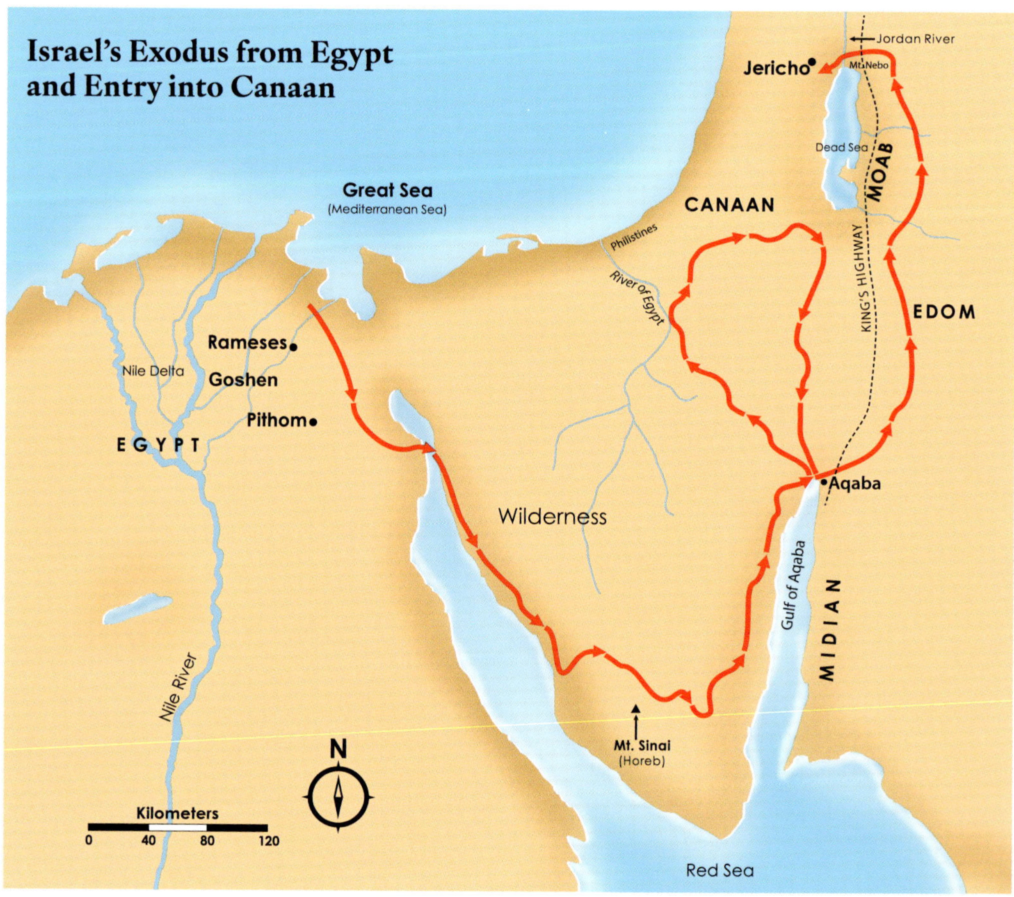

Traveling North

Moses wanted to lead the Israelites north along the King's Highway. Their relatives, descendants of Esau known as the Edomites, ruled over an early section of the highway. Moses asked permission to pass through their land, but the people of Edom refused and the Israelites were forced to go a different way.

Victory

As Moses led the Israelites toward the Promised Land, he asked permission for them to pass through different lands. However, the local kings in those areas refused to allow them to pass through in peace. One by one, the kings advanced their armies to attack the Israelites. One by one, God gave the Israelites victory in battle (see Num. 21).

Blessing the Twelve Tribes

Over the years, the generation of people who had been enslaved in Egypt died, including Miriam, Aaron, and Moses. Before Moses died, he gave each of the twelve tribes of Israel a blessing. Over time, these blessings became associated with a symbol for each tribe.

Borders of the Promised Land

Before Moses died, God laid out the borders of the Promised Land. To the east was the Jordan River. To the west was the Mediterranean Sea. To the south was the Wilderness of Zin. To the north was the Euphrates River. God told the Israelites, "It is not because of your righteousness or the uprightness of your heart that you go in to possess their land, but because of the wickedness of these nations that the LORD your God drives them out from before you, and that He may fulfill the word which the LORD swore to your fathers, to Abraham, Isaac, and Jacob" (Deut. 9:5).

God chose Joshua, the assistant of Moses, to lead the Israelites into the Promised Land. Before they entered, the people camped on the plains of Moab, east of the Jordan River. Joshua sent men across the river to spy out the land and the city of Jericho.

Rahab

Fear. Courage. Faith. A woman named Rahab heard about the Israelites and their God. She chose to turn away from the false gods of the Canaanites and put her trust in the God of Israel. She hid the spies from Jericho's king. The spies said they would save Rahab and her family on the day they attacked Jericho if she put a scarlet cord in her window (Josh. 2).

Gibeon

Gibeon was one of the largest cities in Canaan. Northwest of Jerusalem, it was like a royal city. The king lived in his palace inside the city walls, and men of Gibeon were trained as warriors. When the people of Gibeon heard about the Israelites and their God, they were afraid. They decided not to fight like all the other cities that were destroyed. They tricked the Israelites by pretending they came from far away so they could work as servants instead of being destroyed (Josh. 9).

Battle of Jericho

God told Joshua He would fight for the Israelites. He told the priests to join a seven-day march around the walls that surrounded the city of Jericho. On the seventh day, the priests blew their trumpets and the Israelites shouted. The walls of Jericho fell to the ground! The Israelites saw the scarlet cord hanging in Rahab's window, so as they destroyed the city, they kept Rahab and her family safe.

Shiloh

God chose Shiloh as the holy place for worship, so the Israelites set up the tabernacle there. Joshua and Eleazar the high priest met at the tabernacle with the leaders of each of the tribes. The leaders cast lots (like flipping a coin or drawing straws) to determine God's decision on how to divide up the land. Instead of getting land, the Levites (priests) lived among the tribes and represented God to the people.

Judges

After Joshua died, the Israelites worshiped the false gods of the Canaanites. God removed His hand of protection, and their enemies attacked. When they realized their sin and cried out to God, He raised up judges to lead them.

Othniel

Othniel became the first judge of Israel. He was Caleb's son-in-law, and he led the Israelites into battle against their enemies—and won! Most of all, he brought the people back to God. Israel experienced 40 years of peace during Othniel's leadership.

Deborah

In a pattern repeated throughout their history, the Jews turned their back on God. King Jabin of Canaan oppressed them. God raised up Deborah as their judge, so everyone in Israel came to her to hear their cases. Barak, the commander of Israel's army, went to battle against Sisera, the commander of Jabin's army. Deborah went with them and praised God for the victory He gave to the Israelites.

Other Judges

Gideon led Israel to defeat the Midianites. **Samson** led Israel to defeat the Philistines. **Samuel**, the boy prophet, became the last judge of Israel.

Rahab's Family Tree

- What happened to Rahab? After Israel conquered Jericho, she married a man named Salmon of the tribe of Judah. They had a son named Boaz.
- Boaz married Ruth, a widow from Moab. Together they had a son named Obed, who had a son named Jesse.
- Jesse was the father of David—the famous David who became the great king of Israel and was the ancestor of Jesus Christ.
- Rahab is listed in the family tree of Jesus!

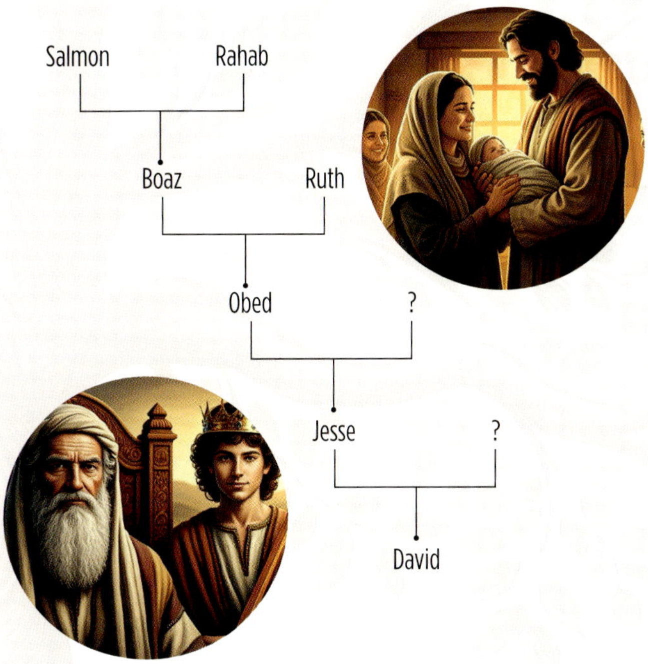

SEA PEOPLES

c. 1276–1178 B.C.

Crashing waves. Sails flapping in the gusty ocean breeze. Shouts of war. They attacked from the sea. Around the coast of the Mediterranean Sea, no settlement was safe. No empire was secure. Raiders known today as the Sea Peoples launched surprise battles against their foes.

History of the Sea Peoples

Where did they come from? Greece? Crete? Other islands in the Aegean or Mediterranean Seas? No one knows for sure. The history of the Sea Peoples is shrouded in mystery and much debate. Their impact, however, can be found among the dusty records of the past.

Philistines

One tribe of the Sea Peoples landed on the shores of Canaan along the coast of the Mediterranean Sea. They conquered local kings, settled in, and took over this coastland territory about the time Joshua led the Israelites across the Jordan and into the Promised Land. In the Bible, this group was known as the Philistines.

Ancient Greece

The Sea Peoples conquered the Greek city of Mycenae. Survivors of the attack fled to other regions. As a result, the Mycenaean civilization declined.

Hittite Empire

The Sea Peoples conquered the Hittites, and their powerful empire collapsed. Its destruction was so complete, the history of the Hittites was lost until modern archaeology uncovered it.

Egypt

The Sea Peoples attacked Egypt. Pharaoh Ramses II fought them off and Pharaoh Ramses III fought them again. Details of these fierce battles can be found carved on the walls of Egyptian temples and tombs.

Strong Cities

The Philistines occupied five major cities along the western coast of Canaan. Gaza was in the south. Ashkelon and Ashdod were north of Gaza. The cities of Ekron and Gath were inland. This area became known as Philistia.

The Secret of Iron

Iron spears. Iron swords. Iron chariots. When the Philistines arrived in Canaan, they brought with them the secret of forging iron. They had learned this skill from the Hittites. The Philistines were the only people in Canaan who knew how to make things from iron. Since iron weapons were the strongest of that time, the Philistines became the most powerful force in the region.

Goliath

The Philistines became Israel's neighbors after Joshua led the Israelites into the Promised Land. Aggressive and warlike, they fought many battles against their neighbors. One of the most famous Philistines was a warrior named Goliath. From the city of Gath, Goliath was a giant of a man. Some say he stood over nine feet tall!

End of the Philistines

Under Israel's King Saul, a young boy named David fought Goliath—and won! After David became king of Israel, he defeated the Philistines. Years later, around 604 B.C., King Nebuchadnezzar of Babylon conquered the Philistines, deported them to other regions of the ancient world, and they disappeared from history.

♦ Peleset warrior, one of the Sea Peoples groups

A New Name

The Roman Empire eventually conquered Israel and most of the land around the Mediterranean Sea. They divided their empire into different provinces, or regions. The province that included the Jewish homeland was named Judea. In A.D. 135, Emperor Hadrian destroyed the city of Jerusalem and plowed it into the ground (Emperor Titus had leveled Jerusalem the first time in A.D. 70). Hadrian banished Jews from Jerusalem. To anger the Jews even further, Hadrian renamed the province Palestina (after the Philistines). The name Palestinians applied to Jews, Christians, Muslims, and Arabs—anyone who lived in the Roman province of Palestina at that time.

The Canaanites lived in the land of Canaan along the eastern shores of the Mediterranean Sea. The Sea Peoples conquered the southern coastland and later became known as the Philistines. The surrounding territory was known as Philistia. The people of God conquered the Promised Land, and their territory became known as Israel. The Canaanites still living along the coast north of Philistia became known as the Phoenicians. The Greeks called their territory Phoenicia.

Ship Builders

Towering cedar trees covered the Lebanon mountains like a thick carpet. The Phoenicians chopped down these trees and built some of the most famous ships of the ancient world. Trading vessels were packed from stem to stern with rich cargo. Warships known as biremes were powered by two rows of oars. These two ships traveled together to provide protection for the trade ships from pirates on the seas and wars at the ports of trade.

Phoenicia

Phoenicia was on a narrow strip of coastal plain sandwiched between the Lebanon mountains in the east and the Mediterranean Sea to the west. Only about 20 miles wide, it stretched north and south for about 200 miles. Phoenicia was in the modern-day country of Lebanon.

Trade Network

Skilled navigators, the Phoenicians sailed to the far corners of the ancient world. They established trading ports on islands and coastlands of the Mediterranean Sea. Confident explorers, they also sailed to the British Isles. They were the first to navigate around the continent of Africa. Some scholars think the Phoenicians sailed to South America long before the days of Christopher Columbus.

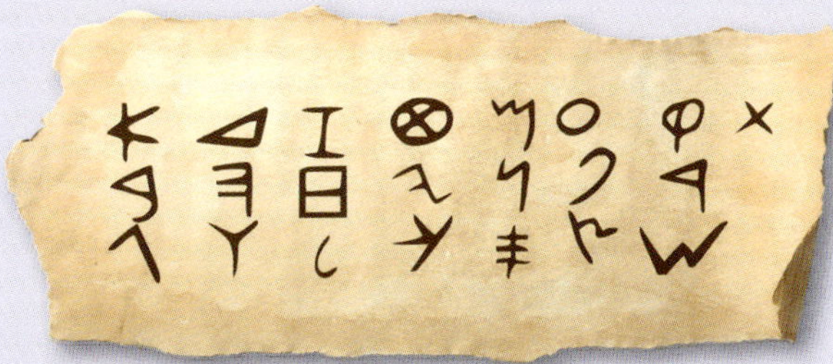

Manufacturers

Phoenicians are credited with the invention of glass blowing. They traded their valuable glass bottles in the port cities they established. Phoenicians also discovered the secret of crafting purple dyed from rare murex shellfish found along the shores of the Mediterranean. Purple fabric dyed in Tyre and Sidon was so expensive and so prized that it was only worn by emperors, kings, and elite wealthy nobles in Greece or Rome.

The Alphabet

Far-flung traders, the Phoenicians needed a quick, easy way to record trading accounts around their vast network. Cuneiform and hieroglyphics required too much memorization and used too many confusing symbols. The Phoenicians invented 22 consonants written as crude letters they used as their alphabet. They carried this system throughout the ancient world. The Greeks added vowels to these letters, and the Romans fine-tuned their appearance. The resulting 26 letters became the foundation of the English alphabet.

Carthage

The most famous trading port built by the Phoenicians was in Carthage on the northern coast of Africa. According to legend, it was founded by a Phoenician princess named Dido. Long after Alexander the Great conquered Phoenicia in 332 B.C., Carthage still flourished. The magnificent city was finally destroyed by the Romans in 146 B.C.

Phoenicia in the Bible

As neighbors to the north of Israel, the Phoenicians interacted with the Israelites. The Bible records how Joshua divided up the Promised Land among the tribes of Israel. Asher's border extended as far north as the Phoenician cities of Sidon and Tyre. Hiram, king of Tyre, sent cedar trees to King David for building his palace. When Solomon was king, Hiram supplied Solomon with cedar, cypress, and gold to build the temple. In later years, the prophets spoke of God's judgment on Phoenicia's great city of Tyre because the city rejoiced when Jerusalem was conquered.

The Bible as a History Book

Historic facts found in the Bible regarding the Phoenicians show how the Bible is a book of history. We can trust the Bible's accuracy on historic events from creation to the prophets to the life, death, and Resurrection of Jesus Christ and beyond.

The tabernacle was at Shiloh. Eli was high priest, and his sons served as priests. But Eli's sons did not know God and led the people of Israel to sin. As a result, God raised up a man, Samuel, who would seek the Lord.

Samuel

Samuel's mother Hannah dedicated him to God (1 Sam. 1:1–28). When he was young, she took him to serve at the tabernacle. Samuel grew up as a Nazarite like Samson. His hair was never cut. One night, the boy Samuel heard the voice of God. He gave Samuel a message of impending judgment for Eli and his wicked sons (see 1 Sam. 3:1–14). Samuel's ministry as a prophet had begun.

King Saul

Israel's people demanded a king instead of being led by God (1 Sam. 12:12). God chose a young man named Saul as king. The prophet Samuel anointed Saul as the first king of Israel. Over time, Saul became disobedient to God, and He responded by saying, "Because you have rejected the word of the LORD, He also has rejected you from being king" (1 Sam. 15:23b). God told Samuel to anoint a different king.

♦ Olive trees produce a heavy crop of olives one year, followed by a significantly lighter crop the next. This is called a biennial bearing cycle. Olives were crushed and then pressed to harvest the oil.

♦ A ram's horn was often used to hold oil.

Defeat!

The Israelites marched in battle against the Philistines. The priests, Eli's sons, carried the ark of the covenant with them into the battle. The Philistines defeated them all! They killed the priests and took the ark. That day, Eli and his sons died. Samuel became both priest and judge of Israel. He set up his court in the town of Mizpeh.

Shepherd Boy

David was a youth tasked with tending his father's sheep. He had a heart that loved God, and he played the harp and sang worship songs to God. Many of David's songs can be found in the Book of Psalms in the Bible. God told Samuel to anoint David, the shepherd boy, as the next king. He would take the throne around 15 years later.

David and Goliath

King Saul led the army of Israel against the Philistines. There was one big problem—Goliath. He was a giant of a man! Everyone in Israel's army was afraid to fight Goliath—except David. He knew God helped him protect his sheep from lions and bears, so he knew God would help him protect Israel from Goliath. David used his sling and stones and killed the giant!

Mighty Warrior

As David grew up, he became a mighty warrior. Everyone in Israel sang his praises. King Saul became jealous of David and tried to kill him. David hid from Saul and assembled an army of his own.

The New King

Another battle raged between the Philistines and Israel. King Saul and most of his sons died in battle. David was anointed a second time, making him king of his tribe of Judah. After Saul's last son was murdered, David became king over all of Israel, uniting the 12 tribes.

Jerusalem

A new king needed a new capital. David conquered the city of Jerusalem. Known later as the City of David, he built his palace inside the city walls. He brought the ark of the covenant and the tabernacle into the city, making Jerusalem the political capital and spiritual home of Israel. Even more, God chose Jerusalem as the city He loved.

Iron

David led Israel in victory over the Philistines, who knew the secret of working with iron. David then led Israel to conquer Edom. They had rich deposits of iron ore. With these two victories, Israel could make iron weapons and iron chariots for their army for the first time. Israel became the most powerful kingdom in the land.

How did King David unite the 12 tribes of Israel?
Ending civil conflict Anointed king over Judah after Saul's death
Winning the people's loyalty Showed mercy to Saul's descendants and gained favor
Becoming king over all Israel Anointed king by elders of the tribes, ending division
Choosing Jerusalem as the capital Captured the neutral city and made it the political center
Making the ark the spiritual center Brought the ark of the covenant to Jerusalem

♦ Ancient spearhead

♦ Iron dagger with ivory handle

Eternal King

Riches. Power. Faith. King David had it all. He wanted to build a temple in Jerusalem to honor God, but David had sinned. He had murdered Uriah the Hittite and married his wife, Bathsheba. Even though David repented and God forgave him, God told David that his son, Solomon, would build the temple instead. Then God gave David a special promise: One day, David's descendant would be king forever! This was God's promise to send Jesus as the eternal King.

♦ Tel Dan Stele

Myth or History?

David was a mighty hero! Bible skeptics claimed David was just a myth or a nice story to read because no evidence outside the Bible ever mentioned King David. But in 1993, archaeologists found a stone at Tel Dan (an excavation site) in northern Israel. The writing on it told about a king "of the house of David." Discoveries like this show the Bible can be trusted for historical accounts.

Late in King David's life, trouble brewed over who would become the next king. His older son, Adonijah, declared himself king. When David heard about it, he anointed Solomon, Bathsheba's son, as the official king of Israel.

Wisdom

In the beginning of Solomon's reign, he asked God for wisdom. God said He would bless Solomon with wisdom along with riches and honor. He became known as one of the wisest men in the ancient world. He was an expert in botany (the study of plants) as well as zoology (the study of animals). He spoke over 3,000 wise sayings (1 Kings 4:32), many of them gathered and collected into one book—the Book of Proverbs in the Bible. He also wrote 1,005 songs and the Song of Solomon in the Old Testament.

Solomon's Kingdom

King Solomon expanded Israel. It extended from the border of Egypt in the south to the Euphrates River in the north. His mighty army was made of 12,000 horsemen and 1,400 chariots. He kept 4,000 stalls for his horses.

Queen of Sheba

The fame of King Solomon spread far and wide, including Sheba, a country in southern Arabia. Camel caravans from Sheba carried spices and gold to places along a vast network of trade. The Queen of Sheba heard of King Solomon's wisdom and traveled with her caravan of camels to meet him. Showering the king with the finest products of her land, the queen was amazed at Israel's king and the court he kept.

Marriage Agreements

It was common practice among nations to arrange marriages between the leaders to guarantee peace between them. But God commanded the Israelites not to marry people from other countries because it would tempt God's people to worship their false gods. However, to establish his kingdom and have peace along his borders, King Solomon married women of other nations. He even married Pharaoh's daughter from Egypt. This helped Israel be at peace with its neighbors, but it led Solomon to worship false gods.

But King Solomon loved many foreign women . . . from the nations of whom the LORD had said to the children of Israel, "You shall not intermarry with them, nor they with you. Surely they will turn away your hearts after their gods." Solomon clung to these in love . . . For it was so, when Solomon was old, that his wives turned his heart after other gods; and his heart was not loyal to the LORD his God, as was the heart of his father David.
–1 Kings 11:1a, 2, 4

♦ Dr. Joe Greene stands at a palatial residence and capitol of the biblical Edom.

Fact or Fiction?

For many years, Bible critics claimed David was a myth and that ancient Edom was a desert wasteland, useless for settlement. However, in 2019, archaeologists announced the discovery of ancient copper mines in Edom (part of modern-day Jordan). This supported the existence of Edom as a nation during early Bible times. Discoveries like this show the Bible is accurate historically. Our faith is founded on fact!

Hiram of Lebanon

Hiram, king of Lebanon, had been friends with King David. North of Israel along the coast of the Mediterranean Sea, Lebanon was home to the Phoenicians. With mighty forests of towering cedars and miles of coastland, Phoenicians were famous for shipbuilding and the trading posts they established all around the Mediterranean Sea.

Solomon's Fleet

An alliance with the Phoenicians had its advantages. Using Phoenician sailors to operate his ships, Solomon assembled a great fleet. Israel was part of the wealthy trade network of the ancient world. Solomon's ships sailed to Tarshish and brought back to Israel the resources and products of the known world. They sailed to far away regions like Ophir and returned with expensive spices, precious gems, and quantities of gold. Solomon ruled Israel during its Golden Age.

Construction

Building projects were King Solomon's passion. Throughout Israel, he built fortified cities surrounded by walls where people would be safe during an attack. In Jerusalem, he built a magnificent palace that included the House of the Forest of Lebanon, the Hall of Pillars, and the Hall of Thrones. He also built a palace for Pharaoh's daughter, one of his wives. His most monumental building project was the construction of the temple in Jerusalem.

Supplies

King David conquered the Philistines and learned their secret of working with iron. He conquered the Edomites and took over their copper and iron mines. He acquired vast amounts of silver and gold as he subdued other nations. King David collected large stockpiles of material to use for building the temple.

Work Begins

King Solomon also formed an alliance with King Hiram of Tyre. Known for their woodworking skills, Hiram's men floated rafts of cedar and cypress logs down the coast of the Mediterranean Sea from Lebanon to Israel. Solomon hired many of Hiram's workers to help build the temple.

King David hadwanted to build a holy house to worship God. God chose the site of Mount Moriah in Jerusalem. This was the place Abraham had journeyed when God told Abraham to sacrifice his son Isaac (see Gen. 22:1–19). Previously used as a threshing floor, King David had bought the land and set it apart as the place to build the temple.

Solomon's Temple

House of God

It took Solomon's workers seven years to build the temple. It followed much of the original design of the Tent of Meeting. Only the priests ministered in the temple and its courtyard to carry out their holy duties. Levites performed all the necessary jobs to take care of the temple.

Foundation Stones

Construction of Solomon's Temple required giant foundation stones. Solomon appointed a labor force of more than 100,000 workers from Israel. These men helped the Phoenicians move the logs, quarry massive stones, and bring the necessary supplies to the construction site.

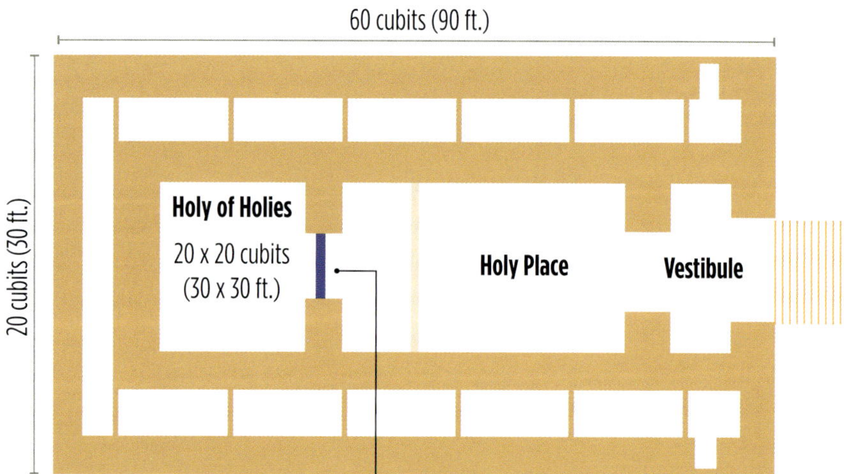

Courtyard

People came to worship God and offer their sacrifices in the large courtyard that surrounded the temple.

Curtain

This veil served the same purpose as in the tabernacle, maintaining the separation between the Holy Place and the Most Holy Place.

♦ Israelites followed God's laws and brought their sacrifices and offerings to burn on the altar in the courtyard of the temple.

The veil shall be a divider for you between the holy place and the Most Holy.
—Exodus 26:33b

Dedication of the Temple

After the temple was finished, King Solomon gathered all the leaders and people of Israel for a special celebration. The ark of the covenant was brought into the temple. The presence of the Lord filled the temple with a cloud of glory. It was a day of great prayer, worship, and rejoicing!

Inside the Temple

The furniture inside the temple was similar to the tabernacle furniture made by Moses after the Exodus. Unlike temples of pagan religions, there were no idols to worship.

- Ten seven-branched lampstands, or menorahs, gave light to the room.

- The altar of incense burned sweet smelling spices to worship God.

- The ark of the covenant found its home in the Holy of Holies.

- The table of showbread held 12 holy loaves of bread that represented the 12 tribes of Israel.

Holy of Holies

Just as in the tabernacle, a smaller room inside the temple was known as the Holy of Holies. The ark of the covenant was kept here, featuring the mercy seat on top between the wings of two cherubim. This represented the place God granted forgiveness for the sins of the people.

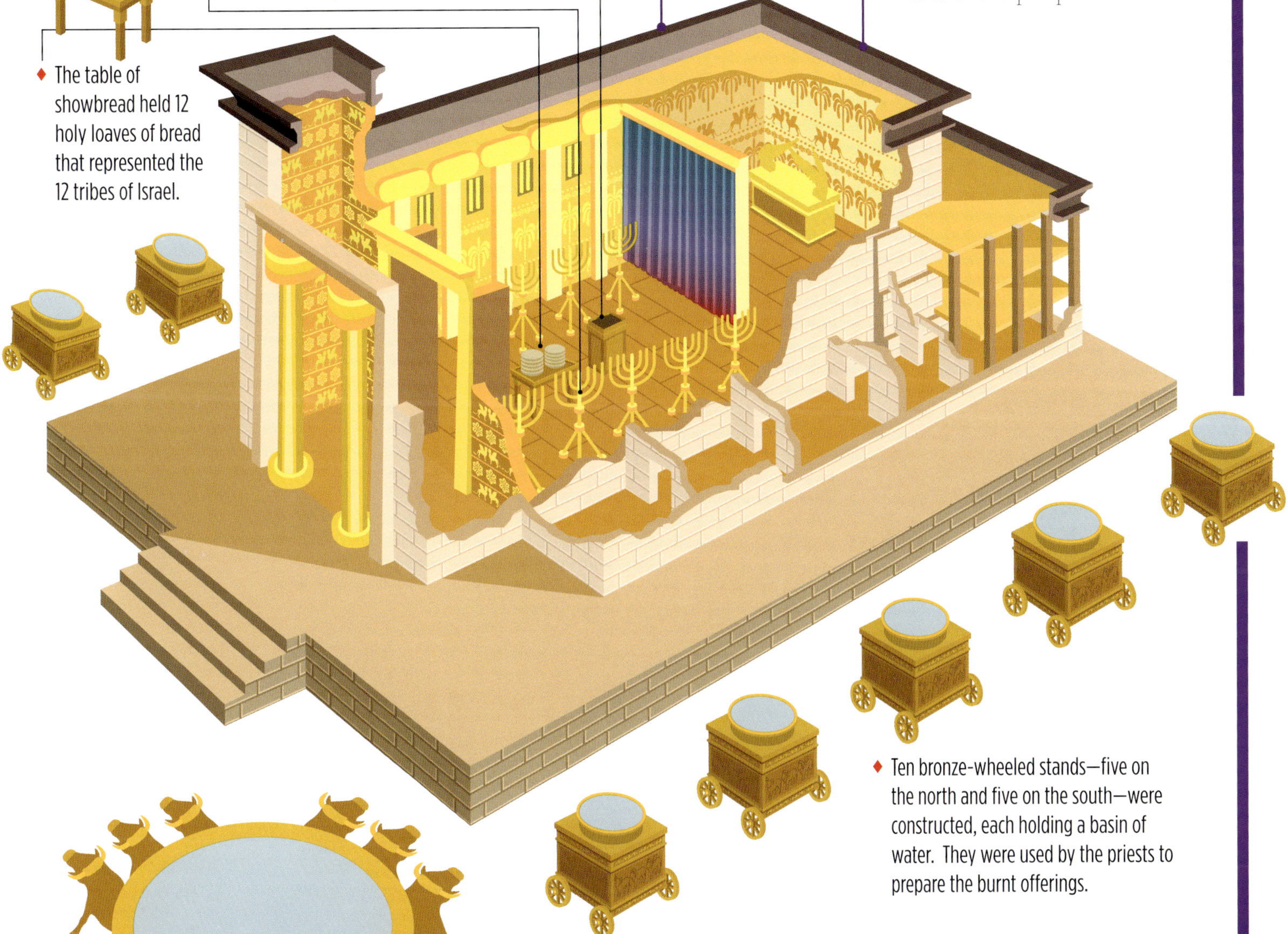

- Ten bronze-wheeled stands—five on the north and five on the south—were constructed, each holding a basin of water. They were used by the priests to prepare the burnt offerings.

- A large bronze basin full of water was placed in the courtyard for the priests to use in ceremonial washing.

Where is one of the driest, hottest, and richest places on the planet? The Arabian Peninsula! Also known as Arabia, temperatures can soar up to 125° F. The Arabian Desert is one of the largest deserts on earth, covering about 900,000 square miles—roughly the size of Alaska and Texas combined! In ancient days, it was famous for its exotic spices and gold. Today, it supplies an abundance of oil to the world. The Arabian Peninsula lies in Southwest Asia near Egypt, Jordan, and Israel.

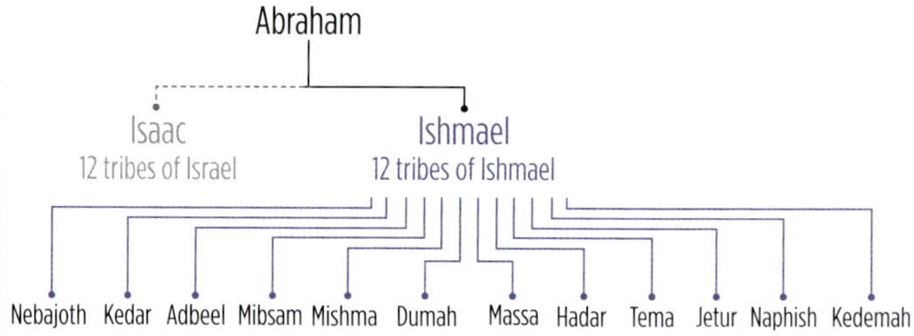

Ishmael

Abraham had two sons, Isaac and Ishmael. Isaac became the ancestor of the 12 tribes of Israel. Ishmael became the father of 12 princes (Gen. 25:13–16) and a daughter who married Esau. The Ishmaelites lived in the deserts of northern Arabia. As nomads, many of their tribes became known as the Bedouins. Their homes were tents made of goat hair. They followed their flocks of sheep and goats to find grazing land in the barren wilderness. Merchants known broadly as the Ishmaelites carried on a prosperous trade with Egypt. Their camel caravans carried spices, balm, and myrrh.

And these were the names of the sons of Ishmael, by their names, according to their generations: The firstborn of Ishmael, Nebajoth; then Kedar, Adbeel, Mibsam, Mishma, Dumah, Massa, Hadar, Tema, Jetur, Naphish, and Kedemah. –Genesis 25:13–15

Dromedaries

Dromedary camels are also known as Arabian camels. Tribes in northern Arabia domesticated them and used them to carry heavy loads. These camels have one hump and can go for long periods of time without needing water. When they find water, they can drink massive quantities all at once. Their padded feet walk effortlessly over the shifting sand. With a double row of eyelashes that protect their eyes and the ability to close their nostrils, they can withstand the frequent sandstorms of the desert.

Arabia's Incense Road

Arab tribes developed carefully guarded routes across the Arabian Peninsula to carry incense, spices, gold, and precious jewels to key trading centers. Long caravans of camels trekked across the hot desert sands, stopping at settlements around large oases where they found food and water. Trading ports along the coast linked Arabia with East Africa, India, and even China.

Saba/Sheba

In the mountains and rich coastal plains of southwest Arabia was the kingdom of Saba. Some scholars associate this region with Sheba in the Bible. Located in modern-day Yemen, it controlled trade in this region of the world by 700 B.C. Incense, one of its main exports, was highly valued for use in religious ceremonies. It was also a good way to hide unwanted smells of daily life (like manure).

Petra

Stunning structures carved into cliffs! The fortress of Petra was famous for its magnificent architecture cut into walls of red sandstone cliffs. It lies south of the Dead Sea in modern-day Jordan. Founded in the mid-400's B.C., Arab tribes known as the Nabataeans took over the region after it had been abandoned by the Edomites (descendants of Esau). Petra controlled overland trade routes connecting northern Arabia with the Mediterranean Sea.

1. Palace Tomb
2. Corinthian Tomb
3. Silk Tomb
4. Urn Tomb
5. Treasury

The climate changed dramatically in different parts of the globe after the Flood in Noah's day and the resulting Ice Age. Even the Sahara Desert in Africa was not yet the dry barren wasteland that it is today. Cave art, fossils, and artifacts show a region where ancient people lived, tending their flocks of sheep, goats, and cattle as they grazed on the lush, green grasslands. Elephants, hippopotamuses, and other wild animals lived along the rivers and in the valleys. As the Ice Age came to an end and the shifting sands of the Sahara took over, people and animals migrated south to other grasslands or north toward the coast.

Africa is a magnificent land.

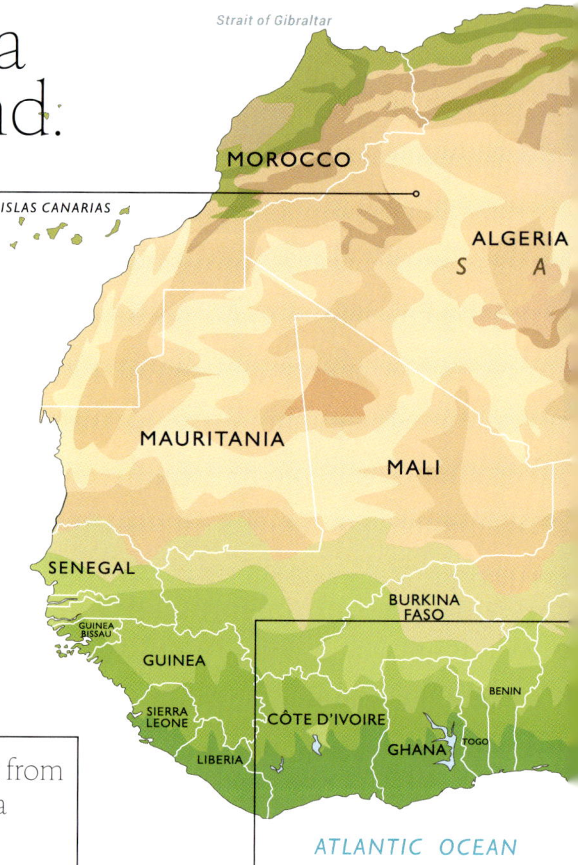

The Sahara Desert
The world's largest hot desert, it covers 3.6 million square miles over a large region of the northern part of the continent.

The equator
The equator runs through the continent from east to west, giving much of this region a tropical climate.

Congo Basin
Sitting along the equator in the heart of Africa is the Congo Basin. The Congo River waters this area of the continent on its journey to the Atlantic Ocean. Covering 1.2 million square miles, the basin's rainforest is about the size of Texas, California, and Montana combined! As the second largest tropical rainforest in the world, it plays a key part in regulating the earth's climate. It is home to gorillas, chimpanzees, and leopards.

African Savanna
Over half the continent of Africa is covered by the African Savanna. Miles and miles of grassland are dotted with trees and bushes. During the summer wet season, it can get 15-25 inches of rain each month. With winter comes the dry season, when the savanna hardly gets any rain at all. Big cats hunt here, including lions and cheetahs. Antelope, zebras, and rhinoceroses thunder across the plains. Elephants, giraffes, and hippopotamuses share waterholes. The Serengeti Plains, the most famous savanna region in Africa, witnesses the great migration of wildebeest each year as they follow the seasonal rains.

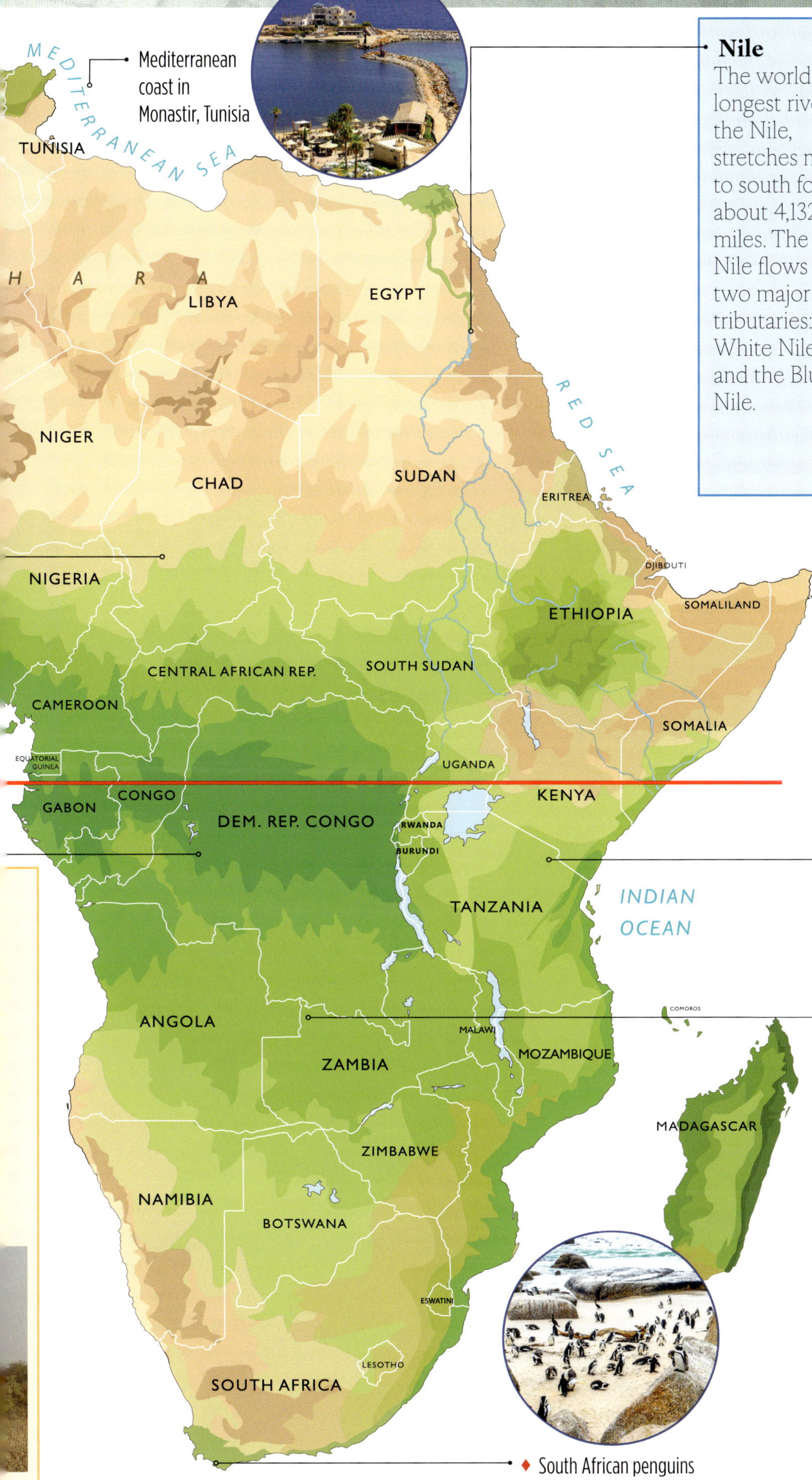

Mediterranean coast in Monastir, Tunisia

Nile

The world's longest river, the Nile, stretches north to south for about 4,132 miles. The Nile flows to two major tributaries: the White Nile and the Blue Nile.

Mount Kilimanjaro

A quest for hikers, Kilimanjaro towers over the land with its snow-capped peaks at about 19,341 feet above sea level.

Victoria Falls

Cascades of water gush down the cliffs at beautiful Victoria Falls at over 132.1 million gallons every minute in peak season.

♦ South African penguins

Evolutionary theories teach that people evolved from ape-like ancestors in Africa and were not smart enough to farm or herd flocks until they had evolved enough to do so. We can trust the Bible's account about the history of ancient people because it is God's Word. And, many of its other historical accounts have been proven true.

Prehistoric People?

Most encyclopedias, school textbooks, science books, and museums claim that prehistoric people had ape-like pre-human ancestors that lived in Africa millions of years ago. However, creationists believe there is no such thing as "prehistoric" because history started with the events written in the Bible when God created the heavens and the earth. There is no such thing as "prehistoric people" because the Bible says that on the sixth day of creation God created Adam and Eve, the first people to ever live. The theory of prehistoric people coming from Africa millions of years ago is based on mistaken evolutionary theories. It is not what the Bible teaches.

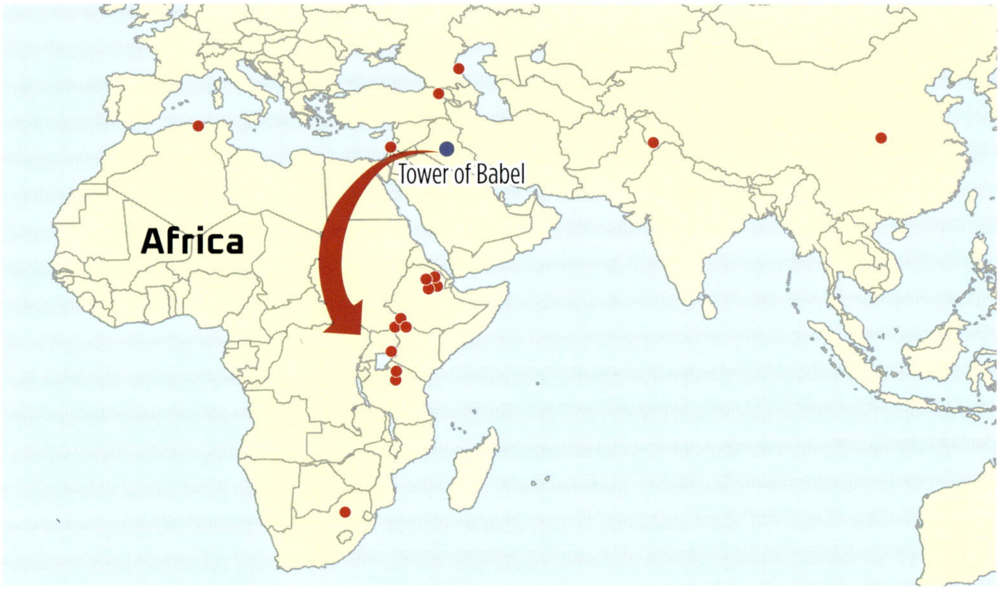

♦ The earliest definitive evidence of humans has been found in regions far from Babel. These tools and remains appear in rock layers that creationist geologists date to the period after the Flood but before the Ice Age. This indicates that the earliest known human settlements likely developed after the Tower of Babel event as people migrated to Africa and other regions.

A Choice

Creation scientists and evolutionary scientists look at the same evidence. Evolutionary scientists create theories that support the ideas of Charles Darwin, a man who created the theory of evolution. Creation scientists form theories based on what the Bible says—that God created Adam and Eve around 4004 B.C. and placed them in the Garden of Eden to live. It is up to each of us to choose whether we believe what God's Word teaches or what evolutionists teach, many of whom do not believe in God.

Created in God's Image

The Bible teaches that Adam and Eve were created in God's image. They were smart from the start. Adam was a farmer, and his sons had flocks and herds. Evolutionary theories teach that people evolved from ape-like ancestors in Africa and were not smart enough to farm or herd flocks until they had evolved over hundreds of thousands of years. We can trust the Bible's account about the history of ancient people because many of its other historical accounts have been proven true. We can choose to believe what the Bible says because it is God's Word. That is called faith, and our faith is founded on fact.

Africa's Rock Art

Ancient paintings have been discovered in a very unlikely place—in parts of the Sahara before it became a desert! This rock art can be found in other parts of Africa as well. Painted in caves and carved onto rocks, these ancient pictures show families with their round huts and large herds of cattle, along with hunters carrying bows.

Bantu Speakers

Africa is a huge continent. Various tribes lived south of the Sahara Desert on the savanna in West Africa. They each spoke different dialects of the same Bantu language. As farming communities, these people ate grains such as millet, sorghum, and rice. Melons, peppers, and onions grew in their fields. They worked with iron to make better farming tools. Their herds of goats, sheep, and cattle grazed on the grasslands. Iron weapons gave them strength against their enemies.

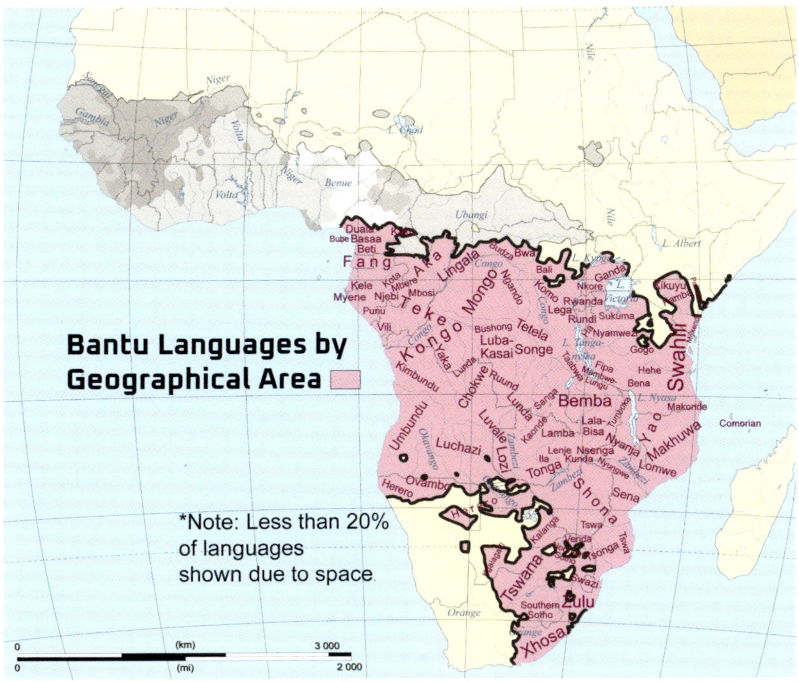

The Bantu Migration

Around 1500–1000 B.C., some of the Bantu speakers began to move away from their homeland near the Niger River in West Africa. Conditions may have become crowded, or they may have been looking for new farmland. This began one of the greatest migrations in history. Spreading southward and eastward, they migrated over the next thousand years to settle nearly the entire subcontinent of Africa south of the Sahara. They carried with them their knowledge of metalworking and farming. Even to this day, different tribes across Africa can trace their dialect back to the Bantu family of languages.

Noah's grandson Mizraim settled Egypt. Another grandson, Cush, settled in the region south of Egypt. In the Bible, this land is called Cush. It is also known as Kush, or part of the kingdom of Nubia. The ancient Greeks called this region Ethiopia. It was located along the Nile River in modern-day Sudan.

♦ Main pyramid at El-Kurru, a royal cemetery

Pharaohs from Cush

For centuries, Egypt ruled over the land of Cush. Eventually, strong leaders rose to power. They conquered their conquerors and became known as Egypt's 25th Dynasty. This dynasty is also known as the time of the Black Pharaohs (to indicate their specific ancestral roots), and they ruled over Egypt for nearly a hundred years from about 750 B.C. until around 656 B.C.

King Piye

Piye (Piankhi) was king of Cush. Around 750 B.C., he left his capital city of Napata with his armies. He invaded Egypt from the south and conquered the entire land up to the Mediterranean Sea. His victory stele, carved on a stone of granite, tells of his military success. Afterwards, Piye sailed back to Napata to rule over his newly combined kingdom, carrying treasures of gold, riches, and clothing. After his death, Piye was buried in an Egyptian-style pyramid as his tomb.

♦ Piye Stele

The 25th Dynasty of Egyptian Pharaohs

After Piye died, his brother Shabako (Shabaqo) became Pharaoh of Egypt. He founded the 25th Dynasty, a period when Black Pharaohs ruled the Nile. It was a renaissance of architecture, art, learning, religion, and culture from Egypt's glorious past. They revived the use of pyramids as the tomb of kings. More than 200 pyramids from this era still survive in modern-day Sudan.

These statues are Cushite (or Kushite) pharaohs of the 25th Dynasty. They ruled both Nubia and Egypt during the 8th–7th centuries B.C.

The statues are black granite with gilded details, symbolizing their "divine" kingship, as they claimed to be gods.

Kashta was the first Cushite king to extend influence into Egypt.

Piye (Piankhi) conquered Egypt around 750 B.C.

Shabaka consolidated control and established the dynasty firmly in Egypt.

Shebitku continued Cushite rule.

Tirhakah was one of the most famous Cushite pharaohs; he fought the Assyrians.

Tanutamani (Tantamani) was the last Cushite ruler of Egypt before being pushed back to Nubia.

Pyramids of Meroë in Sudan

Pharaoh Tirhakah

The most famous pharaoh of the 25th Dynasty was Tirhakah (also known as Taharka, Taharqa, or Taharqo). Ruling from his magnificent capital at Memphis, he ordered ancient Egyptian monuments to be restored to their former glory. He built many new temples and shrines bearing the cartouche (hieroglyphic royal symbol) of his name or image. Artifacts such as stunning sculptures, beautiful pottery, and exquisite jewelry have been found from his reign. With his successful military conquests, he established a wider network of trade.

King Hezekiah

The kingdom of Judah was in trouble! Sennacherib, king of Assyria, marched toward Jerusalem, conquering cities in Judah. King Hezekiah agreed to pay tribute money to Assyria. Assyrian leaders then mocked Hezekiah for trusting in Egypt and his God. Hearing a report of Pharaoh Tirhakah's military advance, Hezekiah made an important decision: he would trust in God and God alone. The prophet Isaiah delivered a powerful message to Hezekiah, saying that God would save Jerusalem. And He did! These events are recorded in 2 Kings 18:13–19:37 and Isaiah 36:1–37:38.

Assyrian Conquerors

The Assyrian army invaded Egypt and conquered its capital city of Memphis. Tirhakah retreated to Napata, and the 25th Dynasty of Egyptian Pharaohs came to an end. When Tirhakah died, a large pyramid served as his tomb. The capital of Cush was eventually moved to Meroë (in modern-day Sudan). Over the next thousand years, Cush was a wealthy kingdom, working with iron and exchanging goods on the trade network stretching between India and the Mediterranean Sea.

Amulet found at Gebel Barkal mesa in Cush. From the 25th Dynasty.

Granite ram of Amun (an ancient Egyptian deity) featuring King Tirhakah

A stamped bulla (clay seal) of King Hezekiah

King Ashurbanipal continued Assyrian control of Egypt

The advanced cities of Harappa and Mohenjo-Daro thrived in the Indus River Valley. Their network of trade connected them with the ancient world. Over time, they began to decline, likely because of environmental changes, shifting river patterns, and social factors. Around 1500 B.C., a group of people called Aryans (which meant "noble") began migrating to India through mountain passes in Central Asia. These nomads introduced new cultural practices, languages, and technologies.

Hinduism

The Aryans believed in the Hindu religion. They worshiped many false gods, including animals. Hindus believe in reincarnation, the idea that when a person dies, they are reborn as a different person or an animal. Cows are worshiped as the most sacred animal of all. Hindu priests are called Brahmins. The caste system is deeply intertwined with Hinduism.

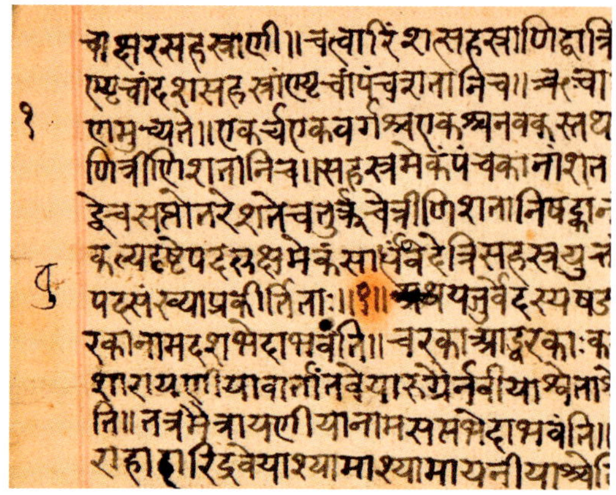

The Vedas

Rituals. Prayers. Hymns. The beliefs of the Hindus were passed down by memory from generation to generation. Eventually, these sacred texts, now called the Vedas, were written down in an ancient language called Sanskrit. The Vedas are India's earliest written texts.

Caste System

Was it because of religious beliefs? Was it to keep the indigenous people of India separate from the Aryans? Historians aren't exactly sure why the Aryans made strict rules about which jobs different groups of people could have. The most important people were priests and scholars. Beneath them were the soldiers. Merchants and businessmen were less important. Workers, laborers, and servants held some of the most needed jobs of all, but the Dalits were considered the lowest class of all. Whichever class children were born into (what their father did for a living) is where they stayed for the rest of their lives. If people tried to break out of their class, they were labeled "untouchables" and became outcasts.

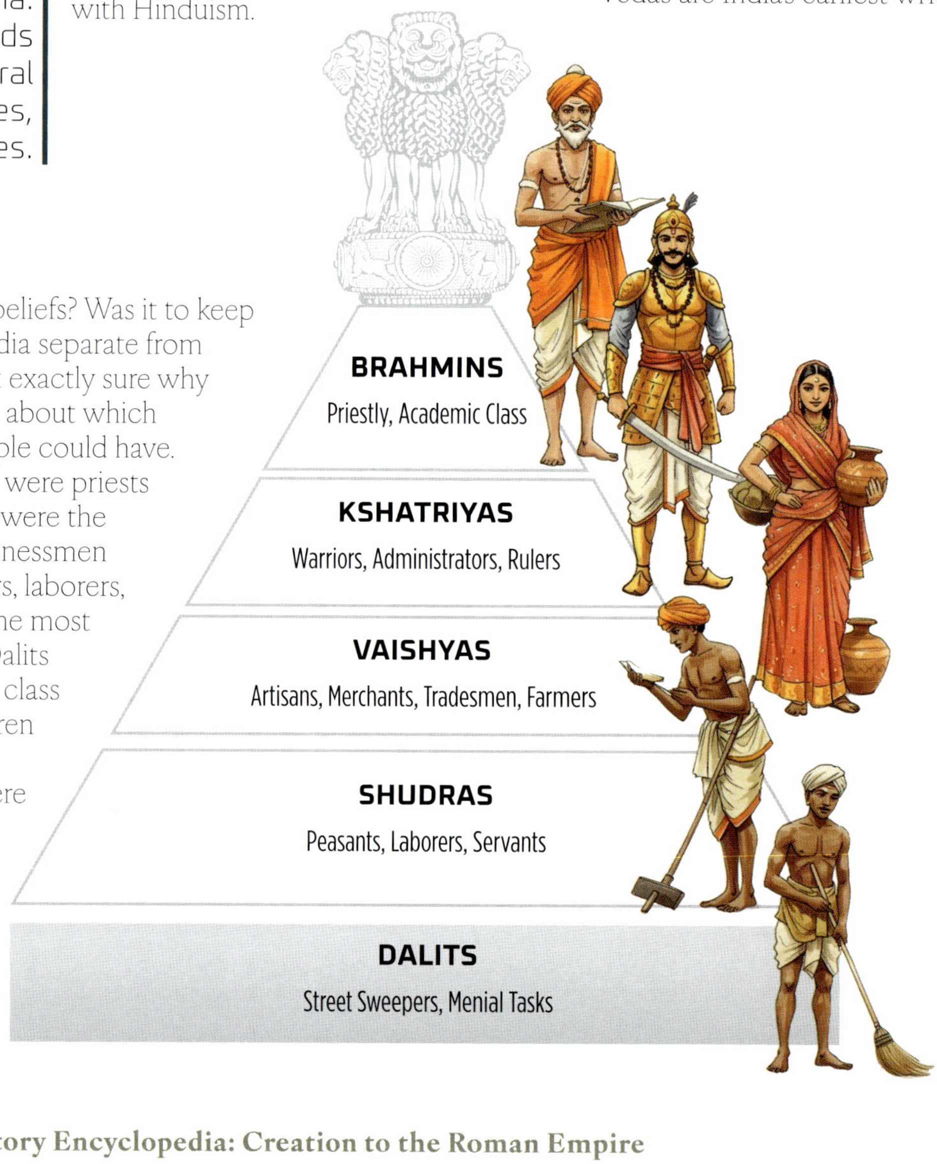

Buddhism

A wealthy prince named Siddhartha Gautama grew up and saw the misery of people living in poverty. Around 500 B.C., he started a new religion called Buddhism. It offered hope to people in the lowest castes of Hinduism. He traveled around India to share his teachings, and his followers began to worship him as Buddha (along with other false gods). After he died, Buddhism eventually faded out in India, but it had already spread to many parts of the globe. It has become one of the largest false religions in the world.

Alexander the Great

Alexander the Great, king of Macedonia, set out to conquer the world. About 326 B.C., he invaded northern India. Warriors riding on elephants tried to push back the Greek soldiers but lost. Alexander returned home but left some of his generals to govern. India became the eastern border of his vast empire.

India's First Empire

After Alexander left, warriors from India quickly drove out his generals. About 324 B.C., Chandragupta Maurya rose to power. He united most of northern India to form the Mauryan Empire. His grandson Ashoka became one of the most famous emperors to rule India. He devoted his reign to improving life in his country. The government provided aid during emergencies, built a better transportation system, and established universities for students to study science, art, and medicine.

Imagine standing in a wide, grassy plain and seeing giant stones arranged in a perfect circle. That's a henge—famous ancient monuments found all over the world. People often wonder: Who built it? Creative and intelligent humans made in God's image!

What is a Henge?

A henge is an ancient circular structure made from earth. It has a raised bank and a ditch, usually on the inside of the bank. People often built other things inside henges, like stone circles, wooden posts, or large standing stones, probably used for a variety of reasons.

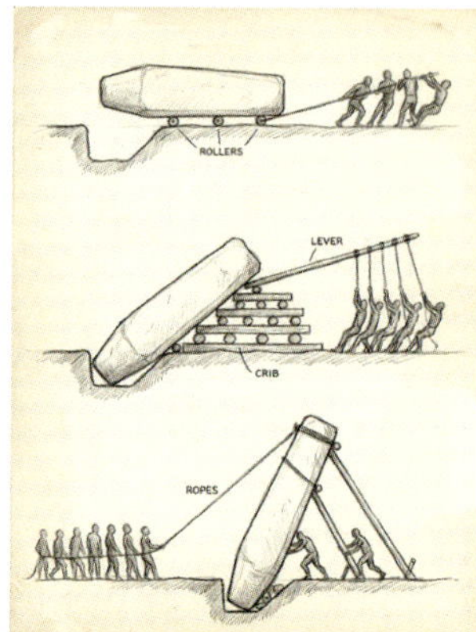

♦ Illustration of a henge construction

A Giant Calendar

How did ancient civilizations keep track of the seasons? How did people track the sun, moon, and stars as they moved across the sky throughout the year? Some scholars believe henges were early calendars. Many of these ancient monuments or stone circles were constructed in line with the rising and setting of the sun and moon. They were also carefully marked to keep track of the first day of summer and winter.

The Most Famous Henge

Built in southern England, Stonehenge is one of the most well-known henges. Bluestones were quarried in Wales and moved over 150 miles to the site. Each weighed about four tons, the average size of one elephant. Sarsen stones were much larger, weighing an average of 25 tons. These were brought from about 20 miles away. Both types of stones were arranged to stand up, forming an inner and outer circle.

Worldwide Henges

Henges have been discovered all around the world. They have been found in the Amazon rainforest as well as the state of Illinois! More than a hundred were built on the British Isles alone. One of the oldest known stone circles is in Nabta Playa, Egypt, built directly on the Tropic of Cancer. A stone henge in Sweden was designed in the shape of a ship. In 1967, the Wheel of the Giants, or Gilgal Refaim, was discovered on the Golan Heights in Israel. This ring of circles was constructed using over 40,000 tons of rocks, or roughly the weight of 8,000 elephants!

Intelligence of the Ancients

The Bible says people were created in God's image, smart from the start. After the worldwide Flood, humans figured out the mathematical calculations and engineering required to build the Tower of Babel. God stopped the construction of the tower and its false religion. Ancient people then spread out around the world, taking their knowledge of stupendous building projects with them.

Questions and Answers

Who built the ancient colossal henges found around the world? How did people move the ginormous stones? When did they build the henges? Why were they built? These are all questions that historians try to answer. Many theories have been suggested, but nobody knows for sure. What we do know is that human beings are capable of building complex structures, including skyscrapers today.

♦ An illustration showing how henges could have been constructed

♦ Illustrations showing how the massive stones could have been carrried from one place to another

Accuracy of the Bible

According to the historical account found in the Bible, Stonehenge and other monuments had to be built after the Flood in 2348 B.C. They would never have survived the deluge. Scientists who believe in evolution, however, claim that the construction of Stonehenge started around 3000 B.C., which was before the Flood.

The Authority of the Bible

Along with primary source accounts, archaeological finds, scientific discoveries, and more, the Bible's accuracy has been proven time and time again. Unfortunately, many people lack understanding, adopt mistaken scientific theories, and choose to ignore God. They decide to believe in evolution. The very first people, created in God's image, were intelligent beings from the very beginning. Their ancient monuments built with unbelievable precision and engineering show us this is true.

BRITISH ISLES

A group of islands known as the British Isles lie to the west and north of the continent of Europe. England, Scotland, and Wales are all located on the island of Great Britain. Ireland is made up of the nation of Ireland and the upper section called Northern Ireland. England, Scotland, Wales, and Northern Ireland together make up the nation known today as the United Kingdom. Other islands, including the Hebrides, Orkney Islands, and Shetland Islands, are part of Scotland. More than 5,000 smaller islands are also part of the British Isles. Key players in the history of the world, the British Isles have an ancient past.

Great Britain

Today, the island of Great Britain is made up of Wales, Scotland, and England. But long before these modern political divisions existed, ancient peoples lived there—peoples we now remember mainly through the massive stone monuments they left behind. Among the most impressive of these are Stonehenge and the nearby stone circles at Avebury. As part of the same complex, Silbury Hill—a huge man-made mound—is the largest earthen structure in Europe built by an early civilization.

Ireland

Known as the Emerald Isle, Ireland is famous for its lush green lowlands in the center of the island. Bays and inlets from the Atlantic Ocean cut deep into its western coast. High rocky cliffs and mountains rise up along its shores. Its earliest settlers probably arrived from the continent of Europe and stayed to farm in this mild, rainy part of the world.

Descendants of Japheth

After the worldwide Flood and the Tower of Babel event, the descendants of Noah's three sons spread out and populated the world. Some of the descendants of Noah's son Japheth migrated north and west around the Mediterranean Sea, settling in Europe. Of these descendants, different groups from Europe were probably the original settlers of the British Isles.

Ring Forts

Long ago, clans in Ireland were led by local kings, many of whom built circular stone forts called ringforts. The remains of these forts still dot the Irish countryside. The clans also buried their dead in large cemeteries marked by megalithic tombs—some possibly older than Stonehenge or the Great Pyramid of Egypt. One of these is the Newgrange Burial Mound, which is perfectly aligned with the rising sun during the winter solstice (shortest day of the year). It is considered one of the most impressive megalithic tombs in Europe.

♦ Newgrange entrance

♦ Newgrange Burial Mound

Mines and Quarries

Great Britain is home to some of the oldest mines and quarries. A quarry for making axe heads and hammerstones was found in Wales. Mines were dug to find flint, the valuable stone used for arrowheads, knives, and saws. Copper and tin mines, providing essential resources for working with bronze, made Great Britain part of the vast trade network of the ancient world.

♦ Gold cup from Rillaton, Cornwall, England, c. 1800-1600 B.C.

♦ Collection of copper alloy tools: six socketed axes, two gouges, two knives and one socketed hammer

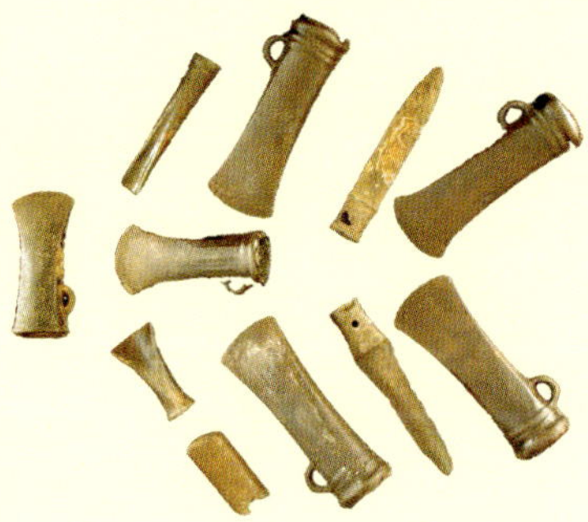

♦ Copper alloy spearhead, c. 1200–800 B.C.

♦ Cast bronze (copper alloy) flat axe, c. 2000-1700 B.C.

Copper, Bronze, and Gold

Metalworking was highly prized in early Ireland. In 1854, workers constructing a new railroad track near an ancient hillfort dug up a stunning collection of golden bracelets, jewelry, and collars. Known as the Clare gold hoard, it is evidence of the fine metalwork of early days. Ireland exported copper, bronze, and gold items to Great Britain and Europe in trade.

♦ Celtic life and dress

The Celts

With the arrival of the Celts, life began to change on the British Isles. New religious practices, ways of governing, and ways of life became the norm.

♦ Shield found near Battersea Bridge in London

Deep in the ancient forests of Europe, people banded together into separate tribes. These tribes first appeared around 700 B.C. in a region known as Hallstatt in modern-day Austria. The people shared a common lifestyle, religion, and language. They became known as the Celts.

Life at Home

Celts were farmers, iron workers, and storytellers. Many Celtic families grew wheat and barley. They also kept small herds of pigs, cows, and chickens. They built round houses from timber or stone with thatched roofs made of grass and reeds. The Celts also crafted iron cauldrons for cooking and gold jewelry to wear. They held great feasts where they told epic stories of their bravery and conquests in their history.

Fierce Warriors

Different Celtic tribes attacked each other. Perhaps because of natural disasters, population growth, or dwindling resources, tribes began to spread across Europe, conquering villages and cities as they went. Some spread east to Galatia in modern Turkey. Others, known as Gauls, settled in France and Italy. They sacked and burned Rome around 387 B.C. and attacked Delphi, Greece, around 279 B.C. Some tribes migrated as far as the British Isles and settled there over time. Fierce warriors, some painted their bodies blue or decorated themselves with blue patterns and designs. Some bleached their hair white and combed it into tall spikes to look more fearful. They announced their attack with loud trumpet blasts and fought with strong iron weapons.

British Isles

The Celts arrived on the shores of the British Isles around 500 B.C. Chiefs built hillforts where the commoners (farmers) could gather to trade or seek protection during an attack. When Julius Caesar conducted brief raids in Britain in 55 B.C., he faced fortified Celtic settlements and fierce resistance. Full Roman occupation occurred later under Claudius in A.D. 43. Today, the Celtic language is still spoken among people in Wales, Scotland, and Ireland.

Patterns

Ancient Celtic artists were famous for the patterns they designed and integrated into their crafts. Metalworkers carved patterns into swords and shields. Weavers wove wool into bright patterns for clothes and blankets. Knots, leaves, clovers, braids, and geometric designs were some of the favorite patterns found among Celtic items.

♦ Celtic knot

♦ Druids

Druids

Druids were the religious leaders of the Celts, who followed after false gods. With no written language, they were the storytellers, passing down their history from one generation to the next. Druids often performed their religious practices in groves of oak trees or near a lake or river. They would throw valuable weapons or treasures into the water as a sacrifice to their false gods.

♦ Celtic cross

Rise of Christianity

As the Roman Empire grew in strength, its armies conquered most of the Celtic tribes across Europe. With the spread of Christianity, many Celts eagerly accepted the message of the gospel. Paul the apostle wrote a letter to the church in Galatia, home to former Celtic tribes. This letter became the Book of Galatians in the Bible. A man of deep faith named Patrick took the gospel to Ireland. Commoners, druids, and chieftains alike accepted Jesus as Savior and Lord.

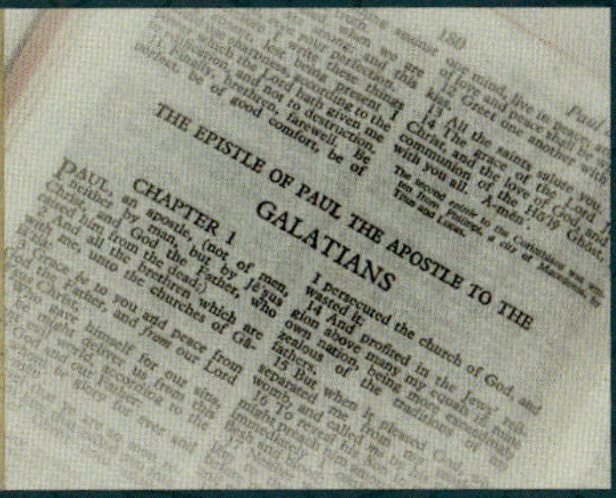

Deep, dark forests covered the hills and hamlets of early Europe. As family groups moved in and settled there, they chopped down trees to build houses and barns. They cleared land for farming and hunted deer, elk, bear, and other forest animals. The clear bubbling streams and refreshing rivers provided fish for them to eat.

♦ The Eurasian steppe belt stretched roughly 5,000 miles and historically facilitated migration, trade, and cultural exchange between East and West.

Ancient Europe
Early Europeans found unique climates and natural resources based on where they settled. They used stone where it was plentiful, and they harvested trees to build homes, tools, and other necessities. In marshy, wet places, they built wooden tracks on which to walk.

Eurasian Steppe
The continents of Europe and Asia are neighbors. For 5,000 miles, vast grassy plains called steppes stretch from north of the Black Sea across central Asia and into Mongolia and China. In ancient times, this Eurasian Steppe (or the Steppe of Steppes) was home to wandering tribes migrating from season to season to find the best grazing land for their herds.

Eastern and Western
Geographers divide the far-reaching Eurasian Steppe into two regions. Its western region is wetter and greener with lusher pastures for grazing herds. Its eastern region has more extreme temperatures, with winters being more frigid and summers being much hotter. This region is drier because it receives less rainfall.

Kurgans
How do you build a monument when there is nothing but grass for as far as the eye can see? With dirt! When a chief or king died, they buried him with his riches underneath a big mound of dirt called a kurgan.

♦ A suit of armor, called the Golden Cataphract, consists of thousands of gold pieces; it was found by chance in 1969 during the construction of a road at the Issyk burial mound in the south of Almaty, Kazakhstan.

The Scythians

Wearing felt caps, riding their horses, and carrying their tents, the Scythians dominated the steppes north of the Black Sea beginning in the seventh century B.C. They were nomadic tribes, wandering from grassland to grassland to graze their large herds of cattle, sheep, and goats. They traded with the Greeks and other neighbors, and they became very rich.

Warriors

Experts with bows and arrows, Scythian warriors could attack while on horseback. The invention of stirrups gave them the ability to shoot while riding. They were a threat to the Assyrian Empire. Eventually, in the second century A.D., they were overthrown by a group known as the Sarmatians, who in turn were eventually conquered by the Huns.

Master Riders

The Scythians loved to race their horses, tails streaming in the wind. Excellent riders, they seemed to float above the rolling grass that surrounded them like the ocean, with wide open skies above them. Around 700 B.C., horses became the favorite transportation across the steppes, and their riders exhibited amazing skills.

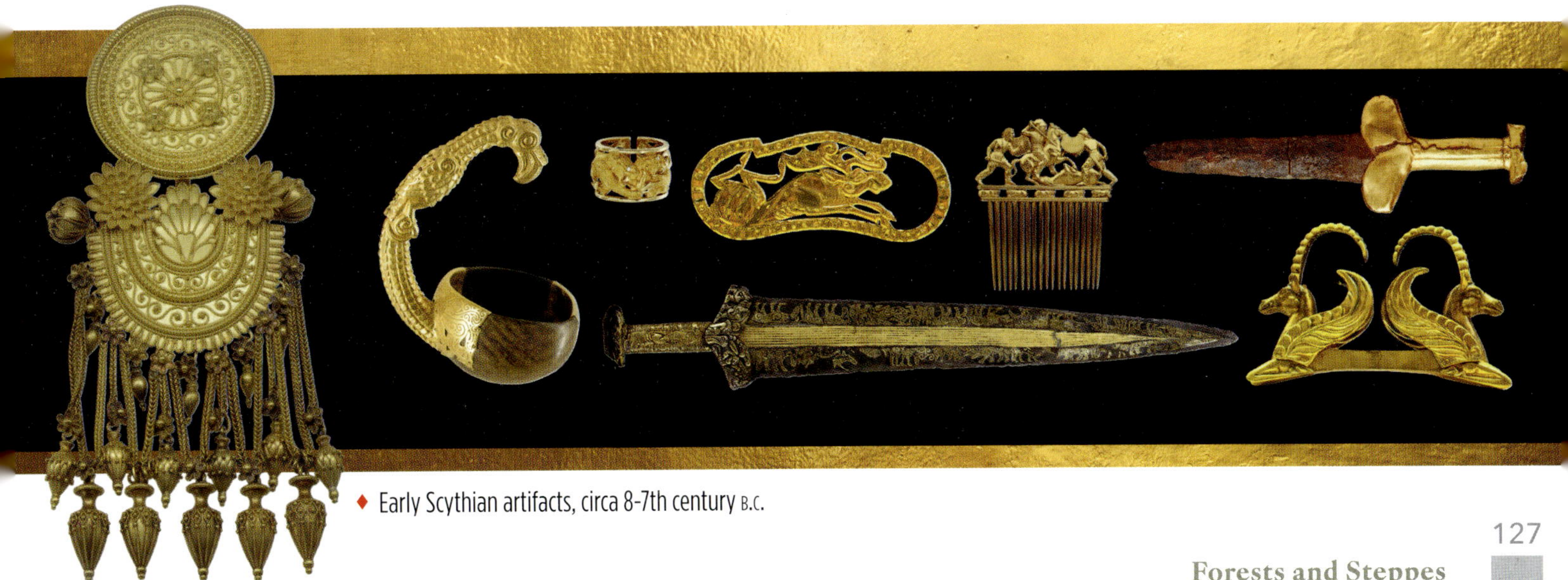

♦ Early Scythian artifacts, circa 8-7th century B.C.

The Zhou Dynasty ruled China for nearly 800 years, longer than any other government in its history. Iron was introduced to China during this era. It became widely used to make farming tools (like plows) and weapons.

Feudal China

China developed into a feudal society during the Zhou Dynasty. In this system, large landowners built up their own armies and offered protection to the people who lived on their land. These different lords, who controlled various regions, fought back and forth with each other. This became known as the Warring States period.

Philosophers

For years, there was political unrest and fighting among the regional lords in China. A philosopher named Confucius tried to bring peace during this period. His teachings focused on moral obedience to family members and rulers. His beliefs became known as Confucianism, and it influenced art, education, and politics in China for centuries to come. Other philosophers came up with ideas for different ways to stop all the fighting. In time, some of these teachings became the foundations of different false religions.

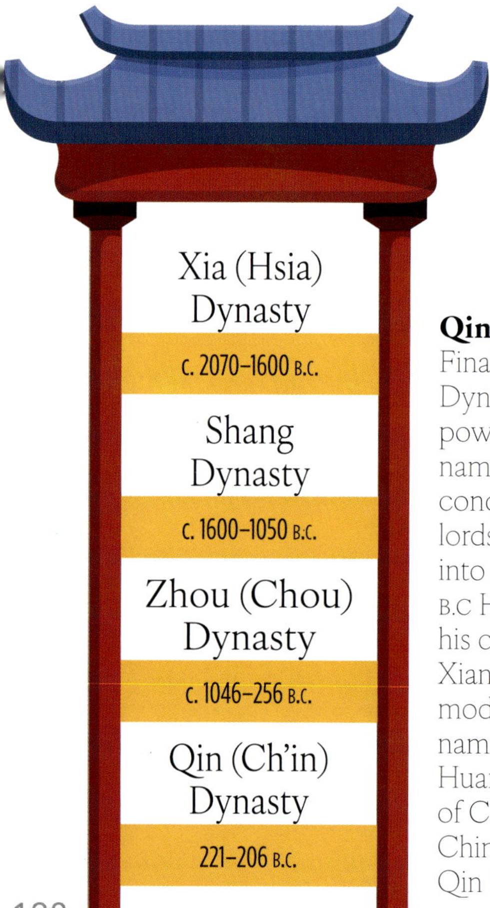

Qin Dynasty

Finally, the Qin Dynasty rose to power. A warlord named Zhao Zheng conquered the other lords and united them into an empire in 221 B.C He established his capital city at Xianyang near modern-day Xi'an. His name became Qin Shi Huangdi, first emperor of China. The name China comes from the Qin (Ch'in) Dynasty.

Shi Huangdi

Qin Shi Huangdi sought to unite all of China. He built roads and canals to connect the villages and cities. He made trade easier with a standard money system and a standard unit of weights and measures. He even standardized the Chinese system of writing. Unfortunately, in his aggressive policy to enforce equality, he burned many scholarly texts, especially of Chinese history and philosophy. He killed hundreds of scholars who disagreed with him and his philosophy of Legalism.

Legalism

Emperor Qin Shi Huangdi supported the philosophy of Legalism, which emphasized strict laws. This system also gave the emperor authoritarian rule and centralized power. No laws protected the citizens; harsh punishments were often given out. Secret police enforced the absolute rule of the emperor and his leaders. Many of these principles still influence the government of China today.

China's Great Wall

Horses thundered across the grasslands, carrying fierce warriors to the north of China as they fought their way to power. The riders of the Mongolian steppes were a threat to the Qin Empire. Qin Shi Huangdi had a plan. He decided to build a wall so tall and so wide that it would keep China's enemies out. Construction on the Great Wall of China began. It is thought that some 30,000 laborers died while working on this dangerous project, their bodies buried into the wall. China's famous wall was rebuilt and enlarged by other rulers over the years. Today, it is 5,500 miles long.

Terra-Cotta Army

Could Shi Huangdi live forever? While he searched for the secret of immortality, he ordered the construction of his own tomb. A colossal mausoleum, it even contained a model of his empire. Nearby stood an army of more than 7,500 warriors to protect him after death. Each life-size soldier was made of terra-cotta, the same clay used to make pottery. The discovery of the terra-cotta warriors became one of the most stunning archaeological finds of modern history.

Liu Bang grew up among the common peasants. He led a group of rebels who defeated the harsh rule of the Qin Dynasty. In 206 B.C., he was declared Emperor Gaozu of the Han Dynasty. His family ruled China for the next 400 years.

♦ Emperor Wu (Wudi) of Han

Han Dynasty
206 B.C.– A.D. 220

Six Dynasties Period
A.D. 220–589

Sui Dynasty
A.D. 581–618

Tang (T'ang) Dynasty
A.D. 618–906

A Bigger Empire

North. South. West. Emperor Wudi imagined a larger China. Chang'an was his capital city. Armies rode north and took over the northern peninsula of Korea. Soldiers headed south to conquer as far as modern-day northern Vietnam. The Silk Road opened to the west for the first time in history. It connected Chang'an with Rome. Silk and jade from China traveled by camel caravan to find its way to the courts and villas of the Roman Empire.

Government Exams

Rather than simply appointing family members to his court, Emperor Wudi provided an education for people who wanted to work in the government. They studied classic literature from China with a focus on the teachings of Confucius. Students who passed their exams were given important positions in the government.

Two Great Empires

The Han Empire ruled the Far East. The Roman Empire ruled Western civilization, almost equal in size. The Silk Road connected them both in a vast network of trade.

♦ Silk weaving in modern China

♦ Tomb banner from the Western Han period (206 B.C.–A.D. 25). Found at the Mawangdui archaeological site in Changsha, China.

Buddhism
Under Wudi's rule, Buddhist missionaries from India arrived in China along with caravans carrying cinnamon, ivory, and precious gems. The peasants and common laborers accepted the new ideas brought by Buddhist monks. They felt that the teachings of Confucius were for the educated upper class and government officials. By 100 A.D., Buddhism was declared an official religion and became one of the largest false religions in China.

River of Sorrow
In 11 A.D., the Yellow River raged against the walls built along its banks by different emperors during their rule. Breaching the river's dikes, waves of mud and silt flooded the land, causing mass destruction in its path. With a mind of its own, the Yellow River cut a new path until it swept into the sea 100 miles away from where it had gone before. It was nicknamed the "River of Sorrow."

Later Han Dynasty
The Han Dynasty is divided into its early and later periods. In A.D. 25, the capital city was moved to Luoyang, marking the beginning of the later Han Dynasty. It was an era of scientific and technological achievement. Paper was invented. *Shuo Wen*, one of the world's oldest dictionaries, was written. Trying to replace the books burned during the Qin Dynasty, scholars wrote detailed histories of China's past. Both poetry and prose were written with a new style that became a famous part of China's literature.

Reform
For a short time, Emperor Wang Mang tried to establish his own Xin Dynasty. He urged extreme government reform to break up the power of the large landowners and divide their massive plots among the peasants. In A.D. 23, the Han overthrew Wang Mang and reestablished themselves as rulers of the empire.

Han Dynasty Inventions

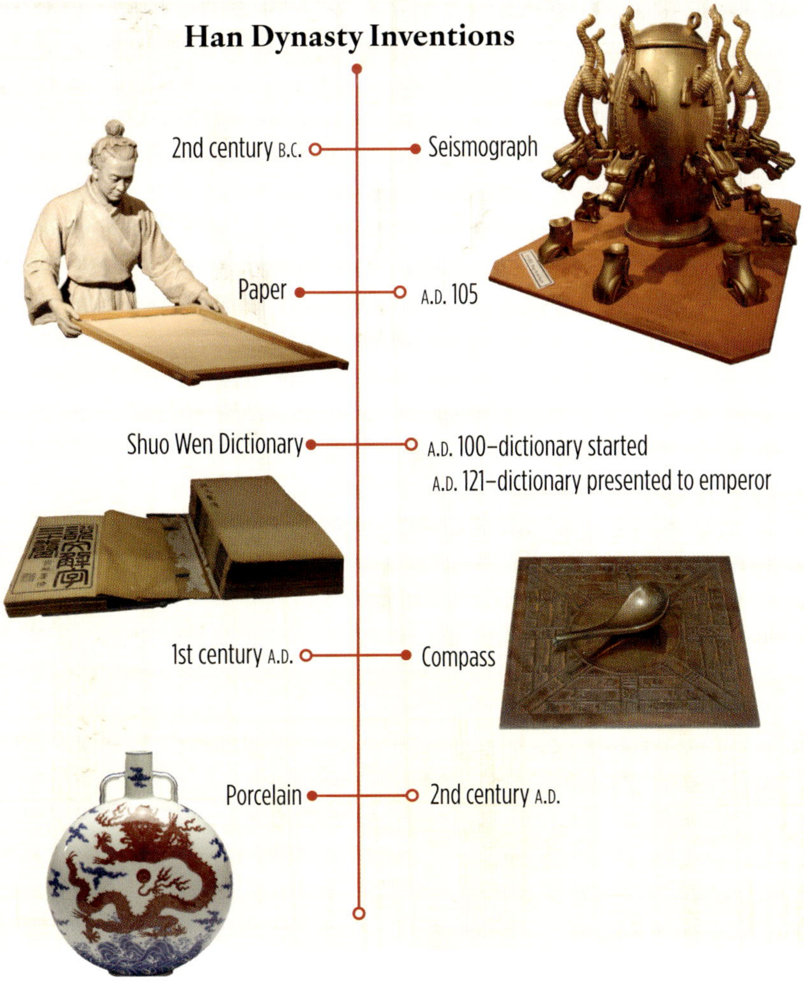

Known as the Land of the Rising Sun, Japan lies in the North Pacific Ocean, east of Russia, China, and Korea. Made up of thousands of small islands, its four main islands include Hokkaido, Honshu, Shikoku, and Kyushu. Rugged mountains slope down to narrow coastal plains. Numerous volcanoes shake the island nation with earthquakes that sometimes cause giant tidal waves of tsunamis to flood its shores.

Early Settlers

Some of the earliest people to settle Japan are thought to be the Ainu. With their distinctive facial features and men's full beards, the early Ainu appeared to have different roots than later groups who settled in Japan. Clay pots from ancient Japan were found with rope-like designs pressed into them. These are linked to a culture called Jomon, meaning "cord-marked." The Jomon are considered ancestors of the Ainu and were hunters who also fished in Japan's many lakes and along its coastlines.

♦ Jomon vase

Yayoi

Around 300 B.C., the Yayoi migrated from the mainland of Asia to Japan. They pushed the Ainu (indigenous people group) north, where they settled on the large island of Hokkaido. The Yayoi people built villages and became the dominant tribe in Japan. They irrigated their fields and planted rice. Craftworkers made items like bells, tools, and weapons from bronze and iron.

♦ A woodblock print portraying the legendary first emperor Jimmu, who witnessed a sacred bird flying away during his expedition to eastern Japan.

Yamato

The Yamato tribe rose to power in Japan in the second century. According to legend, Jimmu became Japan's first emperor around 660 B.C. The people believed he descended from the sun goddess (a false god). His descendants ruled as future emperors. Considered a representative of the gods, the Yamato line of emperors still holds a ceremonial position today. The Imperial Family of Japan is the longest continuous dynasty among all the nations of the world.

♦ Torii Gate (sacred gateway) of Shinto religion, Lake Biwa, Japan

Religion

The Yayoi introduced the Shinto religion to Japan. It is a mixture of ancestor and nature worship. Shrines were built as holy places. Small figurines represented good luck. Eventually Buddhism arrived from China, and practices from both religions intermingled by the eighth century.

Sacred Tombs

What riches are buried deep inside Japan's mysterious and ancient tombs? Known as *kofun*, stone coffins were buried under mounds of dirt and soil often built in the shape of a gigantic keyhole. Small clay warriors called *haniwa* stood guard around each one. Some of the biggest tombs in the history of the world, the *kofun* contain items that remain a mystery because they have never been excavated. That is because these ancient structures are considered holy. The Yamato period (A.D. 250–710) is also known as the *kofun* period, when more than 160,000 *kofun* were built.

♦ Burial site of Prince Shotoku

The Great Reform

A central government. A system of writing. Culture. Around A.D. 600, Prince Shotoku used China's Tang Dynasty as a model and brought many new traditions with a new way of life to Japan. It was a period marked by developing towns, building temples, and appreciating the arts.

Imperial Capital

The first permanent imperial capital of Japan was set up in the city of Nara around A.D. 710. By now, the emperor had become more of a religious figure than a government leader. Officials and monks struggled against each other to hold power over the land. In A.D. 784, the capital was moved to the city of Nagaoka-kyō, marking a new era in Japanese history.

They crossed a bridge. A land bridge, that is. After the worldwide Flood in Noah's day and the incident at the Tower of Babel, people scattered and populated the earth. Sea levels were lower from the effects of the Ice Age. A 50-mile bridge of dry land surfaced in the Bering Strait between Siberia and North America. Animals wandered across. Hunters and their families followed. People migrated in all directions, settling throughout North and South America. They used the natural resources in the distinct regions they settled and used them for food, housing, and clothes.

Arctic and Subarctic

This polar region of ice and snow stretches from present-day Alaska, across Canada, and to Greenland. The ancient Aleut Unangan people hunted seals and whales near their homes on the Aleutian Islands. On the mainland, herds of caribou thundered across the tundra on their seasonal migrations, followed by family groups who hunted them for meat and hides. Below the treeline, evergreen forests carpeted the rugged land. Moose, elk, and deer provided food. Tribes also fished in the abundant lakes and streams.

Pacific Northwest

Tribes living along the coast in the northwest hunted salmon with fishing spears. Thick forests provided plentiful wood for building plank houses and large seaworthy canoes that could hold up to 60 people at a time.

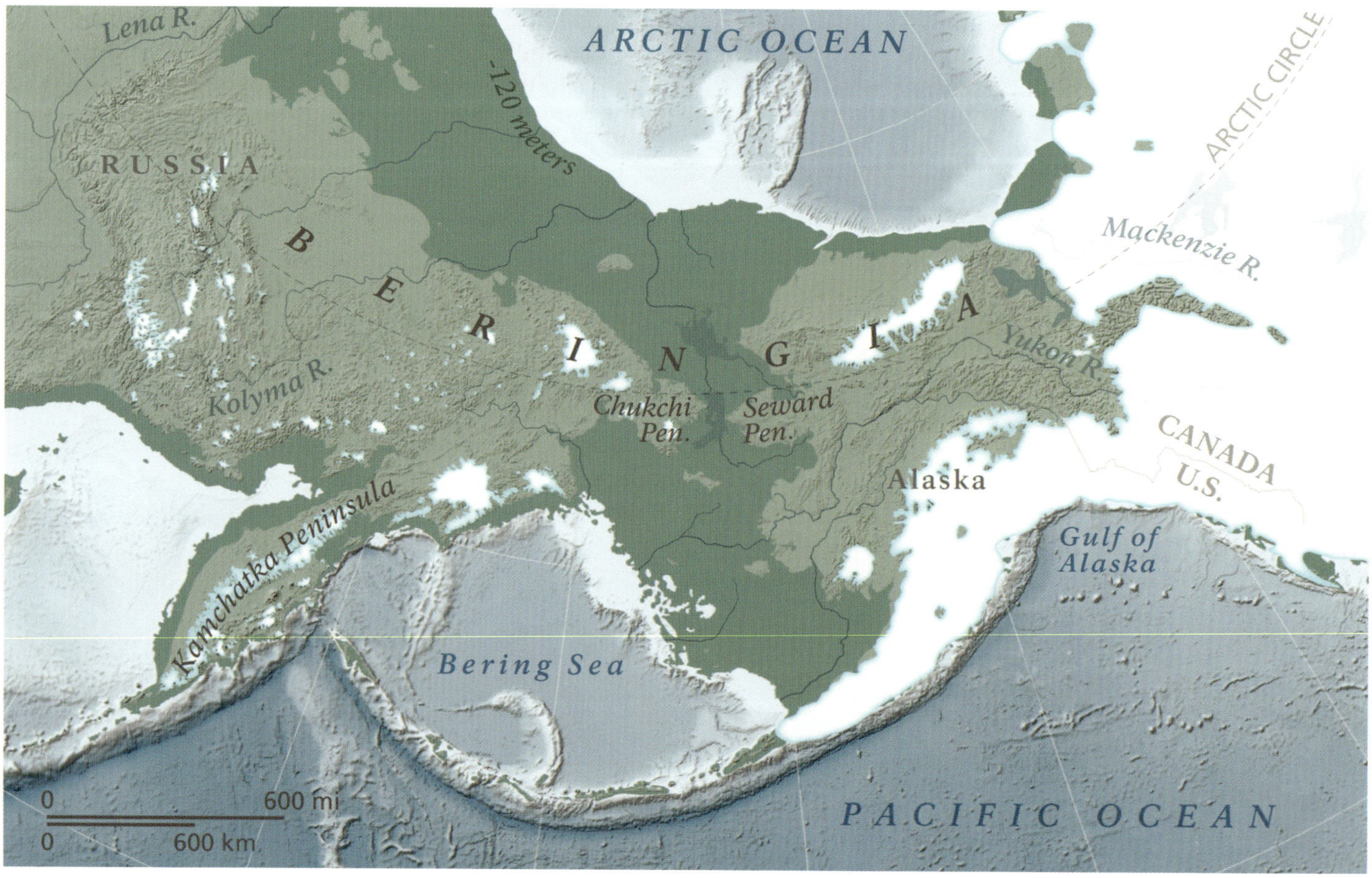

Northeast

♦ Hopewell pottery shard

People settling in the northeast utilized the rich resources of the forest. Many of their homes were built from wood, branches, and bark. They made clothes out of deerskin and rabbit fur. The Adena people (ancient North American Indians) lived in present-day Ohio and Indiana. While pharaohs built pyramids in Egypt, Adena tribes built massive mounds of earth. They held religious services, ceremonies, and burials on these large earthworks. The Hopewell, an ancient indigenous culture of the east-central area of North America, continued to use some of these mounds to bury their honored dead.

West and Southwest

Villages formed along the rivers and streams of the grasslands and plains. Hunters carrying spears stampeded herds of buffalo over cliffs. Early family groups lived in Danger Cave in the desert region of present-day Utah. They hunted local animals and gathered pine nuts and seeds for food. They left behind many artifacts, including tools made of animal bone or wood. Tribes in California ground acorns on grinding stones and fished along the coast.

♦ Woven basket from Danger Cave

Southeast

Mounds. Ridges. Pits. Around 1700 B.C., a Native American civilization rose up near the Mississippi River in Louisiana. They moved the earth into rows of half-circle ridges while digging pits and heaping large mounds of dirt nearby. Known as Poverty Point today, the excavated area 260 miles northwest of New Orleans has produced thousands of artifacts. Hunters chipped stone points for the end of their *atlatls*, or spear throwers. They fired clay into small, decorated balls that were heated and then placed in an earth oven for cooking. They carved bowls from soapstone brought in from quarries in other states. Several thousand people probably lived in this community, developing a network of trade that possibly extended far to the north.

♦ Pottery

♦ Pump-drill

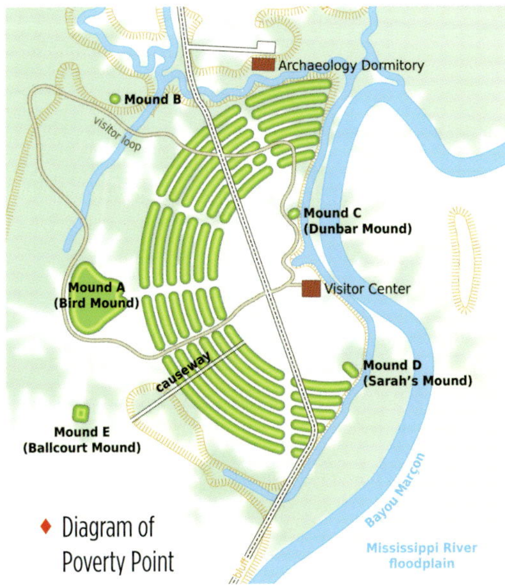

♦ Diagram of Poverty Point

Dating Systems

Both evolution and creation scientists agree that the earliest people to live in North America migrated from Asia and survived in different regions and climates by using the natural resources around them. However, scientists disagree on the system used to date these settlements and ancient civilizations. Evolutionists use faulty dating methods to fit their data on the evolutionary timeline thousands and thousands of years before the biblical account of creation. Creation scientists show how archaeological findings support a post-Flood migration that occurred after the Tower of Babel incident around 2247–2242 B.C.

Mesoamerica is a narrowing strip of land at the southern tip of North America that connects it with Central and South America. The first inhabitants started planting and growing maize, an ancient form of corn, in this region. Corn, beans, and squash were commonly planted together. Through trade and travel, cultures up and down North and South America began to grow these three main crops.

The Olmecs

Massive. Enormous. Colossal. Giant heads carved from stone boulders became the signature of the Olmecs, the earliest advanced civilization in Mesoamerica. Quarried miles away, some of these stone heads were up to 9 feet high and weighed 40-50 tons. How did they move them? No one knows for sure. The history of the Olmecs is still shrouded in mystery.

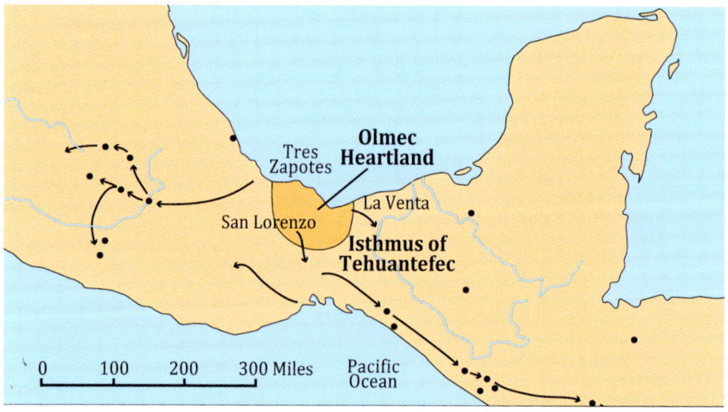

♦ Other Mexican civilizations are thought to have developed from the roots of this ancient people. They were likely based near the southern Gulf of America, though their impact reached many areas all over the country.

♦ El Castillo, or Kukulkan, the main pyramid at Chichen Itza, an ancient city in Mexico

Original City Planners

The Olmecs built their first capital near the Gulf of America at San Lorenzo around 1200 B.C. By around 900 B.C., their new capital became the nearby city of La Venta. In both locations, the Olmec people constructed large mounds of earth by carrying baskets of dirt and emptying them in one area. Using poles covered with thatch, they built their houses on top of these manmade hills. Olmecs used this same method to build temples, ceremonial buildings, and monuments. An open marketplace, or plaza, was in the center of the structures. In later years, the Olmecs built large earthen and stone pyramids. Their civilization eventually died out, but later cultures used the Olmec city planning model to design similar towns.

♦ Artifact found in La Venta, the primary center of Olmec culture

The Continent

South America is a varied continent. It is home to the Amazon River and the world's largest tropical rainforest. The Andes Mountain range, running north and south for about 4,500 miles, is the longest on earth. At 22,835 feet above sea level, Aconcagua is the highest mountain peak in the Americas. The Atacama Desert gets some of the lowest amounts of rain anywhere in the world.

Tierra del Fuego

At the southernmost tip of South America lies an archipelago, or group of islands, known as Tierra del Fuego, meaning "Land of Fire." It is at the end of the Andes Mountains. Topped with glaciers that carve fjords (long, narrow inlets) deep into the sea, this island group is a frigid, harsh land of freezing rain, bitter winds, and snow.

Yahgan

Few ancient cultures survived in the frigid region of Tierra del Fuego. These tribes kept many campfires burning to help keep warm. The Yahgan people lived along the coast. Families moved from site to site, gathering berries, wild celery, and shellfish along the shore. They often lived for days in their canoes, hunting seals. The hides of the seals provided capes for clothing, moccasins, and temporary tents.

Ona

The Onas lived inland on the large island of Tierra del Fuego. This tribe ate berries, shellfish, and a seafaring bird called the cormorant. Their main food source was the guanaco, an animal like the llama. As nomads, the Ona people followed the guanaco herds to hunt them. Using branches that they covered with hides, they built temporary shelters against the extreme weather.

Modern-day Peru lies along the west coast of South America. A large desert, drier than the Sahara, stretches out across its coastal plain. Rivers flow from the highest peaks of the Andes Mountains, across the desert, and to the Pacific Ocean. They provide water for farming. At an altitude of over 12,500 feet above sea level, Lake Titicaca is the highest lake in the world. On the eastern side of the Andes, the Amazon River runs through lush rain forests and thick jungles.

♦ Traditional *totora* reed boat on Lake Titicaca

First Villages

Family groups in ancient Peru domesticated the llamas of the Andes. The people used them for their meat and milk. Their wool was good for weaving blankets, capes, and clothes. Llamas were also used to carry heavy loads on steep mountain trails between villages. People farmed corn, squash, and lima beans, adding spicy chili peppers to the traditional crops. High in the peaks of the Andes, the world's first potatoes were harvested, cooked, and eaten.

♦ Llamas are still vital to life in Peru, as they are used to carry items such as building materials, water, and goods across the steep and uneven terrain of the Andes mountains where vehicles cannot go.

Chavín Culture

The earliest known South American civilization was the Chavín culture, emerging around 900 B.C. They built an impressive stone temple complex at Chavín de Huántar, over 10,000 feet above sea level, near mountain passes linking the desert coast to the Amazon rainforest. The purpose of its maze-like tunnels and interconnected rooms remains unknown. Like many South American cultures, the Chavín likely worshiped the jaguar, a powerful symbol common in their art. They were also the first in the Americas to recognize gold's value, as indicated by the many intricate gold artifacts uncovered by archaeologists there.

♦ Underground tunnels within the main temple of Chavín de Huántar

Paracas People

In southern Peru, the Paracas culture developed on the Paracas Peninsula. They were known for the beautiful and exquisite textiles woven from llama wool and cotton. Each was an amazing work of art. As coastal people, they gathered shellfish, fished, and hunted sea lions. The Paracas people turned their barren desert homelands into lush green farmland by building massive irrigation channels. Music was an important part of the Paracas people, and many of their musical instruments have been found.

◆ Paracas bowl, c. 300–100 B.C.

◆ A zampoña (pan pipe)

◆ Ceramic bottle with a feline face

In elite families, the Paracas wrapped wooden boards around the heads of their infants to form elongated skulls as they grew.

When people died, their bodies were treated and mummified. The deceased were wrapped with layers of intricately embroidered textiles.

◆ Above-ground Nazca aqueduct for channeling water

Nazca Civilization

Around 200 B.C., the Nazca people lived as neighbors to the Paracas, with many similar customs and crafts. After the Paracas disappeared, the Nazca civilization continued to thrive. They hunted seals and otters from the sea, and they raised llamas, alpacas, and guinea pigs for food. Farmers grew potatoes, sweet potatoes, and peanuts on terraces cut into the hillsides. Irrigation channels, underground aqueducts, and cisterns kept water available even during drier seasons. Skilled craft workers, they developed unique pottery, including colorful double-spouted jugs, masks, and panpipes.

Nazca Lines

A monkey, hummingbird, and spider. Triangles, rectangles, and trapezoids. The Nazca people created art of a colossal size by etching hundreds of humongous geoglyphs in the dirt and sands of the desert floor. Because of low rainfall levels, these large-scale images have not washed away, even after nearly two thousand years. The purpose of their construction remains unknown. Most images are so large that they are best seen by plane!

King Solomon was dead. His son Rehoboam stepped up as the next king. But Solomon had burdened his kingdom with heavy taxes to pay for all the luxuries of Israel's Golden Age. Led by Jeroboam, a delegation arrived at Rehoboam's courts. They asked for lower taxes. Rehoboam refused. Jeroboam then led a rebellion. The ten northern tribes split away to form their own kingdom and named themselves Israel. Rehoboam was left with his own tribe of Judah and part of the tribe of Benjamin. In 975 B.C., the Hebrew kingdom became divided—Israel in the north and Judah to the south (see 1 Kings 12:1–20).

Israel

Dan and Bethel

King Jeroboam was worried that his new kingdom did not have Solomon's Temple in Jerusalem. He set up two golden calves as centers of worship, one in the city of Dan and one in Bethel. He led God's people in the terrible sin of idolatry (see 1 Kings 12:28–29).

Samaria

Omri, an officer in the army of Israel, was crowned its new king in 929 B.C. He moved the capital to Samaria. His former ally, King Ben-Hadad of Damascus, turned against him and laid repeated sieges against the city. Omri's son, Ahab, then became king. Ahab married Jezebel, the evil Phoenician princess from Tyre. The terrible worship of the false god Baal filled God's holy land (see 1 Kings 16:29–33).

975 B.C.

Kings	PROPHETS
Jeroboam I	Ahijah
Nadab	
Baasha	Jehu
Elah	
Zimri	
Omri	Micaiah
Ahab	Elijah
Ahaziah	
Jehoram	
	Elisha
Jehu	
Jehoahaz	
Jehoash	
Jeroboam II	Jonah
Zechariah	Amos
Shallum	Hosea
Menahem	
Pekahiah	
Pekah	Obed
Hoshea	

c. 721 B.C.

Fall of Israel

God sent prophets—including Elijah, Elisha, Amos, and Hosea—to the Northern Kingdom of Israel to call the people to repent and turn back to Him. But the people refused. During the Divided Kingdom period, not one king of Israel listened to the prophets' call for repentance, obedience, and worship of God alone. So, God allowed enemy armies to attack Israel. In roughly 721 B.C., the Assyrian Empire conquered the Northern Kingdom of Israel, and the citizens of Samaria were carried away into captivity (see 2 Kings 17:5–6). King Sargon II of Assyria colonized Samaria by bringing in foreigners from such regions as Babylonia to settle the land. They intermarried with the remaining Israelites left behind. Their descendants became identified as the Samaritans, still known in New Testament times.

Judah

Kings

Prophets

975 B.C.

Prophets	Kings
Shemaiah	Rehoboam
	Abijah
Azariah, Hanani	Asa
Jehu, Jahaziel, Eliezer	Jehoshaphat
	Jehoram
	Ahaziah
	Athaliah (queen)
Joel, Zechariah	Joash
	Amaziah
Micah, Isaiah	Uzziah
	Jotham
	Ahaz
	Hezekiah
	Manasseh
	Amon
Nahum, Zephaniah, Habakkuk, Huldah, Uriah	Josiah
	Jehoahaz
	Jehoiakim
	Jehoiachin
	Zedekiah
Jeremiah, Ezekiel, Obadiah, Daniel	
Haggai, Zechariah	
Malachi	

588 B.C.

Judah

The Southern Kingdom of Judah extended the dynasty of King David down through its line of rulers. Some wicked kings led the people to idolatry, while some faithful kings, such as Jehoshaphat, Hezekiah, and Josiah, led great revivals to return the Hebrew people back to God. Judah continued the Levitical priesthood who served at the temple in Jerusalem. Judah's territory was smaller than Israel's with less rainfall and much less farmland. But Judah was not on the main trade route to Egypt like Israel was. This resulted in being attacked less than Israel.

♦ Solomon's Temple

Peace and Prosperity

At first, Judah and Israel fought against each other. At various times, however, they joined together as allies to fight against enemy attacks. For a short while, both kingdoms even experienced a time of peace. In Israel, under the rule of King Jeroboam II, the upper class grew more prosperous. Farms flourished, trade increased, and the nation's wealth multiplied. In Judah, King Uzziah dug many wells to increase their supply of water for their livestock and crops. He conquered neighboring territories and fortified his cities. He built up his armies, providing them with state-of-the-art armor and weapons, including an invention that catapulted stones and arrows against their enemies. Both nations thought a Golden Age had returned to God's people, but the prophets said otherwise. Amos, Hosea, and Isaiah warned them—gaining riches without honoring or worshiping God would lead to their ruin.

Fall of Judah

Assyria, Egypt, and Babylon attacked the small kingdom of Judah. When the people looked to God for help, He kept his hand of protection over them and fought their battles for them. But many of Judah's kings led the people to turn away from the true God of Israel and to worship the false gods of other nations. The prophets called Judah to return to God, but again, the people refused to repent and suffered the consequences. King Nebuchadnezzar led the Babylonian Empire against Judah. Hebrews were carried off as captives to Babylon, including the prophet Ezekiel and Daniel and his friends. In 588 B.C., the Babylonians sacked Jerusalem. Its wall was breached, the city was destroyed, and the glorious temple was burned to the ground. More captives were deported to Babylon. Foreigners resettled Judah's cities, but there was one ray of hope. God promised to return His people to their land.

After King Solomon's death, Israel split into two kingdoms: the Northern Kingdom of Israel and the Southern Kingdom of Judah. Many kings in both kingdoms led the people into idol worship. God sent His prophets to call His people to repent and turn back to Him.

Kings

Prophets

King Ahab

Ahab is known as one of the most evil kings of the northern kingdom of Israel. His marriage to Jezebel, the pagan Phoenician princess, added greatly to his downfall. She encouraged him to kill the prophets of God and destroy the holy places set aside to worship God. Ahab built a temple for the fasle god Baal and led his people into terrible sin.

Elijah

Elijah was a prophet during King Ahab's reign. Elijah challenged Jezebel's 850 prophets of Baal and Asherah (false gods) to meet him on Mount Carmel for a showdown of sorts. The prophets and Elijah built an altar, and the one true God sent fire down from heaven to consume the offering. Jezebel's false gods did nothing. When Elijah prayed, God sent fire from heaven that consumed the sacrifice. The people declared, "The Lord, He is God!" (1 Kings 18:20–39b). Elijah did not die but was carried up to heaven in a chariot of fire (2 Kings 2:11). Years later, Elijah appeared with Moses on the Mount of Transfiguration and spoke with Jesus (Matt. 17:1–13).

Elisha

After Elijah was taken into heaven, his assistant Elisha took over Elijah's ministry. God performed many miracles through Elisha, including healing Naaman from leprosy (2 Kings 5:1–14). One time, when an enemy army surrounded Elisha, God sent a vast army of horses and chariots of fire to protect him (2 Kings 6:8–23). Elisha's ministry in the Northern Kingdom of Israel lasted more than 50 years.

King Jehoshaphat

Judah's fourth king was Jehoshaphat. Like his father, King Asa, Jehoshaphat was a godly king. He continued his father's plan for reform, destroying pagan worship centers. He sent priests and Levites throughout his kingdom to teach the people about God. During enemy attacks and times of trouble, Jehoshaphat prayed and turned to God for help. Even though he made an alliance with King Ahab, Jehoshaphat tried to obey God's commandments and required his judges to make decisions based on the justice of God (see 2 Chron. 17—20).

King Josiah

Josiah was crowned king of Judah when he was just eight years old. Deeply devoted to God, Josiah led the nation to reform, repair, and revival. He removed pagan altars, idols, and people who practiced witchcraft from the land. He repaired the aging and forgotten temple. When the Book of the Law was found in the temple, Josiah led his kingdom in a great revival to return to obedience and worship of the one true God. Like no other king in the history of Israel or Judah, Josiah led the people in a great celebration of Passover.

Isaiah

Around 759–698 B.C., the prophet Isaiah called the people of Judah to return to God. His message included warnings of punishment and judgment for Judah's continuing sin of idol worship. Known as the Messianic Prophet, much of Isaiah's message was a word of hope for the coming Messiah. His ministry took place during the reigns of Uzziah, Jotham, Ahaz, and Hezekiah.

Jeremiah

Jeremiah was a prophet during the reign of the last five kings of Judah (c. 629–588 B.C.). After King Josiah's death, the kingdom of Judah once again turned its back on God and turned to idol worship. Jeremiah's message was often a sad one, warning of punishment if the people did not repent. He witnessed the fall of Judah, the conquering of Jerusalem, and the destruction of the holy temple by King Nebuchadnezzar and the Babylonian Empire.

What was one of the world's first great empires? The Assyrian Empire! The kingdom of Assyria was located along the Tigris River in northern Mesopotamia in modern-day Iraq. For centuries, it conquered its neighbors or was conquered. At the height of its powerful empire, it ruled over the entire Fertile Crescent, including Babylonia, Phoenicia, Israel, and Egypt.

Daily Life

Much of what we know about the Assyrian empire comes from ancient clay tablets unearthed from its royal library at Nineveh. These artifacts tell us that both men and women wore long robes called tunics. Important men sported long beards squared off at the bottom. Their palace complexes, temples, and courts were magnificent, surrounded by lush gardens. Colorful bricks and massive stone carvings decorated buildings in their cities. Villages and farming communities brought water to the fields with complex irrigation systems and canals.

♦ Ancient Assyrian lamassu (guardian sculpture), 9th-7th century B.C.

♦ Ashurnasirpal II after a successful military campaign, c. 865-860 B.C.

War

Horses. Chariots. Skilled archers. The Assyrians were fierce warriors known for their skill in conquering fortified cities. They built towers on wheels to put into position and climb over city walls. Often, they carried captives away to live in other parts of their empire and settled foreigners in their place. The Assyrians divided their empire into provinces, requiring heavy taxes and tributes to be paid to their king.

Tribes of Israel

The Assyrians laid siege to Samaria, capital of the Northern Kingdom of Israel. They conquered Israel in 721 B.C. and deported the ten tribes to all points of the empire, where they seemed to disappear from history. These captives became known as the Ten Lost Tribes of Israel. Later, King Sennacherib led the Assyrians to lay siege to Jerusalem, capital of the Southern Kingdom of Judah. But King Hezekiah turned to God for help. With a great miracle, God saved Judah. He sent an angel to kill 185,000 enemy soldiers, and the Assyrian army abandoned their siege (see 2 Kings 18:13–19:37).

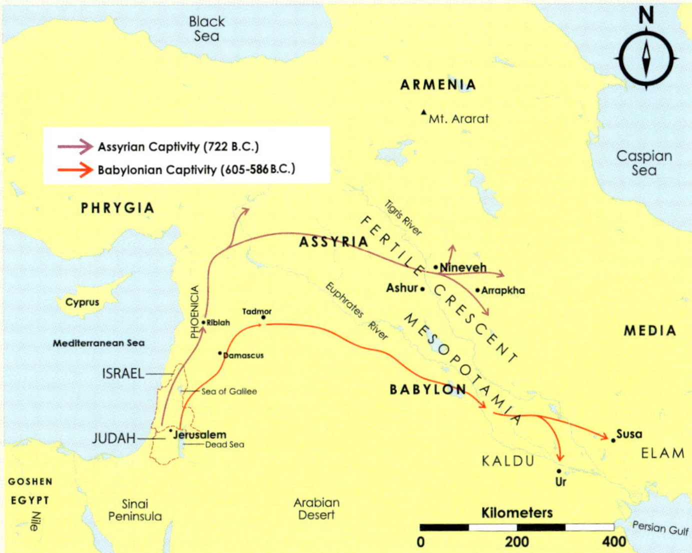

Lost Tribes included:

- Reuben
- Simeon
- Issachar
- Zebulun
- Dan
- Naphtali
- Gad
- Asher
- Ephraim
- Manasseh

Jonah

The Assyrian Empire worshiped many false gods. They believed their kings were like gods, creating giant stone sculptures of the king's face on the body of a bull or lion with wings. God sent Jonah, a Hebrew prophet, to call Assyria's capital city of Nineveh to repent. From the king to the commoner, everyone listened to God's warning and repented. God forgave them and spared the great city from destruction.

♦ Gilgamesh Dream Tablet

Royal Library of Nineveh

Ashurbanipal was one of the latest and greatest kings of the Assyrian Empire. A patron of literature and the arts, he accumulated vast amounts of clay tablets in his royal library at the capital city of Nineveh. Each tablet was written in cuneiform, an ancient type of writing used in Mesopotamia at this time. Topics including history, medicine, religion, and science were catalogued and stored.

♦ Sculpted relief depicting King Ashurbanipal hunting lions, c. 645-635 B.C.

End of an Empire

After the death of Ashurbanipal in 631 B.C., the Assyrian Empire weakened. Together with the Medes, the Babylonians rose up and destroyed its capital. They burned the palaces, temples, and royal library of Nineveh to the ground. While nearly everything else was destroyed, the library's baked clay tablets survived the fire. Forgotten for 2,000 years, over 30,000 of these tablets have been recovered from the library's ruins.

A new king. A new era. A new heart for the people. In 726 B.C., Hezekiah became king of Judah. He was 25 years old. One of the first things he did as king was reopen the doors of the temple. He cleansed the temple from idol worship and led the people back to the worship of the Lord.

Siloam Tunnel (Tunnel of Hezekiah), used to supply water to ancient Jerusalem in case of siege

Remains of the wall built around Jerusalem during Hezekiah's reign

Assyrians Attack

In 721 B.C., the Assyrian Empire conquered Samaria. It was the end of the Northern Kingdom of Israel. To protect the Southern Kingdom of Judah, Hezekiah made the wall around Jerusalem stronger. He built a tunnel to protect the city's water supply. The Assyrians marched into Judah and conquered all its fortified cities. To slow the advance of the Assyrian army toward Jerusalem, King Hezekiah agreed to pay tribute. Sennacherib demanded eleven tons of silver and one ton of gold. Hezekiah paid this amount by stripping the gold off the doors of the temple and emptying the silver out of the palace and temple treasuries (2 Kings 18:13–16).

Siege of Jerusalem

The Assyrians also laid siege to Jerusalem. When Hezekiah cried out to God for help, God sent an angel to destroy the Assyrian army. Sennacherib abandoned the siege and returned to his home where he was assassinated by his own people (see 2 Kings 19).

Sennacherib Prism

A two-foot-tall, hexagonal clay monument known as the Sennacherib Prism is now housed at the British Museum. A record of Sennacherib's conquests, it boasts that the Assyrians conquered 46 cities in Judah and laid siege to Hezekiah like a "caged bird" in his royal city of Jerusalem.

Babylonian Empire

The Babylonians conquered the Assyrian Empire. Then, Nebuchadnezzar enlarged his Babylonian Empire. He set his sights on Jerusalem. God sent the prophet Jeremiah to call his people back to Him and warned that their sins would be punished if they continued in their idol worship. Led by their last four kings, the nation of Judah refused to repent.

First Deportation

Around 606 B.C., Nebuchadnezzar led his armies into Judah. He laid siege to Jerusalem and plundered treasures from the temple to put in his own pagan temple in Babylon. Daniel and his friends, along with other nobles and elite descendants of Judah's kings, were deported and carried off into captivity. Daniel, Shadrach, Meshach, and Abednego were trained to serve in Babylon at the palace of the king.

Jerusalem Destroyed

Horses and chariots thundered across Judah once again. King Nebuchadnezzar and his armies camped outside the walls of God's holy city. For two and a half years, the people inside Jerusalem perished with barely any food or water. Finally, around 586 B.C., the terrible siege came to an end. The walls of Jerusalem fell. Babylonian soldiers set fire to the houses, palaces, and the temple. Captives were carried away to Babylon. Only the poorest and weakest people were left to farm the land.

Prophets in Exile

God did not abandon His people. He punished their sins but promised to heal them and bring them back to their land. The prophet Jeremiah said God would bring them back home in 70 years (see Jer. 29:10). The prophet Ezekiel gave them visions of a new temple where God would live with His people (see Ezek. 40–48). The prophet Daniel told the people about their conquering King who would one day rule forever (Da. 2:44).

TIMELINE: 600 B.C. – 30 B.C.

500 B.C. — 400 B.C. — 300 B.C.

- Second temple built by Jews in Jerusalem 516 B.C.
- Birth of democracy in Athens c. 507 B.C.
- Yo-yos created c. 500 B.C.
- Ezra returns to Jerusalem 467 B.C.
- Nehemiah rebuilds Jerusalem's wall c. 454 B.C.
- Parthenon built In Greece 447 B.C.
- Peloponnesian War 431-404 B.C.
- Sparta conquers Athens 404 B.C.
- Catapults used for military c. 400 B.C.
- Gauls sack Rome 390 B.C.
- Alexander (the Great) is Aristotle's student 343 B.C.
- City of Alexandria founded in Egypt 331 B.C.
- Rise of Mauryan Empire (India) c. 324 B.C.
- Greek Empire is divided 323 B.C.
- Yayoi period in Japan c. 300 B.C.
- Septuagint, Greek version of Old Testament, written 277 B.C.

- 509 B.C. Roman Republic established
- c. 500 B.C. Founding of Buddhism
- c. 490-449 B.C. Persian Wars
- 460 B.C. Birth of Hippocrates, Father of Medicine
- c. 450 B.C. Phidias sculpts Statue of Zeus at Olympia
- c 432 B.C. Pythagoras theorem measures the right triangle
- 407 B.C. Plato becomes pupil of Socrates
- c. 400s B.C. Fortress of Petra carved into cliffs (Jordan)
- c. 397 B.C. Malachi prophesies; last book in Old Testament
- 367 B.C. Aristotle is Plato's student
- 336-323 B.C. Alexander the Great expands the Greek Empire
- c. 326 B.C. Alexander the Great attacks India
- 323 B.C. Death of Alexander the Great
- 305 B.C. Ptolemy I of Greece becomes pharaoh, founding Ptolemaic dynasty in Egypt
- 284 B.C. Library of Alexandria
- c. 272-232 B.C. Emperor Ashoka rules (India)

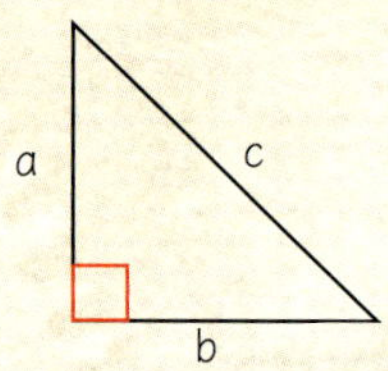

Ctesibius invents musical water organ c. 270 B.C.

Start of first Punic War 264 B.C.

Eratosthenes measures Earth's circumference c. 240 B.C.

Terra-cotta army guards Emperor Qin's tomb 210 B.C.

Rosetta Stone 196 B.C.

Han Dynasty (China) c. 202 B.C.–A.D. 220

Antiochus (Greece) takes Jerusalem and ransacks the temple 170 B.C.

Antikythera Mechanism, world's oldest "computer," tracks time (Greece) 150–100 B.C.

Fall of Carthage ends Third Punic War 146 B.C.

Rise of Pharisees and Sadducees c. 145 B.C.

Anna starts to serve God at the temple, waiting for the Messiah 88 B.C.

Pompey takes Jerusalem 63 B.C.

Julius Caesar invades Britain 55 B.C.

Adoption of Julian calendar 45 B.C.

Herod the Great appointed king of Judea 40 B.C.

Death of Cleopatra, last pharaoh of Egypt 30 B.C.

200 B.C. — 100 B.C.

260 B.C. First Roman fleet sails the seas

248–226 B.C. Early batteries used (Persia)

221–206 B.C. Qin Dynasty unites China

c. 220–206 B.C. Great Wall of China built

218 B.C. Hannibal crosses the Alps with elephants

c. 190 B.C. Parchment made from animal skin (in Pergamum)

165 B.C. Judas Maccabeus rededicates Jewish temple in Jerusalem

150 B.C. Crates of Mallus makes a globe of the world

146 B.C. Roman Empire conquers Greece

c. 125 B.C. Isaiah scroll written

73–71 B.C. Spartacus leads revolt of gladiators and slaves

58 B.C. Gallic Wars

45 B.C. Julius Caesar becomes dictator of Rome

44 B.C. Julius Caesar assassinated

31 B.C. Cleopatra and Mark Antony defeated in Battle of Actium

Hammurabi wrote his famous code of laws around 1792 B.C., during the first Babylonian Empire. Centuries after it collapsed, Babylonia was conquered by its neighbors to the north and became part of the Assyrian Empire. A hotbed of rebellion, the city of Babylon was destroyed by the Assyrians. Around 625 B.C., Babylonia revolted against its oppressors. A general in the Babylonian army, Nabopolassar, declared himself king of Babylonia. He joined with his neighbor, the Medes (modern-day Iran), to overthrow the Assyrian Empire.

Building an Empire

Power. Riches. Fame. King Nabopolassar and his son Nebuchadnezzar II conquered neighboring kingdoms and enlarged the new Babylonian Empire. They brought riches and laborers from their new conquests back to their capital city of Babylon. They rebuilt the city into a marvel of architecture and beauty until its fame spread around the ancient world.

City of Babylon

The city of Babylon was shaped like a colossal square. Each side was 15 miles long. A massive wall surrounded Babylon. It was so thick that four horses pulling a chariot could gallop along its top. One hundred bronze gates were built all around the wall. The impressive Ishtar Gate with its baked blue bricks and decorations of lions, dragons, and bulls welcomed holiday parades and military marches into the city. The royal palace, throne room, and hanging gardens were at the heart of the city. A tall ziggurat dominated the landscape with steps along its sides leading to a temple shrine at the top. The Euphrates River flowed through the center of the city.

Hanging Gardens of Babylon

King Nebuchadnezzar built beautiful palace gardens for his queen. Terraces and arches were covered with dirt where huge trees and other greenery were planted so that they seemed to be hanging in the sky above people as they walked beneath them. A mechanism, turning like a giant screw or a chain pump, brought water up from the Euphrates River to water the gardens. These palace gardens were so magnificent that they were known as one of the Seven Wonders of the Ancient World.

♦ The "Garden Party" relief depicting Ashurbanipal and his wife relaxing under a pergola of climbing grapevines with hanging grapes, small birds, fruiting date palms, and pine trees.

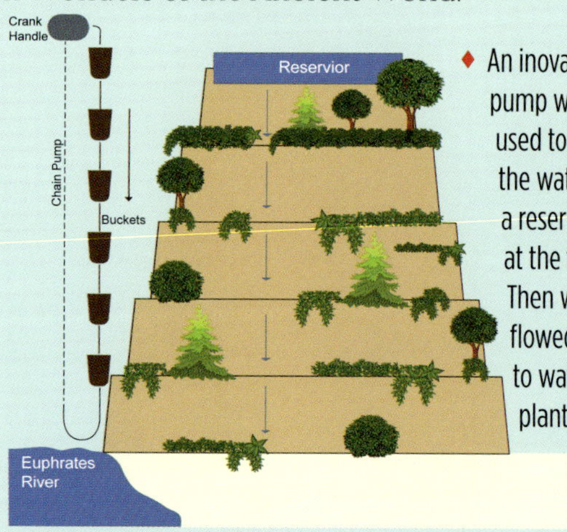

♦ An inovated pump was used to get the water to a reservior at the top. Then water flowed down to water the plants.

Captives from Judah

Nebuchadnezzar marched with his armies against Judah. He took treasures from Solomon's Temple and deported captives back to Babylon. Shadrach, Meshach, and Abednego were later brought to stand before him. They refused to bow down to the king's image of gold! Furious, he had them thrown into the fiery furnace, only to see a fourth man walking with them in the fire. The three friends walked out of the fire unhurt. The king then declared that the God of the Hebrews is the Most High God (see Dan. 3:1–30).

Daniel's Vision

The prophet Daniel interpreted a dream for King Nebuchadnezzar. The interpretation involved nations that would rise and fall in the future (Dan. 2).

Dream	Interpretation
Head of gold	Babylonian Empire
Chest and arms of silver	Persian Empire
Belly and thighs of bronze	Greek Empire
Legs of iron	Roman Empire
Feet of iron and baked clay	In the future

Daniel and His God

God gave Nebuchadnezzar terrifying dreams about future events. When Daniel was called in to interpret these visions, Daniel warned the king to humble himself and give honor to God. But the king was very proud. About a year later, he said, "Is not this great Babylon, that I have built for a royal dwelling by my mighty power and for the honor of my majesty?" (Dan. 4:30). God immediately struck down the king, and he went insane. After a time when his reason returned, Nebuchadnezzar praised Daniel's God as the Most High God who lives forever.

Fall of Babylon

King Nabonidus was gone on a military campaign. His son Belshazzar was left in Babylon to rule in his absence. Belshazzar knew the lessons Nebuchadnezzar had learned. Yet, he dishonored God by using the holy cups from Solomon's Temple to worship his false gods. A hand appeared and wrote on the wall the king's punishment from God. That very night in 539 B.C., Darius the Mede led King Cyrus's Persian troops to enter and overtake the city of Babylon. It was the end of the Babylonian Empire.

How could the king of Persia control his huge empire? By building a Royal Road! This road stretched over 1,600 miles from the capital city of Susa to the city of Sardis near the Aegean Sea. About every 14 miles, the king kept food supplies and fresh horses in reserve. The king's messengers could gallop from one end of the road to the other in just one week. Soldiers were stationed all along the route to protect them. The Royal Road was the main route in a network of roads built across the Persian Empire for trade and travel.

Bible as History

The Bible is a book of faith. It teaches us the truth about God. It is also a book of history. It documents the true history of the world, starting with creation. Many archaeological discoveries confirm the history found in the Bible. The Cyrus Cylinder is just one example of these finds. Our faith is founded on facts!

The Cyrus Cylinder

Ancient Persia was located in modern-day Iran. The king of Media was its ally to the north. In a series of conquests, King Cyrus of Persia eventually conquered the Medes and other neighboring countries. He and his predecessors built an empire that stretched from the Indus River to Egypt, including parts of Greece. The Cyrus Cylinder of 539 B.C., a large, barrel-shaped clay stone with writing on it, documented the conquests and rule of King Cyrus.

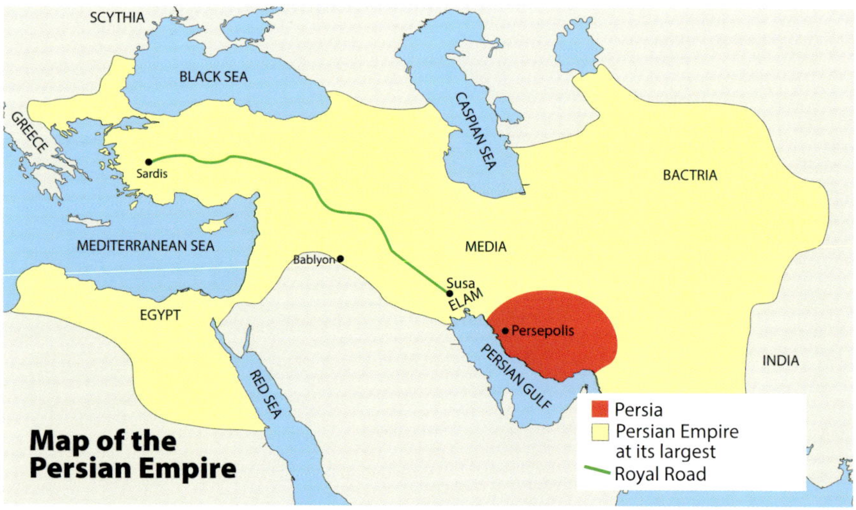

Map of the Persian Empire

King Darius I

Darius I oversaw three governors who oversaw 120 satraps (governors) who oversaw all the provinces in the vast Persian Empire. He organized the government of his empire in an efficient way. He planned to promote the Jewish man Daniel to oversee his governors. But other jealous governors and satraps convinced the king to enact a law against praying to a god other than Darius. Daniel prayed anyway, resulting in being thrown into a lions' den. When an angel saved Daniel from the lions, King Darius issued a decree that everyone in his kingdom must honor and respect Daniel's God (see Dan. 6).

Life in Persia

In ancient Persia, people wore long robes over pants, accented with expensive jewelry. Families could include a husband, several wives, and all their children. A king could have many wives in his magnificent palaces. The king's wives all lived together in a group called a harem. The universal language in the Persian Empire was Aramaic. The official religion was ancient Zoroastrianism, which worshiped gods of nature. Their wise men were known as Magi.

Esther, the Wise Queen

After he banished his first queen, King Xerxes (also known as Ahasuerus) crowned Esther as the new queen of the Persian Empire. A Hebrew, Esther had been raised by her older cousin Mordecai. When Haman, a palace official, proposed a plan to kill all the Jews throughout the empire, God used Esther to save her people. The holiday of Purim is still celebrated among Jewish families today to remember this historic victory for the Jews.

The prophet Isaiah told God's message to the people: One day the kingdom of Judah would be restored. Jerusalem would flourish once again. God would raise up a king named Cyrus who would command that both the city and the temple be rebuilt. When Isaiah gave this prophecy, Judah, Jerusalem, and the temple were thriving, so why would he say those things? His message was about the future!

The Decree of Cyrus

"Thus says Cyrus king of Persia: All the kingdoms of the earth the LORD God of heaven has given me. And He has commanded me to build Him a house at Jerusalem which is in Judah. Who is among you of all His people? May his God be with him, and let him go up to Jerusalem which is in Judah, and build the house of the LORD God of Israel (He is God), which is in Jerusalem" (Ezra 1:2–3).

Cyrus Family Tree

- Achaemenes (King of Persia)
  - Teispes (King of Persia)
    - Ariaramnes (Ruler of Persia)
      - Arsames (Ruler of Persia)
        - Hystaspes (Prince)
          - Darius the Great (King of Persia)
    - **Cyrus I** (Ruler of Anshan)
      - **Cambyses I** (Ruler of Anshan)
        - **Cyrus the Great** (King of Persia)
          - Cambyses II (King of Persia)
          - Bardiya (Prince)
          - Artystone (Princess)
          - Atossa (Princess)

Seventy Years

The prophet Jeremiah had a message from God for the future, too. The people of Judah would be exiled in Babylon. After 70 years, God would bring them back to their land. It happened just as God said it would. King Nebuchadnezzar destroyed Jerusalem and deported its captives to Babylon. Seventy years later, after the Persian Empire conquered the Babylonian Empire around 536 B.C., King Cyrus signed a decree to send the Jewish exiles back home.

Cyrus the Great

As the king of the Persian Empire, Cyrus the Great treated his subjects well. He allowed captives to return to their homelands. He allowed people to practice their own religion. He allowed their temples to be rebuilt. He did this for the people of Judah, just as Isaiah had prophesied nearly two centuries earlier. After King Cyrus died, he was buried in an impressive tomb that still can be seen in Iran today.

♦ Entrance for the Tomb of Cyrus the Great

Return to Jerusalem

Priests. Levites. Singers, servants, and gatekeepers. In 536 B.C., more than 40,000 people made the journey from Babylon back to Jerusalem along with their camels, horses, donkeys, and mules. Led by Zerubbabel, the prince of Judah, they carried 5,400 gold and silver articles from the original temple back with them. After their return, they gathered in Jerusalem with the Jews still living in the land. Zerubbabel and Jeshua, the high priest, built an altar to offer burnt offerings. They celebrated the Feast of Tabernacles together (see Ezra 3:1–4).

Zerubbabel was a descendant of Jehoiachin, the last king of Judah, who was a descendant of King David. Zerubbabel is listed in the genealogy of Jesus. As the prince of Judah, he worked with Jeshua the high priest to start building the second temple. They hired masons and carpenters. They bought cedar logs from Lebanon and had them floated on the Mediterranean Sea from Sidon and Tyre down to Joppa, then brought to the Temple Mount in Jerusalem (see Ezra 3:7).

The cedars of Lebanon were prized throughout the ancient Near East. This aromatic, durable wood was highly desirable for building projects like the temple restoration.

When the builders laid the foundation of the temple of the LORD, the priests stood in their apparel with trumpets, and the Levites, the sons of Asaph, with cymbals, to praise the LORD, according to the ordinance of David king of Israel. And they sang responsively, praising and giving thanks to the LORD,
"For He is good,
for His mercy endures
forever toward Israel."
Then all the people shouted with a great shout, when they praised the LORD, because the foundation of the house of the LORD was laid.
–Ezra 3:10–11

The Foundation

A special ceremony took place as builders laid the foundation of the temple. The priests stood in their holy robes, blowing their trumpets. The Levites played the cymbals, and together they sang praises to God, "For He is good, for His mercy endures forever toward Israel" (Ezra 3:11). Everyone shouted with excitement. Some wept when they remembered the destruction of the first temple, and some rejoiced to see the work begin on the second temple.

Work Stopped

People were living in the region who were not Jews. Years earlier, these foreigners had been captured and brought to live in Israel from other parts of the empire. They worshiped many false gods along with the God of Israel. The Law of Moses had strict instructions and guidelines about who could work on God's holy dwelling and how the work should be done. Zerubbabel and Jeshua would not allow idol worshipers to help. These foreigners persecuted the Jews and frustrated their work. After Cyrus died, the foreigners wrote letters to King Xerxes and later King Artaxerxes. Finally, with permission from the Persian Empire, the foreigners used weapons to force builders to stop work on the temple (Ezra 4–5).

Moreover I issue a decree as to what you shall do for the elders of these Jews, for the building of this house of God: Let the cost be paid at the king's expense from taxes on the region beyond the River. –Ezra 6:8

The Temple Completed

About 20 years later, God sent His prophets Haggai and Zechariah to encourage His people. Despite dangerous threats, Zerubbabel and Jeshua began work on the temple again. Tattenai, the Persian governor of the region, immediately sent a letter of complaint to the new ruler of the Persian Empire, King Darius. The king signed his own decree: Let the Jews build the temple and give them everything they need! In 516 B.C., the people of God finished the temple and dedicated it to Yahweh. Then they celebrated the Passover together with joy (Ezra 6).

When King Nebuchadnezzar leveled Jerusalem, he also destroyed the protective wall surrounding the city. Seventy years later, the first exiles returned to Jerusalem in 536 B.C. and rebuilt the temple. But the wall of Jerusalem had still not been repaired. When Nehemiah heard about it, he was greatly distressed.

Nehemiah

Nehemiah lived in captivity in the Persian capital of Susa (also known as Shushan). He held a very important position as cupbearer to the king. It was his job to taste everything the king ate or drank to make sure it was not poisoned. He asked King Artaxerxes (Queen Esther's stepson) for permission to return to Jerusalem and repair its wall. The king supplied Nehemiah with official passes to travel safely across the empire, along with a military escort on horses so he could get to Jerusalem without harm.

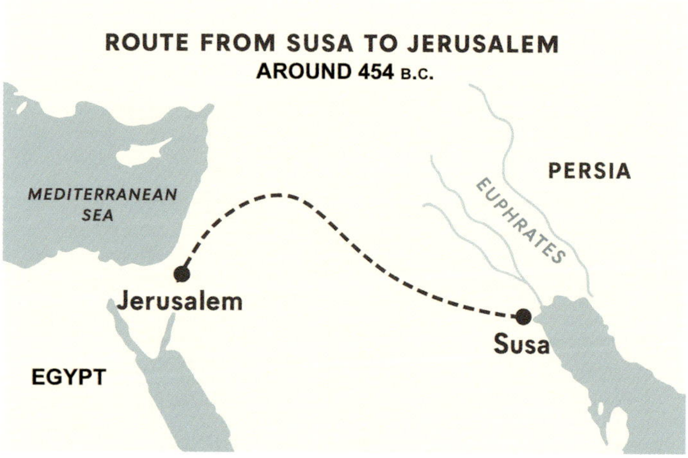

Building the Wall

Once in Jerusalem, Nehemiah enlisted local families of Jews to help rebuild the wall around the city and repair all its gates that had been burned by fire. There was just one problem. Sanballat, the governor of Samaria, and Tobiah, an Ammonite official, were upset at this political move on behalf of the Jews. A rebuilt wall around Jerusalem would strengthen their power and defenses against their enemies. Along with the Arabs, Ammonites, and Ashdodites, they mocked, threatened, and even planned to attack Nehemiah and his fellow Jews while they worked. But with God's help and hard work, the Jewish people rebuilt the wall in just 52 days!

Political and Religious Reform

Nehemiah worked as governor to hold the political leaders accountable to obey God's righteous and just laws (Neh. 13). Ezra worked with the priests to help the people follow God and His ways. Because people in Old Testament times did not have Bibles of their own, Ezra read aloud from the Book of the Law of Moses for everyone to hear. A great revival took place as people realized their sins, repented, and started to follow God's commandments (Neh. 8–10).

So they read distinctly from the book, in the Law of God; and they gave the sense, and helped them to understand the reading. (Neh. 8:8)

And they stood up in their place and read from the Book of the Law of the Lord their God for one-fourth of the day; and for another fourth they confessed and worshiped the Lord their God. (Neh. 9:3)

Elephantine Island

Archaeologists unearthed an ancient set of documents in Egypt on Elephantine Island at a military fortress in the Nile River. A colony of Jews lived there at the time of the Persian Empire. Legal contracts, business accounts, and lists were discovered, including an official letter mentioning the name of Jehohanan the high priest and Sanballat, the governor of Samaria. These very same names appear in the books of Nehemiah and Ezra. This supports the accuracy of historic details included in the Bible, further proof that we can trust it.

♦ Marriage contract between Egyptians

♦ Legal report on the decision of a probate dispute

♦ Receipt for a grain loan

♦ Property transfer document, Ananiah to Yehoishema

After the fall of the Mycenaean civilization, ancient Greece was organized into independent city-states, each with its own government and identity. When the Persian Empire rose to power, it launched attacks against these city-states—sometimes winning, sometimes losing. In response, the Greek city-states united and defeated the Persians, both in the sea and on land. Over time, two city-states emerged as the most powerful: Sparta and Athens.

Sparta

Wrestling. Running. Fighting. Every Spartan boy belonged to the government and left home to enter military training when he was seven years old. Even girls were encouraged to be athletic and strong. Living a simple, harsh lifestyle, Spartans were severe and proud. Only the ruling class were considered citizens. Most others, known as *helots*, farmed the land. The most powerful city-state in Greece, Sparta fought against Athens in the Peloponnesian War, conquering it in 404 B.C.

Athens

Led by its famous statesman, Pericles, Athens grew to be the center of culture and learning in Classical Greece. Stunning architecture dominated the landscape. The study of science, philosophy, history, and mathematics advanced. Democracy was born.

- The birthplace of Greek drama — the theater of Dionysus in Athens, Greece
- Panoramic view of the Acropolis of Athens, Greece, with the Parthenon temple

Greek Architecture

The Persians burned Athens to the ground in the early fifth century B.C. When the Persians were finally driven out, Pericles supported massive construction projects to create one of the most beautiful cities the world had ever seen. The Parthenon, a magnificent temple of elegant white marble, was built on the hill known as the Acropolis, overlooking the city. Rows of marble columns became a signature look in Greek architecture. Three main styles of columns were used: Doric, Ionic, and Corinthian.

♦ Doric ♦ Ionic ♦ Corinthian

Greek City-States

Most Greek city-states had similar features. For protection, they were surrounded by a wall. An acropolis (fortified part of a city) stood on a hill overlooking the city, usually with a temple built at its top. The agora was a central gathering place where people not only bought and traded goods, but also where they met for political gatherings, legal matters, and religious ceremonies. Athletes trained at a gymnasium. Some cities built stadiums with a long racetrack in the center. Theaters were often built into the hillsides with steep rows of seats facing the stage so spectators could watch competitions.

Birthplace of Democracy

Around 700 B.C., nobles in Athens overthrew the king. By 507 B.C., they set up a citizen assembly of free men to decide government matters. Public speeches at the agora (a central public space) addressed political issues, which were decided by vote. This marked the birth of democracy!

♦ Original grounds of the first olympics

Olympics

Every four years, the finest athletes in Greece flocked to the stadium in the town of Olympia to compete and test their skills. Events included: chariot racing and horse racing, boxing and wrestling, running, discus, and javelin events. On the middle day of the festivities, the people offered sacrifices to Zeus, king of the Greek gods. The Olympic Games were so famous that many of its competitions were decorated on vases and other fine pottery for the wealthy class.

The years between the Persian Wars and the Peloponnesian War are often called the Golden Age of Greece. Led by the famous leader Pericles, the magnificent and powerful city-state of Athens became a center of learning, art, and culture. During the middle of the fifth century B.C., the city experienced a birth of great achievements. Athens became known as the cradle of Western civilization.

Philosophy

Who was famous for asking questions? Socrates! He tried to inspire his students to think by starting with a question. His most famous student, Plato, wrote down his ideas. Plato began a school of philosophy called the Academy. His most famous student was Aristotle. Some say Aristotle was one of the smartest people who ever lived.

History

Facts. Fiction. Legends. The Greek historian, Herodotus, included it all. He is known as the Father of History. He wrote about the wars between the Persian Empire and the Greek city-states. Thucydides, another Greek historian, wrote about the Peloponnesian War between Sparta and Athens, keeping his accounts closer to the truth.

Science, Math, and Medicine

Ancient Greeks loved circles and triangles. Two mathematicians, Thales and Pythagoras, calculated theorems (mathematic ideas) to measure geometric shapes. Euclid also studied geometry, and his findings are still valuable today. Hippocrates focused more on the science of medicine, requiring his students to recite the Hippocratic oath (a promise to act ethically and prioritize a patient's well-being). Aristotle was a master in nearly every field of science. Future generations of scientists would build on the work of these great scientists.

Ancient Innovators: Greece's Legacy in Thought and Science

Golden Ratio

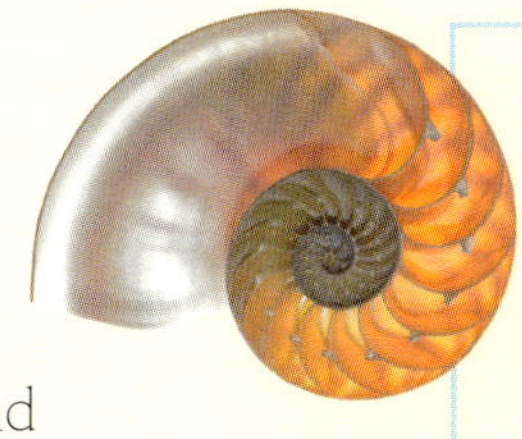

Euclid calculated a ratio of numbers related to each other. Found in nature, this pattern can be seen in the spiral of a seashell, arrangement of sunflower seeds, and design of pinecones. The Golden Ratio is approximately equal to 1.618. In mathematics, its symbol is the Greek letter phi (ϕ). The Greeks said that anything created based on using the Golden Ratio, whether a building or a photo, would be very pleasing to look at.

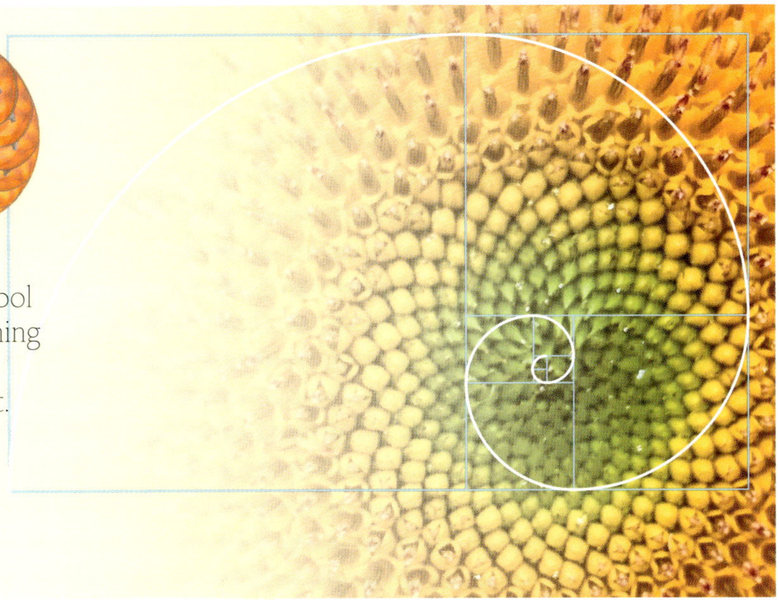

Three-Act Structure

Aristotle wrote a great work called *Poetics* that explained the art of storytelling. It discussed plot, characters, and dialogue. He also said that every story needs a beginning, a middle, and an end. This became the basis for the three-act structure, still used in writing today.

Literature, Art, and Religion

The ancient Greeks worshiped many false gods. Their pagan worship included immoral and shameful acts. Their philosophy, literature, and art contained descriptions and stories featuring these activities. The Bible clearly teaches that God gives everyone the opportunity to know Him. When people refuse to worship the one true God, He will allow them to live with the results of their sinful ways.

For since the creation of the world His invisible attributes are clearly seen, being understood by the things that are made, even His eternal power and Godhead, so that they are without excuse, because, although they knew God, they did not glorify Him as God, nor were thankful, but became futile in their thoughts, and their foolish hearts were darkened. Professing to be wise, they became fools, and changed the glory of the incorruptible God into an image made like corruptible man—and birds and four-footed animals and creeping things. Therefore God also gave them up to uncleanness, in the lusts of their hearts, to dishonor their bodies among themselves, who exchanged the truth of God for the lie, and worshiped and served the creature rather than the Creator, who is blessed forever. Amen. –Romans 1:20–25

Humanism

Instead of pursuing the knowledge that God offers, ancient Greeks pursued knowledge itself as a final triumph. Their scholars, philosophers, and thinkers developed the roots of humanism, the belief that people can be good without God. In fact, humanism denies the existence of anything spiritual or supernatural. Unfortunately, these false ideas became popular and influenced the world for generations to come, even today.

[F]or all have sinned and fall short of the glory of God. –Romans 3:23

Philip II was king of Macedonia, a kingdom north of Greece. He saw how the Peloponnesian War weakened Athens and Sparta, Greece's two strongest city-states. With his army, Philip marched into Greece, and by 338 B.C., he ruled over the land of Greece. He had a son named Alexander.

Tutor for an Heir

Philip II declared Alexander to be his heir to the throne when Alexander was very young. Who would be the best tutor for a future king? Aristotle, of course! King Philip II hired Aristotle to tutor 13-year-old Alexander. He taught Alexander philosophy, Greek literature, mathematics, and medicine. Only the most brilliant tutor in history would be good enough to teach the student destined to become the most brilliant military leader in the world.

Conquering an Empire

In 33 B.C., at age 20, Alexander became king of Macedonia when his father was assassinated by rivals. Alexander set out to conquer it all—Syria, Israel, Egypt, Babylon, Persepolis, and Susa. By 331 B.C., he defeated King Darius, and the Persian Empire was his. Along with his troops, Alexander brought highly skilled workers on his military campaigns to establish his reign. Surveyors planned his routes. Engineers built weapons of warfare to attack each city. Architects planned new cities that he founded. Historians and scientists kept careful records of every new land he conquered.

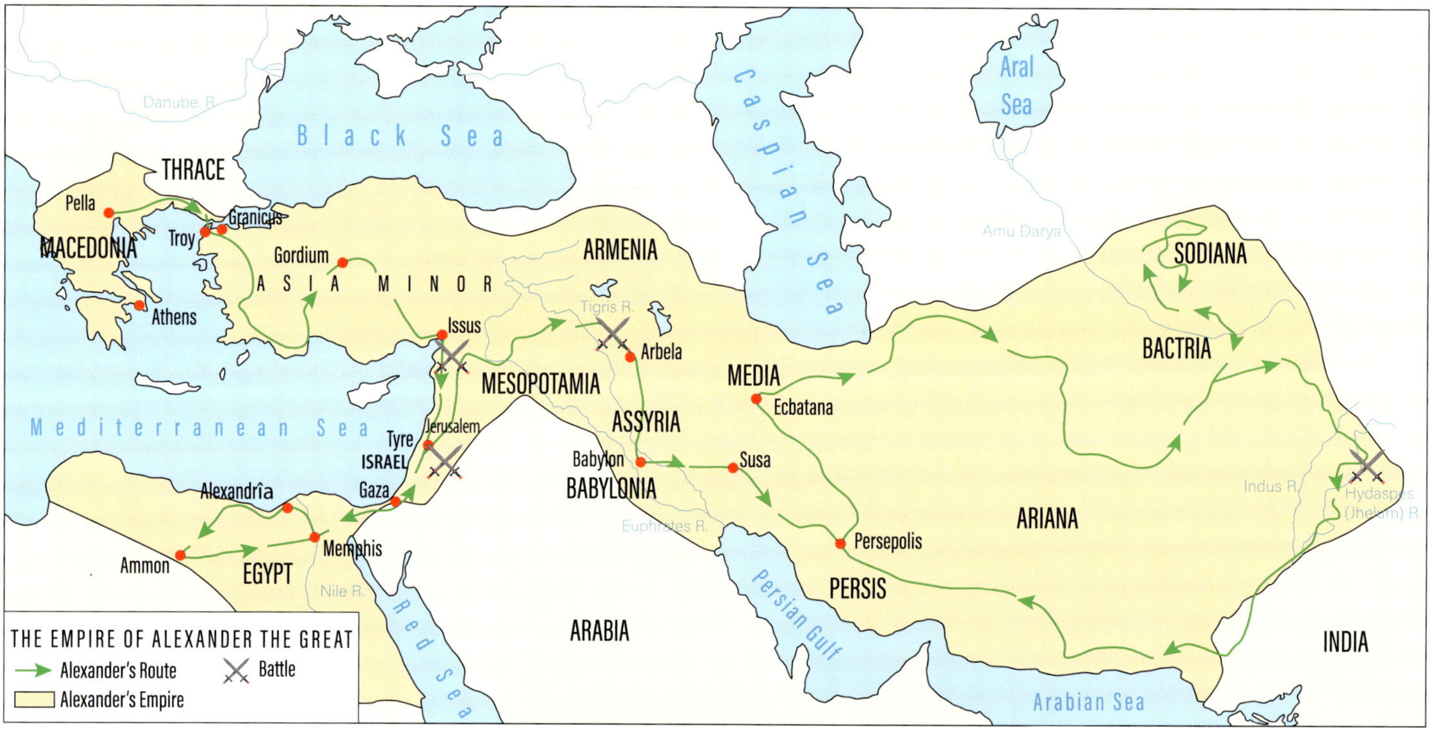

A Decade of Warfare

Labeled a military genius, Alexander led his troops over thousands of miles in his quest to conquer the world. Finally reaching the Indus River in northern India, his exhausted soldiers staged a mutiny and refused to go any farther. After ten years of fighting, Alexander returned with his troops to his capital city of Babylon, king over the largest empire the world had ever known.

Alexandria

Aristotle taught his pupil well. Alexander the Great spread Greek culture in every place he conquered. He built Greek cities throughout his empire. Founded in 331 B.C., the city of Alexandria in Egypt became the most famous of all. A seaport, its fleet of ships dominated trade on the Mediterranean Sea. Its famous library and museum attracted Greek scholars, including Euclid, Archimedes, and Eratosthenes. Alexandria was home to an influential Jewish community, so the Septuagint (the Greek translation of the Old Testament) was probably written here.

Lighthouse of Alexandria

On the island of Pharos at the port of Alexandria, a monumental lighthouse was built. Flames of fire shone out from it each night, guiding ships safely into the harbor. Standing over 350 feet tall, it was known as one of the Seven Wonders of the Ancient World. It stood for over a thousand years.

The Birth of the Hellenistic Age

Alexander the Great died in Babylon at the age of 32, not long after his military campaigns ended. Because he had no strong successor, his top generals fought for control over the vast empire he had built, stretching from Greece to India. Eventually, the empire split into several smaller kingdoms, each ruled by a different general.

Daniel's Prophecy

Daniel, a captive Hebrew serving in the Persian Empire, received a vision from God. The angel Gabriel explained the vision to Daniel. Two hundred years later, part of this prophecy was fulfilled. A ram with two horns (the Media-Persian Empire) was conquered by a goat with one horn (Alexander the Great). The goat's horn broke into four smaller horns (the empire's split after Alexander's death). Once again, historical events support what the Bible, God's Word, says (see Daniel 8:1–27). Only the God of the Bible can know what will happen in the future . . . and it always happens just as He says!

Modern-day Italy is a boot-shaped peninsula that sticks out into the Mediterranean Sea. In ancient times, a powerful group of people called the Etruscans settled there. Greeks built city-states there. The city of Rome was established on seven hills near the Tiber River. According to myth, Rome was founded in 748 B.C. by twin brothers, Remus and Romulus, who were supposedly the sons of the false Roman war god Mars. The legend also says the twins were abandoned as babies and raised by a she-wolf. According to the myth, Romulus killed Remus and named the city after himself.

World's First Republic

In 509 B.C., wealthy Romans banded together to overthrow their king. The world's first republic was formed. The Senate (council of men) made the laws and governed Rome. It led Rome's army to conquer nearly the entire peninsula of Italy.

Social Structure

Three classes of people made up the social structure in Rome. On the highest level, the Patricians were free citizens who were wealthy enough to own land. Only Patricians could become Senators. All other free people were called Plebians. The rest of the people in Rome were slaves, the lowest status in society.

Punic Wars

Rome was a key city in the network of trade. It set its sights on conquering Carthage, a wealthy port city on the northern coast of Africa. The wars between Rome and Carthage became known as the Punic Wars. Heading toward Rome, a Carthage general named Hannibal led his troops riding the backs of war elephants across Spain and into the Alps. Unable to survive in the freezing weather of the Alps, most elephants died. In 146 B.C., Rome destroyed Carthage and became master of the Mediterranean Sea.

Julius Caesar

Hungry for power, Roman generals fought each other to be consuls, the leaders of the Roman Senate. As general, Julius Caesar led his troops to expand Rome into Gaul (France) and then Britain. He returned to Rome and became dictator, only to be assassinated by the Senate the following year in 44 B.C. Octavian, the adopted son and heir of Julius Caesar, first aligned himself with Mark Antony and then fought against him. After a series of military victories, Octavian became the first emperor of the Roman Empire in 27 B.C.

Slavery

Unfortunately, slavery has been practiced in many forms across most cultures and historical periods worldwide. Slavery is the system where a group of people are forced to work for someone, and their freedoms and rights are taken away. For centuries, the Egyptians kept the Hebrews in slavery and used them as laborers to build their temples, pyramids, and cities. The Aztecs captured people from other tribes, made them slaves, and offered them as sacrifices to their false gods. As the Romans conquered more lands, they took more captives as slaves who were forced to help build the empire.

Freedom in Christ

One day, God sent his Son, Jesus, to be born in the town of Bethlehem in the Roman province of Judea. During that time, the Roman Empire ruled the world. The Bible tells us that everyone is equal in God's eyes (see Gal. 3:28) and all people are fearfully and wonderfully made by Him (Ps. 139:14). No form of slavery is justified. Jesus came to set the captives free (see Luke 4:18).

Rome's army was the nation's strength. The Praetorian Guard stayed in the city of Rome and protected the emperor. Made up of Roman citizens only, legions were groups of about 5,000 soldiers. Other soldiers who were not citizens fought as auxiliaries (supporting troops). The Roman military also included doctors, surveyors, and engineers. Troops fought to conquer new territory, defend provinces, and fight Rome's enemies. They also acted as the construction workers for Rome, building aqueducts, bridges, and roads.

Circus Maximus

Rome loved its chariot races. Since the early days of the city's history, Romans gathered at its racetrack, called the Circus Maximus, to cheer on their favorite charioteers and teams of horses. Julius Caesar enlarged the track, and future emperors rebuilt it after fires, each time more grandiose than before. During its most popular period, crowds of 250,000 people in Rome could watch 24 chariot races a day!

Colosseum

Rome's most famous amphitheater, or theater in the round, was the Colosseum. After Roman troops destroyed the temple in Jerusalem in 70 A.D., they took its treasures and many Jewish captives back to Rome. It is said that the temple treasures paid for the materials to make the Colosseum, and about 100,000 Jewish slaves were used to build it. Lions, elephants, giraffes, and other wild animals from as far away as Africa were kept in its underground tunnels and rooms. Gladiators fought each other and the wild beasts in Rome's sporting events. Crowds of 50,000 people cheered from the seats. In 80 A.D., Emperor Titus opened the Colosseum with 100 days of contests and games.

♦ Remains of the Roman Colosseum

AQUEDUCTS

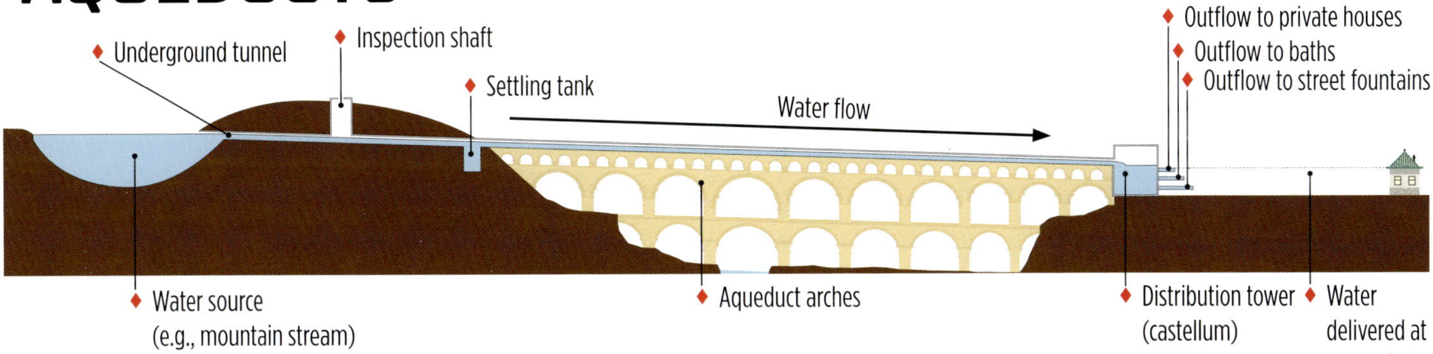

Surveyors surveyed long, straight lines. Workers cut through mountains and leveled valleys. Engineers built giant concrete arches, repeating one after the other across miles of land. All throughout the Roman Empire from Africa to Spain to Rome, Romans built aqueducts to carry water above the heads of its citizens from faraway springs into densely populated cities. The Aqua Virgo, built in 19 B.C., still delivers water to the city of Rome today.

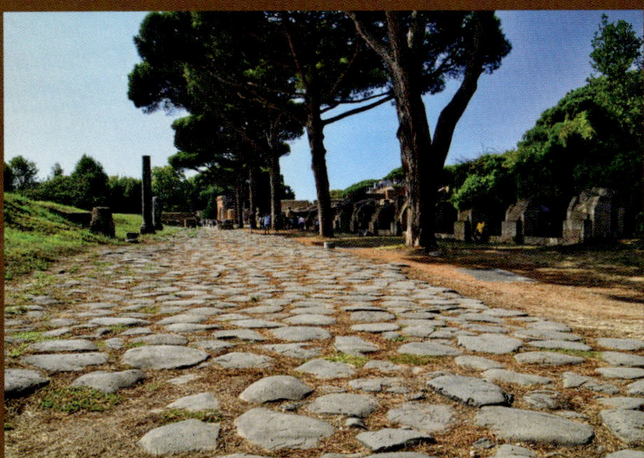

Roman Roads

As soon as Roman troops conquered new territories, they set to work building roads. For 50,000 miles, Roman roads crisscrossed from towns to seaports in provinces all around the Mediterranean Sea and even onto the British Isles. Today, tourists can still walk on portions of the Appian Way, the famous road leading into the city of Rome.

Hadrian's Wall

The northern frontier of the Roman Empire was Britain. Emperor Hadrian built a 73-mile wall coast to coast across the northern section of Britain to protect the Romans from attacks from the north. Much of that wall is still standing today.

Mount Vesuvius

Shake. Rattle. BOOM! Mount Vesuvius was a volcano in Italy. To everyone's shock, it erupted in A.D. 79. Almost instantly, it buried the nearby city of Pompeii in volcanic ash and rock. Buildings, homes, villas, paintings, mosaics, and more have been dug out of the ashes to give us a picture of what life was like in the first century Roman world.

ROMAN EMPIRE RULES THE WORLD

44 B.C–A.D. 476

When Julius Caesar was assassinated, Mark Antony and Octavian both stepped up to rule in his place. At first, they worked together. Then Mark Antony joined with Cleopatra, queen of Egypt, to fight for the ability to rule Rome. They were defeated by Octavian in an epic battle at sea. In 27 B.C., Octavian took the name Caesar Augustus and became the first emperor of the Roman Empire.

Provinces

The Roman Empire was enormous, controlling all the lands around the Mediterranean Sea. At its height, the empire covered 2.5 million square miles and stretched across three continents. It included Egypt and North Africa, Britain, Spain, France, and much of Europe. The empire also extended into parts of Asia and the Middle East. To manage this vast territory, Rome divided it into provinces, each governed by a Roman-appointed official. One of these provinces was Judea, which included Jerusalem and much of the ancient land of Israel.

The Census

Caesar Augustus made a decree. He ordered everyone in every province of the Roman Empire to return to their hometowns to be counted so he could tax them accordingly. Mary and Joseph returned to Bethlehem. In this small town, an event took place that would change the world—and eternity. A baby boy was born. In the night sky, angels sang, "Glory to God!" Shepherds from the nearby fields ran to see the baby. Jesus Christ was born. These historic events are recorded in Luke 2:1–20 and Matthew 2:1–12.

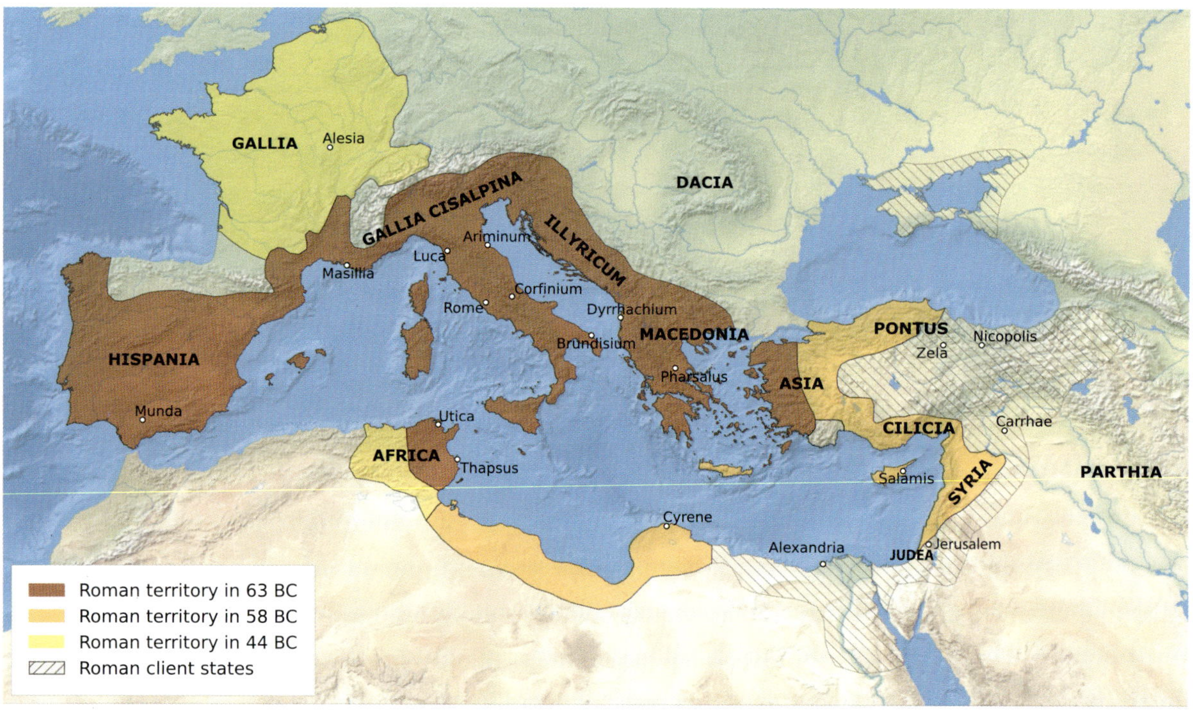

♦ The Roman Empire as it expanded over time. At its largest, it spanned 2.5 million square miles. That's 8 to 9 Texas-sized states!

Law of the Twelve Tables

Twelve bronze tablets. Twelve groups of Roman laws were written in Rome around 450 B.C. When the Gauls sacked Rome in 390 B.C., the tablets themselves were probably destroyed. However, these laws became the model for many civilizations to come.

The Alphabet's Path Through History

Languages of Rome

Rome's earliest settlers were the Latins, who lived in the region of Latium. Latin became Rome's main language, but Greek was also used. Our modern alphabet traces back through ancient civilizations, including Rome. The Phoenicians created an alphabet with only consonants, the Greeks added vowels, and then Romans adapted it into the Latin alphabet we use today.

♦ Gregorian perpetual calendar with the four seasons, created in 1595

The Calendar

Julius Caesar introduced a new calendar, made up of 365 days with an extra day added on leap year. The Julian calendar was used from 45 B.C. up to A.D. 1582. Then the Gregorian calendar replaced it. Names of false Roman gods and emperors such as Juno (June), Julius Caesar (July), and Caesar Augustus (August), were featured on the Gregorian calendar, still used in many parts of the world today, including the United States.

Religion

The Greek people influenced Rome's religious beliefs. The Romans adopted many of the Greek's shameful religious practices. They adopted Greece's false gods and gave them new names of their own. They also began to worship their emperors as gods.

Alexander the Great conquered Egypt, the land of pharaohs and pyramids. He appointed Ptolemy as governor over the region. After Alexander's death in 323 B.C., Ptolemy continued to rule Egypt, establishing a dynasty that lasted 300 years.

Ptolemaic Period

The centuries that Ptolemy's dynasty ruled over Egypt are known as the Ptolemaic Period. All the pharaohs during this time were Greek, not Egyptian. Greeks tried to spread their culture and language in other countries, which is now referred to as Hellenism. The Greeks influenced the culture in Egypt during this time.

Alexandria

During the Ptolemaic Period, the capital of Egypt was moved to the city of Alexandria. With its famous library and museum, this port city on the Mediterranean Sea became the center of Greek learning and culture.

Co-Rulers of Egypt

When Cleopatra was still a teenager, she became co-ruler of Egypt with her father. Her father died when she was 18, and she became co-ruler with her ten-year-old brother, Ptolemy XIII. Her brother's advisors seized power and forced Cleopatra off the throne. She fled to Syria for safety in 49 B.C.

Return to Egypt

General Julius Caesar arrived in Alexandria with his troops. He hoped to ask Egypt for money so he could return successfully to Rome. Cleopatra promised to give him some of the riches of Egypt if he would help her get her throne back. Caesar fought alongside the troops Cleopatra raised, and they won. Caesar's alliance with Cleopatra was part of what is known as the Alexandrian War (48-47 B.C.). Cleopatra returned to Egypt to sit on her throne again, this time as co-ruler with a different brother, Ptolemy XIV.

Egypt Visits Rome

Cleopatra and Julius Caesar had a son named Caesarion. Julius Caesar returned to Rome and became its dictator. Julius Caesar invited Cleopatra, Caesarion, and Ptolemy XIV to join him in Rome. They stayed there for a couple of years. When Caesar was assassinated in 44 B.C., Cleopatra, her son, and her brother fled back to the palace in Alexandria for protection.

Mark Antony and Cleopatra

Mark Antony had first joined forces with Octavian and Lepidus as the Second Triumvirate. Then he fought against them. Antony wanted to rule the Roman Empire. He knew it would take a lot of troops and cost a lot of money to fight Octavian, the heir of Julius Caesar. Cleopatra agreed to give Antony more riches from Egypt. They fell in love and eventually married. They had twins, a boy named Alexander Helios and a girl named Cleopatra Selene. Then they had another son, Ptolemy Philadelphus. Mark Antony agreed to give Cleopatra some of the territory in the Middle East that Egypt had conquered centuries before.

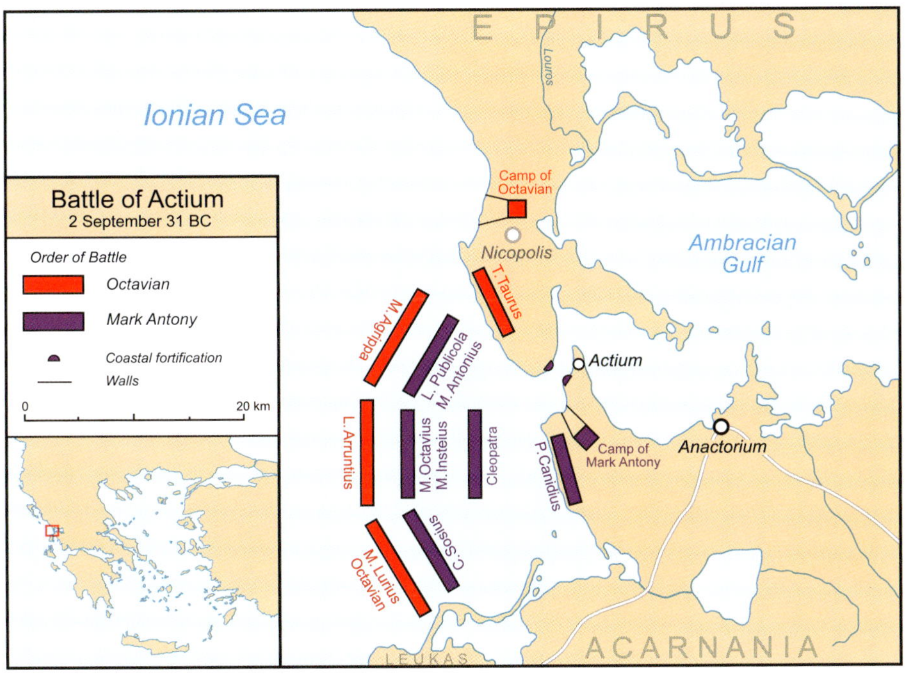

Battle of Actium

War! Octavian and the Roman Senate saw that Antony and Cleopatra wanted to rule the world, so they declared war on Egypt. Cleopatra's fleet of Egyptian warships joined with Antony's fleet of Roman warships at the famous Battle of Actium in 31 B.C. Octavian's mighty ships overpowered them and won. Cleopatra was the last pharaoh of Egypt. After Antony and Cleopatra died, Egypt became part of the mighty Roman Empire. Octavian became the first emperor of Rome in 27 B.C., when he took on the name Augustus, or Caesar Augustus, who was on the throne when Jesus was born.

TIMELINE: 30 B.C. – A.D. 476

20 B.C. | B.C. | A.D. | A.D. 50

Pantheon built in Rome 27 B.C.

c. 27 B.C. Augustus Octavian becomes first emperor of Rome

Herod the Great begins renovation of temple c. 19 B.C.

Birth of John the Baptist c. 5 B.C.

c. 5 B.C. Mary, mother of Jesus, visited by angel Gabriel

5 B.C. Roman census

Birth of Jesus 5-4 B.C.

Wise men visit the Christ 4 B.C.

4 B.C. Anna and Simeon worship Jesus, the Messiah, in the temple

Judea divided among Herod's sons 4 B.C.

4 B.C. Death of Herod the Great

1 Anno Domini (A.D.) Year of our Lord

Rice cultivation in Japan A.D. 2

A.D. 9 Jesus visits the temple in Jerusalem

Pontius Pilate governor of Judea A.D. 26

A.D. 27 Baptism of Jesus by John the Baptist

John the Baptist killed c. A.D. 32

c. A.D. 33 Jesus' crucifixion, Resurrection, and ascension

Stephen is first Christian martyr A.D. 34

A.D. 35 Saul's conversion to the Apostle Paul

Caligula rules as Roman Emperor A.D. 37-41

A.D. 43 London founded

Paul's first missionary journey c. A.D. 47

A.D. 48 Great Library of Alexandria burns

Christian Church at Corinth c. A.D. 50-52

c. A.D. 50s Romans, 1–2 Corinthians, Galatians, 1–2 Thessalonians, James written

Paul arrives in Rome c. A.D. 60

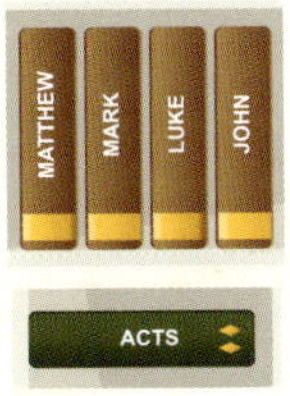

Mark, Matthew, Luke, and Acts written
C. A.D. 60s

Hero (Heron) experiments with steam engines (Alexandria)
C. A.D. 62

The Great Jewish Revolt against the Roman Empire
A.D. 66-70

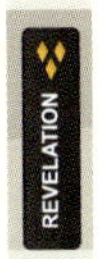

John writes Revelation
C. A.D. 67-95

Rome takes Masada from the Jewish occupants
C. A.D. 74

Pliny the Elder writes *Natural History*
A.D. 77

Mount Vesuvius erupts
A.D. 79

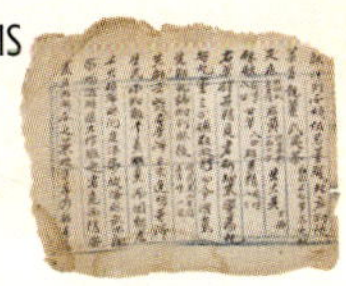

Invention of paper in China
A.D. 100

Hadrian's Wall built (Britain)
A.D. 122

Reign of Emperor Marcus Aurelius ends
A.D. 180

Fall of Roman Empire
A.D. 476

A.D. 100 — *A.D. 150*

C. A.D. 60s
Ephesians, Philippians, Colossians, 1–2 Timothy, Titus, Philemon, Hebrews, 1–2 Peter written

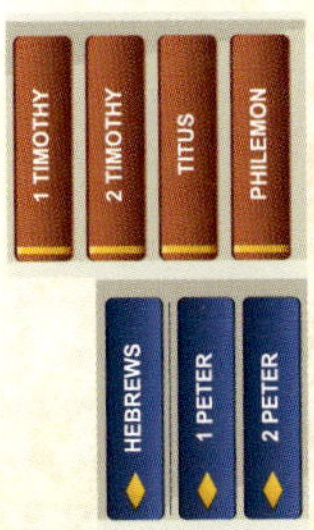

C. A.D. 60-70s
Jude written

A.D. 64
Great Fire of Rome

C. A.D. 67-69
Gospel of John, 1–3 John written

A.D. 70
Titus destroys Jewish temple and the city of Jerusalem

C. A.D. 75
Flavius Josephus writes *The Jewish War*

A.D. 79
Colosseum in Rome finished

C. A.D. 100
Glass blowing

C. A.D. 100-150
Aztec city of Teotihuacán dominates the region (Mexico)

A.D. 135
Emperor Hadrian rebuilds Jerusalem as the Roman city of Aelia Capitolina

A.D. 313
Edict of Milan: Emperor Constantine ends persecution of Christians and rebuilds Jerusalem

The years before Jesus' birth was tumultuous for Judea. King Herod, who was Rome's appointed ruler at the time, expanded the temple but was despised for his brutality. Religious divisions deepened between Pharisees, Sadducees, and Essenes over how God's laws should be followed. Life was hard and scary for God's people. This darkness deepened Israel's hunger for the Messiah, preparing hearts to recognize the Light when He finally came.

Alexander the Great

Josephus was a Jewish historian who wrote about the history of the Jews. He wrote about one instance in which Alexander the Great rode into Jerusalem to conquer the city. The high priest led a procession out to greet him, including priests and citizens dressed in white robes. He also showed Daniel's prophecies to Alexander. Instead of destroying Jerusalem, Alexander offered sacrifices at the temple and permitted the Jews some freedom to continue their worship of God.

♦ Josephus, a Jewish historian

Temple of Zeus

After Alexander died, his empire was split up between his generals. Eventually, the Greek king Antiochus IV took over control of Jerusalem and Judea, the ancient homeland of Israel, around 175-174 B.C. According to Josephus, Antiochus tried to force the Jews to adopt Greek culture and religion. He declared that the Jewish holy temple in Jerusalem would be a temple for the false god Zeus instead. Antiochus sacrificed pigs on the altar, which was a disgrace to the Jewish faith. The Jews revolted, and the family of the Maccabees became their leaders.

Hanukkah

Judah Maccabee raised up an army of devoted Jews and fought against the troops of Antiochus. After a sound victory, Judah led his followers to purify the temple, repair it, and rededicate it to God. At the dedication in 164 B.C., the Jews had only enough oil to light the menorah (a special lampstand) for one day, but the oil burned for eight days. It was a miracle! They agreed to celebrate a festival every year to remember this miracle. It is called the Festival of Lights, Hanukkah, or the Feast of Dedication. Jesus celebrated it, and it is still celebrated today.

3 Major Jewish Groups During the Second Temple Period

	Pharisees	Sadducees	Essenes

Social Class	Middle class — scribes, teachers, merchants	Upper class — wealthy, priestly families	Separatist, communal communities (often near Dead Sea)
Beliefs	Believed in resurrection, angels, and oral law	Rejected resurrection and angels, accepted only written Torah	Believed in purity, angels, end-times, divine judgment
Scriptures	Torah + Oral Law (later Mishnah)	Torah only	Torah and their own strict interpretations
View of Temple	Respected temple but also worshiped in synagogues	Controlled temple worship and priesthood	Separated from temple life, saw it as corrupted
Political Power	Popular with the people, some influence	Aligned with Rome and ruling elite	Little political power, avoided involvement
Lifestyle	Lived among the people, teachers of the Law	Aristocratic, urban	Lived in isolated, disciplined communities (e.g., Qumran)
Famous For	Teaching and interpreting Jewish law	Temple control and political alliances	Strict purity practices, possibly linked to Dead Sea Scrolls
Relation to Jesus	Often opposed His teachings but some sympathetic (e.g., Nicodemus)	Largely opposed Him, involved in temple leadership	Not mentioned directly, but beliefs resembled some apocalyptic teachings of the time

Jewish Leaders

During the years between the Old and New Testaments, three religious groups were formed among the Jews. One group was the Pharisees. These religious leaders followed the Law of Moses in every single detail. The second group was the Sadducees. These upper-class aristocrats often disagreed with the Pharisees and did not believe in the Resurrection of the dead. Scribes from both groups carefully made handwritten copies of the Law of Moses, the books of the Prophets, and the Psalms. A third major group was the Essenes, who lived in separate communities and practiced strict religious discipline.

The Rise of Rome

In 63 B.C., the Roman general Pompey invaded Jerusalem. The city with its surrounding territory became the Roman province of Judea. Herod the Great was appointed to govern part of the region, eventually becoming king of all Judea, including the holy city of Jerusalem.

Come, Messiah, Come!

The Jewish people eagerly awaited the Messiah, the Savior and King that the prophets predicted would come. The Jews had groaned under the heavy weight of their oppressors throughout history, and now they suffered under the fierce Roman Empire. At the temple, in their synagogues, and in their homes, the people cried out in prayer for their Messiah to deliver them.

Jesus Christ changed history more than anyone else who ever lived. Even 2,000 years after His death, He has influenced world events, cultures, nations, and people more than any other person ... ever. No other man or woman has had an impact like Jesus. That's because He wasn't just a servant leader. He wasn't just a great prophet or teacher. Jesus is God incarnate (in the flesh). He is the Savior of the world.

#1 Bestseller

According to the Guiness World Records, the Bible is the best-selling book of all time. From beginning to end, it is the epic true story about Jesus and His love for each one of us. In the Book of Genesis, God promised to send a Savior. The prophets talked about His coming. The four gospel writers documented eyewitness reports about the life of Jesus. The letters of Paul, along with other books in the New Testament, talk about how to live out one's faith in Jesus. And the Book of Revelation promises that one day Jesus will return as the conquering King. The Bible teaches us the truth about who Jesus is!

Evidence

Renowned scholars (and even atheists) have set out on a journey to prove Jesus isn't God, but they find enough evidence to conclude He truly is who the Bible says He is. Famous scholar C.S. Lewis, who did not believe God is real, became a Christian and wrote one of the most beloved children's series of all time, *The Chronicles of Narnia*. Journalist and atheist Lee Strobel became a Christian after investigating the historic evidence and scientific research regarding Jesus. He wrote many books about who Jesus is, including the *Case for Christ for Kids*. Police detective and atheist J. Warner Wallace used his method for solving unsolvable crimes to discover that Jesus really is the Son of God. He wrote *Cold-Case Christianity for Kids*.

Calendar

The Gregorian calendar is the universal standard for dates. It is based on the approximate birth of Jesus Christ.

B.C.	"Before Christ" was born	The date 100 B.C. means 100 years "before Christ" was born.
A.D.	"Anno Domini," which in Latin means "in the year of our Lord"	The date A.D. 100 is 100 years after the birth of Jesus.
B.C.E.	Before Common Era	Even documents that use B.C.E. or C.E. count forward or backward from the birth of Jesus.
C.E.	Common Era	

Christmas

Christmas is the holiday that celebrates the birth of Jesus. Many people in countries all around the world celebrate Christmas. Over the centuries, people in different cultures have developed unique traditions. In the U.S., Christmas traditions include gift giving, singing carols, gathering with family, serving people in need, and a whole lot more.

Art & Architecture
Jesus influenced art. His life and teachings are the subject of countless paintings, sculptures, and other pieces of art. Jesus also influenced architecture. From grand cathedrals to small country churches, buildings all around the world throughout modern history point to Jesus. They also serve as a place for His followers to gather to worship Him and grow strong in their faith.

Jesus, the One to Know
Buddhism. Islam. Confucianism. Many other religions center on following a person who lived, taught an important message, and died. Christianity is different because Jesus lived, died, and came to life again. Jesus is alive! His followers don't just believe in Him and follow His teachings. His followers know Him. His followers have a relationship with Him. His followers love Him because we know He first loved us. When a person decides to become a Christian, they get to know the Creator of the universe, and He becomes their very best Friend. Jesus' followers do what He says because He wants what is best for them.

A Special Invitation
Even today, Jesus invites everyone to follow Him. He invites you! Tell Him you are sorry for your sins and the wrong things you have done and said. Ask Him to forgive you and tell Him that you want to follow Him as your Lord and Savior. Then get ready for an exciting adventure with Jesus. Your life will never be the same!

The birth of Jesus was fit for a King! Angels announced His coming. Wise men brought Him their treasures. Ancient prophesies came true! Remarkably, however, most people living at the time of Jesus' birth did not recognize who He was or the Kingdom He came to establish.

John the Baptist

The angel Gabriel appeared to Zechariah, a priest serving at the temple. Gabriel announced that he and his wife, Elizabeth, would have a son, even though they were too old. The son would be named John. He would be a Nazirite, dedicated to God for His purposes. John, whom we know as John the Baptist (or Baptizer) would prepare the way for the Messiah.

Calculating the Birthday of Jesus

In 46 B.C., Julius Caesar developed the Julian calendar, but it wasn't accurate. In A.D. 525, a monk named Dionysius adjusted it and placed the birth of Jesus as the turning point in history between B.C. (Before Christ) and A.D. (Anno Domini, the year of our Lord). It still had mistakes, so in 1582, a more accurate calendar (called the Gregorian calendar) was made. The corrections pushed the date of Jesus' birth to about 5-4 B.C.

Genealogy of Jesus

The genealogy of Jesus can be found in the books of Matthew and Luke. His ancestors can be traced all the way back to Adam and Eve. God promised their descendant Abraham that all nations of the earth would be blessed through him. God promised his descendant Israel (also known as Jacob) that a King as majestic as a lion would be born into the family line through his son Judah. God promised Judah's descendant, King David, that this majestic King would rule forever. His descendant, Jesus, fulfilled all these promises. He is the Lion of Judah!

Historic Events

In the Bible, the books of Matthew and Luke give many details about the birth of Jesus. Matthew was a disciple of Jesus, so Mary (Jesus' mother) probably told Matthew many of the details. Luke wrote his gospel book later. He said he was reporting events that eyewitnesses shared with him (see Luke 1:1–14). Reports like these give us confidence that we can trust the accuracy of the Bible. The details about the birth of Jesus are not made-up stories or fairy tales. His birth was a real, historical event.

- Matthew's genealogy traces Jesus' legal lineage through Joseph, establishing His right to the throne of David.
- Luke's genealogy traces Jesus' biological lineage through Mary, showing Him as the "Son of Man."
- Both genealogies converge at David, but diverge after. Matthew follows Solomon (royal line); Luke follows Nathan (David's other son).
- Matthew presents the line descending from Abraham > Jesus, while Luke traces backward from Jesus > Adam > God (Luke 3:38).

Matthew Genealogy (Joseph)	Luke Genealogy (Mary)
Abraham	Abraham
Isaac	Isaac
Jacob	Jacob
Judah	Judah
Perez	Perez
Hezron	Hezron
Ram	Ram
Amminadab	Amminadab
Nahshon	Nahshon
Salmon	Salmon
Boaz	Boaz
Obed	Obed
Jesse	Jesse
David	David
Solomon	Nathan
Rehoboam	Mattatha
Abijah	Menna
Asaph	Melea
Jehoshaphat	Eliakim
Joram	Jonam
Uzziah	Joseph
Jotham	Judah
Ahaz	Simeon
Hezekiah	Levi
Manasseh	Matthat
Amon	Jorim
Josiah	Eliezer
Jeconiah	Joshua
	Er
	Elmadam
	Cosam
	Addi
	Melchi
	Neri
Shealtiel	Shealtiel
Zerubbabel	Zerubbabel
Abiud	Rhesa
Eliakim	Joanan
Azor	Joda
Zadok	Josech
Achim	Semein
Eliud	Mattathias
Eleazar	Maath
Matthan	Naggai
Jacob	Esli
	Nahum
	Amos
	Mattathias
	Joseph
	Jannai
	Meichi
	Levi
	Matthat
	Heli
Joseph (husband of Mary)	Mary
Jesus	**Jesus**

Virgin Birth

About 800 years before Jesus' birth, the prophet Isaiah told the Jewish people that a virgin would give birth to a Son called Immanuel, which means "God with us" (Isa. 7:14; Matt. 1:23). In Luke 1:26–38, the angel Gabriel appeared to Mary and told her she would have a Son even though she was a virgin and not married yet. Gabriel told Mary that the Holy Spirit would do a miracle to make her pregnant. An angel appeared to Joseph (her future husband) and gave him the same message (Matt. 1:18–25). Jesus was fully human and fully God—at the same time. Nothing is impossible with God!

Autobiography of Caesar Augustus

Why would a broken piece of stone be important? Because the autobiography of Caesar Augustus is carved on it! It is known as the Res Gestae Divi Augusti, translated as "The Achievements of the Divine Augustus." This broken stone slab tells how Caesar Augustus conducted many a census of the Roman world. Archaeological treasures like this confirm what the Bible says. Luke wrote that a decree went out from Caesar Augustus that everyone had to return to their hometown to be counted for a census (see Luke 2:1–2). To be counted in the census, Joseph and Mary traveled to Bethlehem, where Jesus was born.

Fit for a King?

Bethlehem was so crowded that Mary and Joseph could not find any room at the inn. They stayed in a humble stable, where baby Jesus was born. Mary wrapped baby Jesus in swaddling cloths—strips of clean cloth used as a blanket for a baby. With no crib, Mary laid Jesus in a manger, a feeding trough for the animals. The King of kings came to earth as a little baby in the most humble of circumstances to show His wonderful love for us all.

Heavenly Choir

Shepherds were watching their sheep in the fields outside the town of Bethlehem. Suddenly, an angel, shining bright, stood before them. The angel announced, "Do not be afraid, for behold, I bring you good tidings of great joy which will be to all people. For there is born to you this day in the city of David a Savior, who is Christ the Lord" (Luke 2:10–11). With this news, the whole sky filled with angels rejoicing and saying, "Glory to God!" After the angels left, the shepherds ran into the city and found baby Jesus. When they left the stable, they told everyone about the marvelous things that happened the night Jesus was born.

Jesus was born a Jew. According to Jewish Law, He was circumcised when He was eight days old. Because He was the firstborn son of Joseph, Jesus was taken to the temple in Jerusalem and presented to God as the Law of Moses commanded. This visit caused quite a stir! A man named Simeon had been told by God that he would see the Christ, the Messiah, before he died. Simeon took baby Jesus in his arms and proclaimed, "For my eyes have seen Your salvation" (Luke 2:30). A prophetess named Anna lived at the temple. She rejoiced and told everyone about Jesus!

The Magi

In the ancient Babylonian and Persian Empires, wise men called Magi were counselors to the king. They were Gentiles, not Jews. They studied the stars and the night sky. One night, a new star appeared. They believed that this star announced the birth of a new king of the Jews. The Magi followed the star to the land of Israel. We do not know how many came on the journey or how far they traveled. When they arrived in Jerusalem, they asked, "Where is He who has been born King of the Jews? For we have seen His star in the East and have come to worship Him" (Matt. 2:2).

Micah's Prophecy

Herod the Great was king of Judea. He was worried when the Magi told him there was a new king. Who was he and would he try to take over Judea? Herod gathered the chief priests and scribes to talk about what was happening. They told Herod that the prophet Micah predicted the Messiah would be born in the town of Bethlehem (see Micah 5:2). Herod sent the Magi to Bethlehem.

Worshiping the King

The Magi headed to Bethlehem. The star they had been following stopped over the house where Mary, Joseph, and Jesus were now staying. They worshiped Jesus and gave him valuable gifts of frankincense, gold, and myrrh—gifts one would bring to honor a great ruler.

- **Frankincense** is a dried aromatic resin from the Boswellia tree, burned as incense in worship, symbolizing prayer rising to God.

- **Gold** was a symbol of royalty and wealth. Eastern nobles often traveled with portable gold as tribute or gift.

- **Myrrh** is a fragrant reddish-brown resin from the Commiphora tree, used for anointing, embalming, and perfume. It is associated with burial and priestly anointing.

Flight to Egypt

Danger! Danger! Herod the Great was jealous and angry. He did not want any new king to take over his kingdom. An angel warned Joseph to leave Bethlehem right away because Herod wanted to kill Jesus! Joseph, Mary, and Jesus fled Bethlehem in the middle of the night and traveled to Egypt for safety. Herod tried to kill Jesus, but Jesus had disappeared. Herod ordered his soldiers to kill every boy in Bethlehem two years old and younger. It was a very, very sad time.

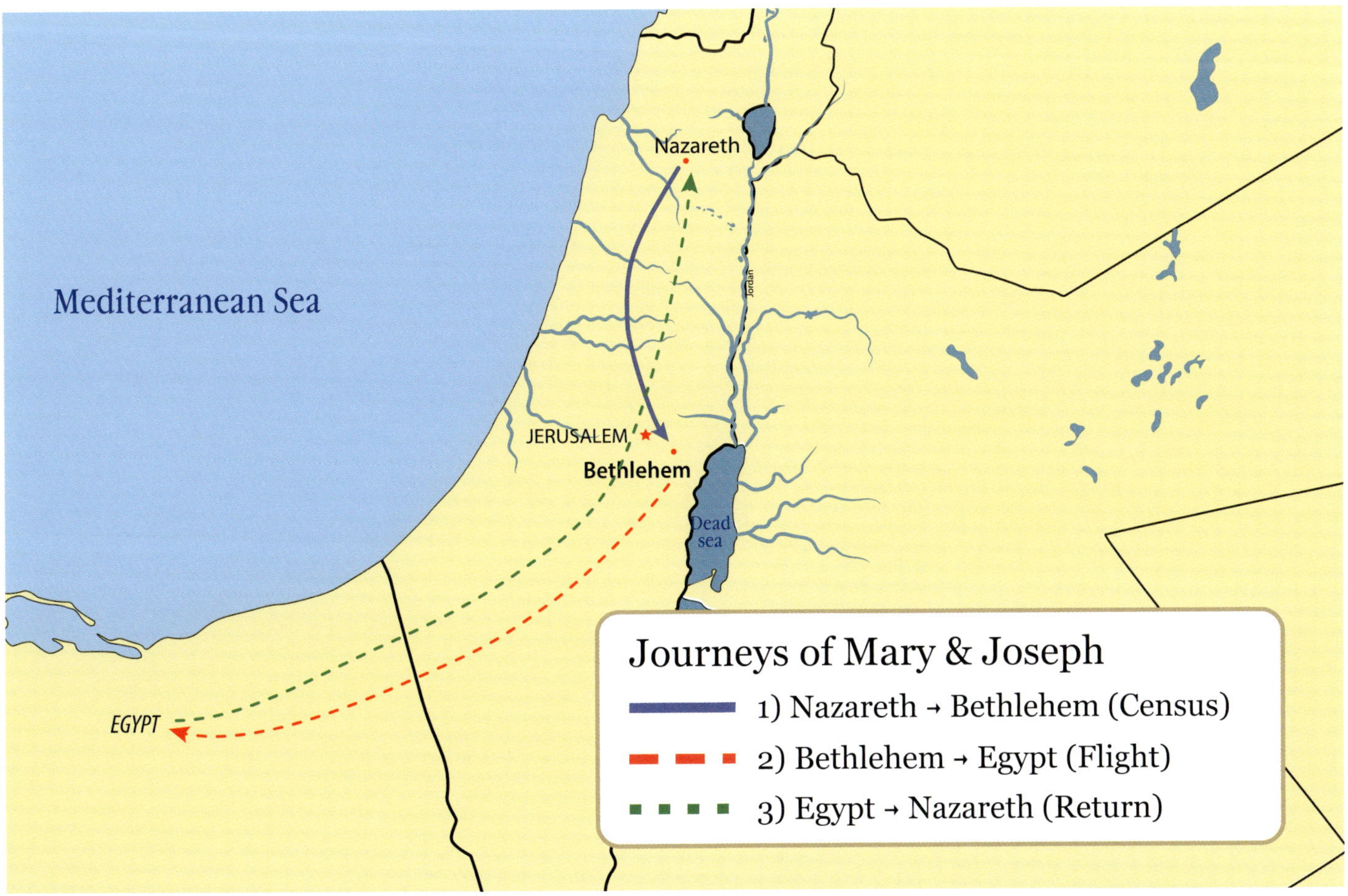

Herod the Great was king of Judea in the land of Israel. He was a descendant of Esau, Jacob's twin brother. Because of jealousy, Esau and Jacob fought as brothers. Their descendants still fought each other when Herod the Great tried to kill Jesus, the newborn King.

Herod's Temple

Herod built massive building projects in his kingdom. His greatest was the temple in Jerusalem, which went under construction in 40 B.C. Its walls shimmered with gold! Like Solomon's Temple but larger, it had one major difference. Behind the curtain, the Holy of Holies was empty. The Ark of the Covenant had been lost long ago. Herod also built a massive courtyard around the temple called the Temple Mount.

♦ Model of the Second Temple on display at the Israel Museum in Jerusalem

♦ Only four retaining walls remain standing today, including the Western Wall.

♦ Stones in the Western Wall in Jerusalem

♦ A large bronze basin full of water was placed in the courtyard for the priests to use in ceremonial washing.

♦ The bronze altar for burnt offerings; measured 15 feet wide by 30 feet long

Why were there so many "Herods" in Jesus' day?

"Herod" was a family name, not just one person. Think of it like a royal dynasty—similar to the Tudors in England or the Caesars in Rome. In addition, "Herod" was also used like a royal title for men in the same ruling family, just like "Pharaoh" or "Caesar."

Herod the Great was the first and most famous. But when he died, his territory was split among his sons, and several of them had "Herod" as part of their name:

Herodian Kings

Herod the Great
37–4 B.C.
King when Jesus was born (Matthew 2)

↓

Herod Archelaus
(Son of Herod the Great)
4 B.C.–A.D. 6
Extremely cruel; Joseph avoided Judea
Matthew 2:22

↓

Herod Antipas
(Son of Herod the Great)
4 B.C.–A.D. 39
Ruled during the ministries of John the Baptist and Jesus
Mark 6 and Luke 23

↓

Herod Agrippa I
(Grandson of Herod the Great)
37 B.C.–A.D. 44
Killed James and imprisoned Peter
Acts 12

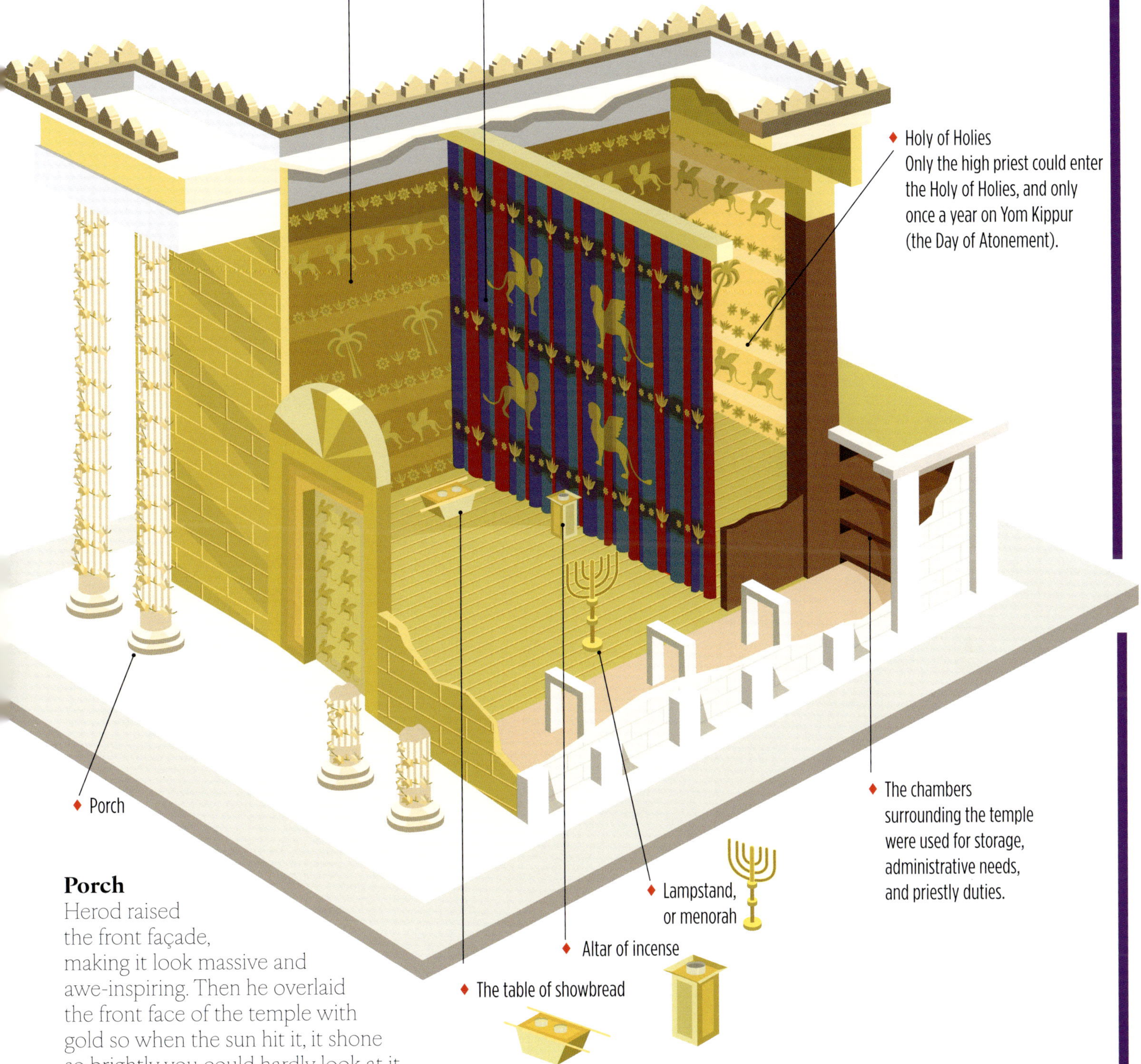

Porch

Herod raised the front façade, making it look massive and awe-inspiring. Then he overlaid the front face of the temple with gold so when the sun hit it, it shone so brightly you could hardly look at it.

HEROD'S TEMPLE COMPLEX

40–4 B.C.

Herod the Great rebuilt the temple building very quickly—in about one or two years—so people could keep worshiping. But the big area around it, called the Temple Mount, took almost 80 years to finish. It was huge and needed enormous amounts of stone. Some were as big as school buses, and they had to be moved and stacked to make the giant platform. Herod's son Antipas continued work after Herod died. Herod's grandson Agrippa I completed the project only a few years before the Romans destroyed the temple in A.D. 70.

	Solomon's Temple	Herod's Temple
Date Built	c. 1012–1004 B.C.	20 B.C., completed c. A.D. 63
Destroyed	586 B.C. by Babylonians	A.D. 70 by Romans
Location	Mount Moriah, Jerusalem	Same site (Temple Mount)
Primary Builder	King Solomon	Herod the Great
Architectural Style	Phoenician–Israelite	Jewish with Greco-Roman influence
Sanctuary Size	60 × 20 × 30 cubits (90 × 30 × 45 ft.)	100 × 60 × 100 cubits (150 × 90 × 150 ft.)
Holy of Holies	20 × 20 × 20 cubits (30 × 30 × 30 ft.)	20 × 20 × 40 cubits (30 × 30 × 60 ft.)
Ark of the Covenant	Present	Absent
Outer Courtyard	Smaller, single level	Vast multi-court system
Temple Mount Platform	Modest enclosure	500 × 300 cubits (~861 × 518 ft.)—or ~36 acres
Pillars at Porch	Named Jachin & Boaz, bronze	Ornamental columns, no named pillars
Altar of Burnt Offering	20 × 20 × 15 feet	48 × 48 × 15 ft.
Bronze Sea	Yes, on 12 oxen	Replaced with laver (wash basin)
Court of Gentiles	Not present	Added — very large
Court of Women	Not separate	Added — 203 × 203 feet
Priests' Court	Present	Expanded, elevated
Ornamentation	Cedar, gold overlay, carvings	Marble, gold, Corinthian columns
Architectural Emphasis	Sanctuary and altar	Grand courts, monumental scale
Height of Porch	180 ft. (possibly tower)	150 ft.
Significance	First permanent temple for Israel	Center of Jewish worship in New Testament era

*These measurements are approximate, as the buildings were measured in cubits. 1 cubit = 1.5 ft

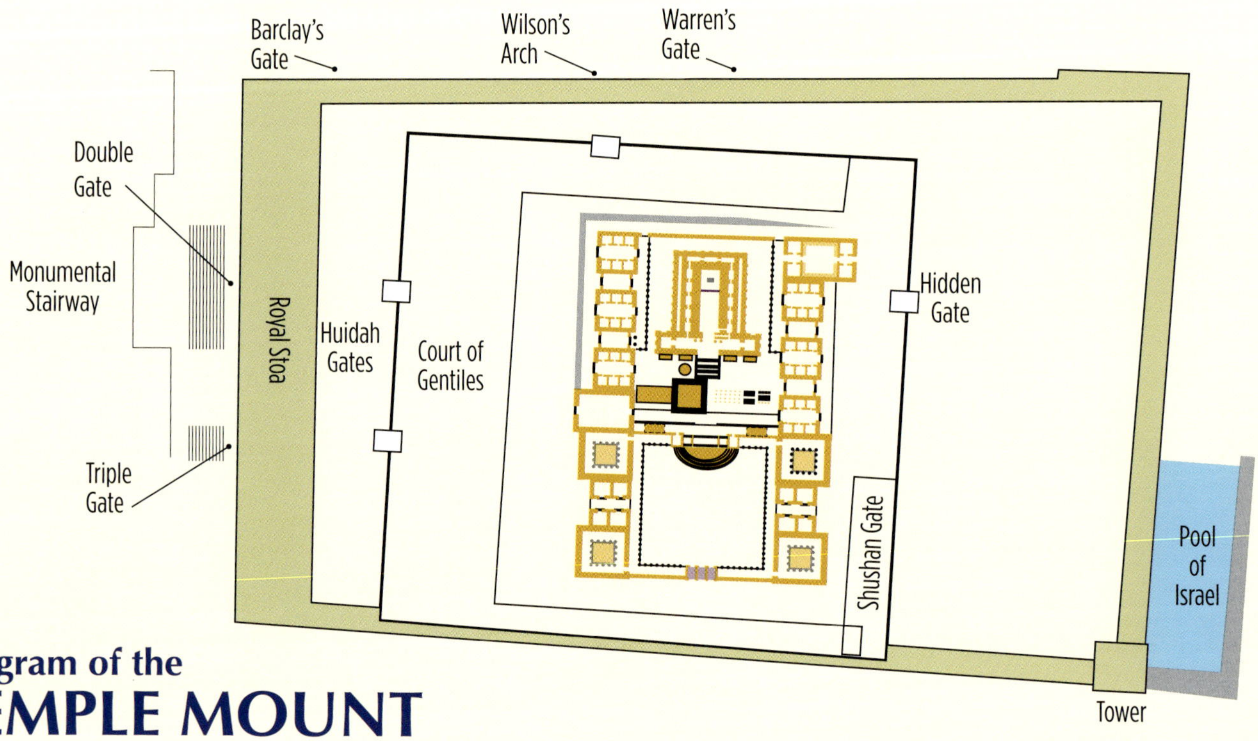

Diagram of the TEMPLE MOUNT

Diagram of the TEMPLE

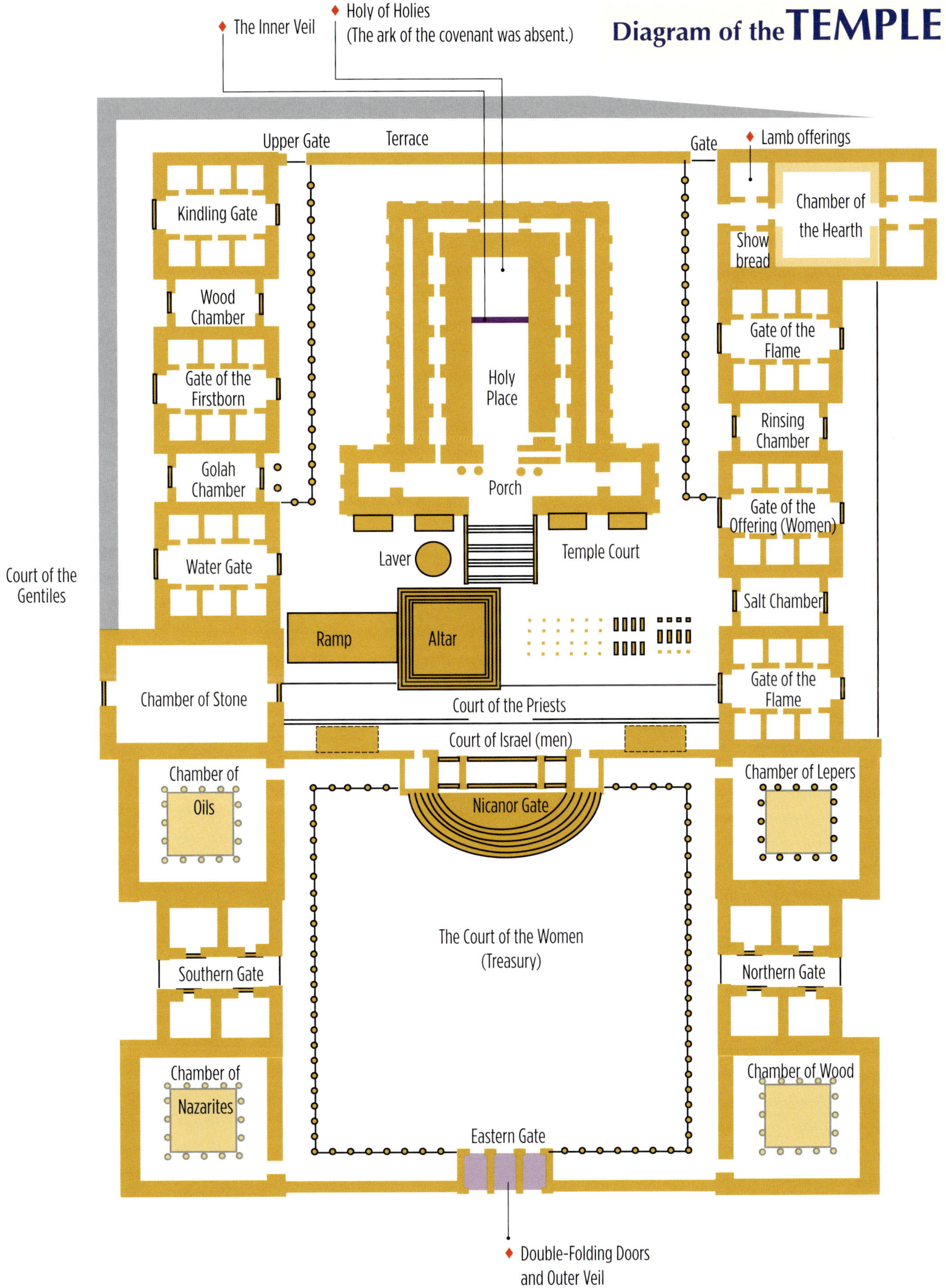

After Herod the Great died, an angel spoke to Joseph in a dream and told him it was safe for them to return to the land of Israel. Herod the Great's son Archelaus was ruling over Judea, so Joseph continued north to the region of Galilee (see Matt. 2:22). Their family settled in the town of Nazareth, where Jesus grew up.

Growing Up in Nazareth

What was it like for Jesus to grow up in Nazareth? Nazareth was a small town, set apart by itself in the hills of Galilee. However, it was near trade routes where camel caravans carried their riches. It was close to Roman roads where soldiers marched past on their way to war. Like other boys His age, Jesus would have been taught to read and write at the local synagogue. Joseph was a carpenter, so he trained Jesus to be a carpenter, too (see Matt. 13:55–56).

♦ Traditional first-century woodworking tools—including an adze, hand plane, hammer, carpenter's square, chisels, and auger bit—similar to those Joseph and Jesus may have used in their carpentry work

Lost!

When He was 12, Jesus and His parents celebrated Passover in Jerusalem with their family and friends. According to the Jewish historian, Josephus, more than two million Jews packed the city during Passover Feast. When His parents left the crowded city to return home, they didn't notice that Jesus was missing until nighttime. They panicked! For three days, they looked for Him! They finally found Him at the temple. Everyone was amazed at His wisdom and understanding. Jesus explained to His parents that He had been doing His Father's business. He returned home to Nazareth with Joseph and Mary. Jesus grew up to be a man of wisdom and favor with both God and the people He knew (see Luke 2:52).

The Baptizer

John the Baptist had an important job. Even before he was born, God set him apart to prepare the Jews to meet the Christ, their long-awaited Messiah. "Repent!" he cried. He made quite a picture. Raised a Nazirite, his long hair was probably never cut. He wore the clothes of a prophet—a scratchy tunic made of camel's hair. Jewish people flocked to hear John's message, confess their sins to God, and get baptized by John in the Jordan River.

Baptism of Jesus

Jesus was about 30 years old when He went out to the Jordan River to see His cousin John. Even though Jesus never sinned, Jesus asked John to baptize Him. When Jesus came up out of the water, the Holy Spirit came down from heaven like a dove and settled on Him. God spoke aloud in a voice everyone could hear, "This is My beloved Son, in whom I am well pleased" (Matt. 3:17b). God the Father, God the Son, and God the Holy Spirit (the Trinity) revealed themselves together at the baptism of Jesus to affirm Jesus as the Messiah.

♦ Visitors of Israel still line up to be baptized in the Jordan River.

Temptation in the Desert

As Jesus prepared for His public ministry, He went through a time of temptation. For 40 days, Jesus fasted, which means he did not eat any food. Three times, Satan then tempted Jesus to sin. The devil tried to get Jesus to use His power as the Son of God for proud and selfish reasons. Each time, Jesus defeated Satan's lies by quoting Scripture verses. Using the authority of the Bible to fight His battles, Jesus won! Satan left, and angels came to take care of Jesus. It was time for His work to begin.

In Bible times, it was common for a rabbi or religious teacher to have a group of students. Jesus chose 12 men as His disciples: Simon (Peter); Andrew, James, John, Philip, Bartholomew, Thomas, Matthew, James, Thaddaeus, Simon, and Judas. The disciples followed Jesus during His ministry. Peter wrote two letters; John and Matthew wrote down eyewitness reports of what Jesus said and did during His ministry. Jesus taught his disciples and other followers about the Kingdom of God, what it means to follow Him, and how to love others.

Sermon on the Mount

Jesus was a teacher and a preacher. One day, He climbed up a mountainside, sat down, and began to speak to His disciples and the crowds who were following Him. He preached a famous sermon known as the Sermon on the Mount. The people were amazed at the authority He had when He spoke. Among other things, He taught them about the blessings they would have if they believed in God and followed His teachings.

The Law and the Prophets

Jesus taught that He fulfilled the Law and the Prophets. The Law of Moses and the Ten Commandments showed people their sins and the need for a Savior who would rescue them from their sins. Jesus taught that He is the Rescuer. The prophets said that God would send a Savior who would be the Messiah, the Christ. Jesus taught that He is the Messiah.

Accepted and Rejected

During His ministry, people believed in Jesus in the region of Galilee and other places where He taught and performed miracles. But when He returned to His hometown of Nazareth, the people rejected Him and His teachings. Jesus accepted sinners, who were the unpopular and mistreated people of His day. He ate with them and taught them about God's forgiveness and love. Jesus rejected many Jewish religious leaders because they were too proud to listen to His message. Many Jewish religious leaders rejected Jesus and looked for a way to condemn Him to death.

Heaven and Hell

Jesus taught about heaven. It is God's Kingdom, where God sits on His throne. It is a perfect place where God's perfect goodness and love exist. There is no pain, sickness, sadness, or death in heaven. Because of His great love, God invites everyone to believe in Jesus as their Savior and live in heaven with Him after they die. Jesus also taught about hell. He described hell as a place of "everlasting fire prepared for the devil and his angels" (Matt. 25:41) and a place of "everlasting punishment" (Matt. 25:46). The Bible also says that God "is longsuffering toward us, not willing that any should perish but that all should come to repentance" (2 Pet. 3:9). To repent means to turn from our sin and turn back to God.

New Birth

Jesus taught that to enter the kingdom of God, you must be "born again" (John 3:3). When a baby is born, it starts to grow and learns to walk and talk. When a person is born again, their heart is changed, and God's Spirit lives in them. That person grows spiritually by becoming more like Jesus over time. That means we show love, patience, kindness, and forgiveness to others. When a Pharisee named Nicodemus asked how it was possible to be born again, Jesus explained, "[W]hoever believes in Him should not perish but have eternal life. For God so loved the world that He gave His only begotten Son, that whoever believes in Him should not perish but have everlasting life" (John 3:15–1).

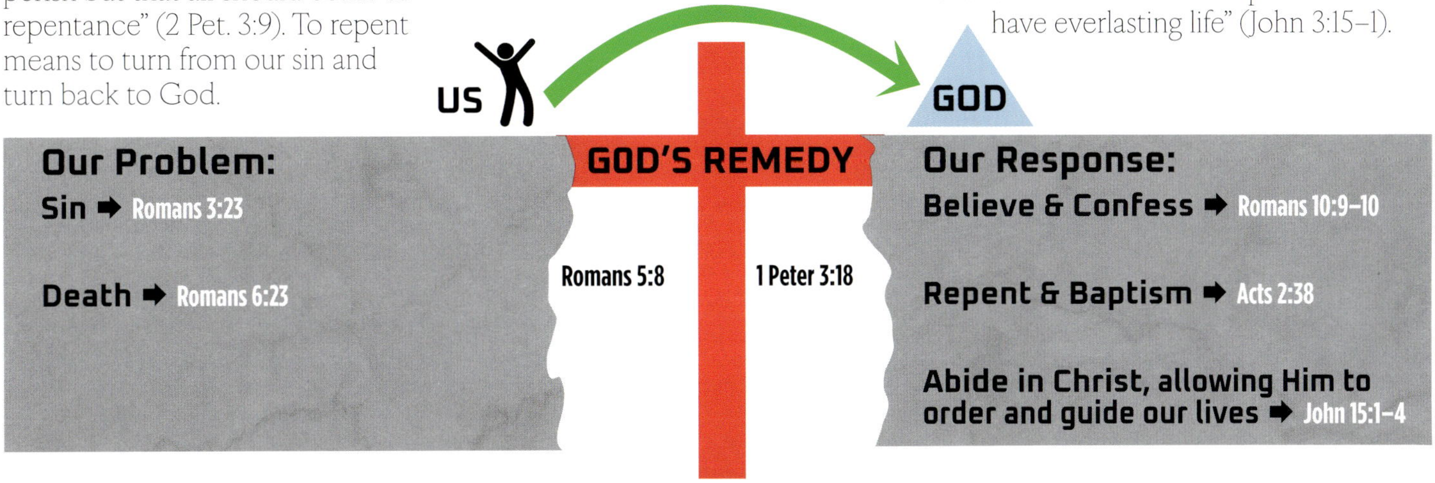

Tradition

Over time, as Jewish leaders passed on the truths of the Torah (the first five books of the Bible) to the next generation, these religious leaders created new rules to explain how to follow God's commandments. And, over time, new traditions took root even though they did not affirm what the Bible says. Jesus taught that it was important to obey the Bible, not the traditions or rules that went against the Bible's teachings.

Jesus was a gifted teacher. He spoke often to the crowds, teaching them about who He is, the Kingdom of God, and their need for a Savior. Jesus liked to teach by telling parables, stories with a hidden truth or word of wisdom. He wanted people to understand what it means to follow Him and obey Him.

Parable of the Pharisee and Tax Collector

In this parable, Jesus taught about the difference between being proud or humble. He told a story about a Pharisee (a religious person) and a tax collector. The Pharisee was proud about doing all the right things, but the tax collector humbly admitted that he was a sinner. Jesus wanted His hearers to know that when people are humble and ask God to forgive their sins, He always will! You can read this parable in Luke 18:9–14.

Parable of the Pearl of Great Price

In this parable, Jesus taught that believing in Him and becoming part of God's Kingdom is the most important thing people could ever do in life. Knowing Jesus is a treasure that lasts forever, worth more than anything else in the world! You can find this parable in Matthew 13:45–46.

Parable of the Talents

In this parable, Jesus taught about the difference between a true Christian and someone who just calls themselves a Christian. A true Christian is someone whose life has been changed because they are born again. They know Jesus as their Savior, Helper, Guide, and forever Friend. They use their talents, time, and resources to tell others about Jesus, too. On the other hand, some may call themselves a Christian, but their heart has not been changed. They may go to church. They might pray. They may even read their Bible. They may do lots of good deeds, but they have never repented of their sins and asked Jesus to be their Savior and to help them follow Him. They are not born again. This parable is in Matthew 25:14–30.

Parable of the Farmer

In this parable, Jesus taught his listeners that the attitude of a person's heart makes a difference. If people have angry, hard hearts, they will refuse to listen to the good news about Jesus. If their hearts are too busy thinking about their worries and doubts, they won't have enough room in their hearts to welcome Jesus into their lives. But people who listen to Jesus with soft, humble hearts that are open to His teachings will find countless blessings. Their lives will be changed forever! You can read this parable in Mark 4:3–8, 13–20.

Parable of the Lost Sheep

In this parable, Jesus talked about a shepherd who would leave 99 sheep to go after one lost sheep because He loved that sheep so much. He wanted people to understand just how much God loves every single person. He doesn't want anyone to live without Him. He wants every person to come follow Him, like a sheep follows a shepherd. You can read this parable in Luke 15:3–7.

Parable of the Good Samaritan

The Samaritan people and Jewish people held a big grudge against each other. They would not even worship in the same place, and they would not help each other. Jesus told a story about a Samaritan who helped a Jewish person, which would be very unusual. He wanted His listeners to know that God loves everyone. Jesus wants His followers to love everyone, even when they are different and don't act like us or look like us. You can read this parable in Luke 10:25–37.

During His ministry years, Jesus performed many miracles. He did things only God can do. These miracles proved to people that He is God. His miracles also showed people God's compassion. Through Jesus, God touched people's lives in a powerful way to show them His great love.

Catching Fish

Jesus told Peter and his fellow fishermen to throw their nets into the lake. They caught so many fish that the net began to break! They had to get help from people in other boats to haul in their catch. Jesus performed this miracle to build the faith of His disciples. He told them to be fishers of men, meaning they would help bring people to Jesus. You can read about this miracle in Luke 5:1–11.

♦ The Ancient Galilee Boat, also known as the Jesus Boat, is an ancient fishing boat from the first century A.D., discovered in 1986 on the northwest shore of the Sea of Galilee in Israel. The boat is 27 feet long, 7.5 feet wide, and has a maximum preserved height of 4.3 feet.

Healing the Paralytic

A group of friends brought a man to Jesus because he could not walk. Jesus said, "Son, be of good cheer; your sins are forgiven." Then Jesus healed him. Jesus did this miracle to show people He had the power to heal people and forgive their sins. This was His purpose. You can read about this encounter in Matthew 9:1–8.

Feeding the People

A great crowd followed Jesus to listen to Him teach. Jesus knew they were hungry but had nothing to eat. He took a boy's lunch of five loaves of bread and two fish, multiplied it, and fed the entire crowd—5,000 men, plus women and children! Jesus did this miracle to show that He will provide everything His followers need. You can read about this miracle in John 6:5–14.

Calming the Storm

Crashing waves! Howling winds! Jesus was asleep in the boat when a terrible storm rose up. They thought they were all going to die. But Jesus commanded the storm to stop. And it did! Jesus performed this miracle to show His followers His power. They could trust Him to take care of them. You can read about this miracle in Mark 4:35–41.

Casting Out Demons
Jesus and his disciples met a man who had many demons. Jesus commanded the demons to leave, and the man was healed! Jesus did this miracle to show that He is more powerful than Satan. Even the demons must obey Him. You can read about this miracle in Luke 8:26–39.

Healing the Centurion's Servant
A Roman centurion (an officer in the military) came to Jesus. He begged Jesus to heal his servant, and Jesus did! Jesus performed this miracle to show that His message of salvation is for everyone, not just the Jewish people. You can read about this miracle in Matthew 8:5–13.

Raising Lazarus from the Dead
Jesus' friend Lazarus was sick. But instead of going to heal him, Jesus waited four days before going to Lazarus' town. By then, he had been dead for four days. Everyone was sad. Jesus was sad, too. Then Jesus commanded, "Lazarus, come forth!" Lazarus came to life again and walked out of the tomb. Jesus did this miracle to teach everyone that He is the Resurrection and the Life. Everyone who believes in Him will have eternal life. You can read about this miracle in John 11:1–44.

Miracles Today
Jesus performed many miracles during His years of ministry, and He is still doing miracles today. He heals people who are hurting emotionally and physically and makes them whole. When we go through tough times, He calms the storms inside our hearts and gives us peace. He loves us, heals us, provides for us, and builds up our faith. He is still the same miracle worker now because He is alive today!

There is a historical Jesus. A real man named Jesus lived and died and was crucified on a Cross during the time of the Roman Empire. Historical records from that time prove this as true. After His death, His followers multiplied and formed churches throughout the Roman Empire. Most people agree that this happened. The question remains—was Jesus a man? Or was He God in human form?

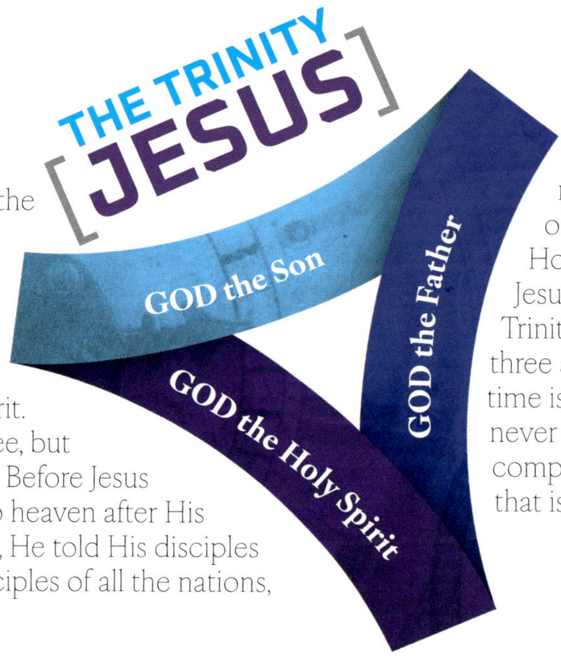

God is God the Father. Jesus is God the Son. The Holy Spirit is God the Holy Spirit. They are three, but they are one. Before Jesus went back to heaven after His Resurrection, He told His disciples to "make disciples of all the nations, baptizing them in the name of the Father and of the Son and of the Holy Spirit" (Matt. 28:19). Jesus was affirming the Trinity. How God can be three and one at the same time is a mystery. We can never quite understand or completely explain it, but that is who God is.

The Bible Points to Jesus as God

What are some examples from the Bible that point to Jesus being God?

The Old Testament prophets said the Messiah would be descended from the root of Jesse, King David's father. Jesus could trace His genealogy back to Jesse, just as the prophets foretold.	**Isaiah 11:10** **Matthew 1:1–16**
When Jesus claimed He is God, the religious leaders reacted by tearing their robes and attempting to condemn Him to death. Their reactions show they understood that Jesus said He is God.	**Mark 14:63–64**
When the family of Jesus heard Him claim to be God, they thought He had lost His mind. Yet after the Resurrection of Jesus, His brothers James and Jude became His followers. James became the leader of the church in Jerusalem. According to tradition, he died as a martyr for his faith. Obviously, Jesus' brothers changed their minds and believed in Jesus' divinity.	**Mark 3:21**
Jesus fulfilled every prophecy about the expected Messiah, and there are over 300! The odds of one person fulfilling eight of those Messianic prophecies is one in one hundred quadrillion, or 100,000,000,000,000,000. The odds of one person fulfilling 48 prophecies in Scripture is one in 10^{157}. That's the number one followed by 157 zeroes!	**Isaiah 53:7** **Matthew 27:12–14**
The books of Matthew and John in the New Testament contain eyewitness reports about the miracles and healings Jesus did that proved He is God. They saw what Jesus did, and they believed that only God could have done such miraculous things.	**Matthew 14:13–21**
When people encountered Jesus, their lives changed. Before the Resurrection, the disciples were fearful and afraid. After Jesus' Resurrection, the disciples were transformed into bold witnesses who were willing to die for their faith. They believed Jesus is God.	**Mark 14:50**

100% God
100% Human

Son of God

Was Jesus an ordinary man? Or is He God's Son who came to earth as 100% God and 100% human being? Many people choose by faith to believe Jesus is the Savior of the world. There are also many people who have examined the evidence and have decided there is proof that Jesus is God.

Seven "I AM" Statements of Jesus

When Moses met God at the burning bush, Moses asked God what His name is. God answered, "I AM" (see Exod. 3:14). In the Gospel of John, Jesus used the same "I am" phrase seven times when talking about Himself. In each of these "I am" statements, Jesus claimed to be God.

John 6:35		Jesus said, **"I AM the bread of life."** Bread feeds our bodies. Because Jesus is God, He can give us life and feed us spiritually.
John 8:12		Jesus said, **"I AM the light of the world."** In the Bible, darkness was a symbol of sin. Because He is the light, He offers a way out of spiritual darkness into the light of God's love and forgiveness. Jesus is the source of truth and our guide in this dark (sinful) world.
John 10:9		Jesus said, **"I AM the door."** Jesus is the only way to know God and go to heaven. People cannot get to heaven by their own good works. If they could, then Jesus would not have had to die on the Cross. Only trusting in Jesus and the sacrifice He offered on the Cross will save us. We must accept His gift of eternal life because no one can come to God except through Jesus (John 14:6).
John 10:11		Jesus said, **"I AM the good shepherd."** People in biblical times knew all about shepherds and sheep. They knew a good shepherd would lay down his life to save his sheep. Jesus is the Good Shepherd who laid down His life on the Cross to save the world from the penalty and power of sin.
John 11:25		Jesus said, **"I AM the resurrection and the life."** Before His death, Jesus knew He would rise from the grave. He knew He would offer the gift of eternal life to everyone who believes in Him as Savior and Lord.
John 14:6		Jesus said, **"I AM the way, the truth, and the life."** Jesus said that believing in Him as Savior is the only way to enter the Kingdom of God. No one can get to God without believing in Him. He said the words He spoke are true. And He offers eternal life to those who repent and turn to Him.
John 15:5		Jesus said, **"I AM the vine."** His followers are the branches. In other words, He is the source of our spiritual life. When we stay connected to Him, our lives flourish. When we disconnect from Him, our spiritual life begins to wilt like a plant without food and water.

Great crowds of faithful Jews were arriving in Jerusalem to celebrate the Passover Feast. In a fulfillment of Old Testament prophecy (Zech. 9:9), Jesus rode into Jerusalem on a donkey, coming in peace as a humble King. As a gesture of worship and honor, the crowd threw their robes on the road in front of him and spread palm branches on the ground. They cried out, "Hosanna to the Son of David! Blessed is He who comes in the name of the Lord!" (Matt. 21:9b).

At the Temple

After entering Jerusalem, Jesus cleansed the temple and drove out merchants who were buying and selling there because it created a noisy atmosphere instead of a respectful one. Not only that, but the merchants were charging higher prices than they needed to. As He taught in the temple, Jesus warned of the upcoming destruction of Jerusalem and told the crowds that He would come back again in a cloud with power and great glory. This future event is known as the Second Coming of Christ.

Anointed at Bethany

Jesus arrived in Bethany at the home of his friends Lazarus, Martha, and Mary. While they were eating supper, another woman named Mary anointed the feet of Jesus with a very expensive jar of perfume. It was an act of love and gratitude for how Jesus had changed her life. Jesus explained that it was also a way to prepare Him for His burial. This story is found in three gospels: Matthew 26:6–13; Mark 14:3–9; and John 12:1–8.

The Upper Room

Every year, the Jewish people celebrate their deliverance from the land of Egypt by having a special Passover meal. As faithful Jews, Jesus and His disciples shared a special Passover meal, but Jesus changed some of it. Today, that meal is known as the Last Supper. He started the tradition of communion (eating bread and drinking juice together) and told His followers to repeat communion together in the future to remember Him. Jesus announced to the disciples that one of them would betray Him. The Bible says that Satan entered Judas, and Judas left the upper room.

Garden of Gethsemane
After supper, Jesus and His remaining disciples walked to the Mount of Olives (groves of olive trees set on a hill) to pray in the Garden of Gethsemane, a special garden on the hill. As the Son of God, Jesus knew His mission would soon be complete when He laid down His life as a sacrifice for the sins of the world. While Jesus prayed in the garden, He sweated drops of blood because He knew how difficult and painful it would be to carry the weight of sin for all humanity. Suddenly an angel from heaven appeared and strengthened Him.

Arrested and Convicted in Court!
Judas betrayed Jesus! He led a group of Roman soldiers and the Jewish leaders to the Garden of Gethsemane to arrest Jesus. His disciples ran away and left Jesus to stand trial before the Sanhedrin, the Jewish supreme court of law. The Jewish leaders accused Jesus of claiming to be God, which was against Jewish law. They then sent Him to stand trial before Pilate, the Roman governor of Judea, because only Roman rulers could put someone to death. Pilate said Jesus was innocent, but the crowd kept shouting, "Crucify Him!" Pilate gave into the crowd and condemned Jesus to the Roman death penalty—crucifixion on a cross.

The Lamb of God
Unblemished, healthy male lambs were being sacrificed at the temple for the Passover celebration. At the same time, Jesus Christ, the innocent Lamb of God, was sacrificed on the Cross. His blood paid the price for the sins of the world, allowing all who believe in Him to be made right with God. The Jewish leaders and the Roman government ordered the death of Jesus, but Jesus chose not to save Himself. The Son of God allowed Himself to be the once-and-for-all sacrifice for the sins of the world.

Death and Burial
When Jesus was crucified, a strange darkness covered the land from 12 p.m. until 3 p.m. At the moment of His death, the massive curtain in the temple was torn in two from top to bottom. The earth shook, rocks split in half, and tombs opened. The Bible also says that "many bodies of the saints who had fallen asleep were raised; and coming out of the graves after His resurrection, they went into the holy city and appeared to many" (Matt. 27:52b–53). One of His followers named Joseph of Arimathea took the dead body of Jesus and buried Him in his new tomb before sundown because he (Joseph) could not do any work on the Sabbath (the next day).

Now after the Sabbath, as the first day of the week began to dawn, Mary Magdalene and the other Mary came to see the tomb. And behold, there was a great earthquake; for an angel of the Lord descended from heaven, and came and rolled back the stone from the door, and sat on it. His countenance was like lightning, and his clothing as white as snow. And the guards shook for fear of him, and became like dead men. But the angel answered and said to the women, "Do not be afraid, for I know that you seek Jesus who was crucified. He is not here; for He is risen, as He said. Come, see the place where the Lord lay." —Matthew 28:1–6

Early Sunday morning, Mary Magdalene, Joanna, Mary (the mother of James), and other women went to the tomb of Jesus. As His followers (and friends), they brought spices to prepare His body for a proper burial. When they got to the tomb, it was empty! They were sad because they thought someone had stolen the body of Jesus. Suddenly, two men dressed in shining garments stood beside them. They announced, "He is not here, but is risen!" (Luke 24:6a)

Missing!
The women who had seen the two angels ran back to tell the disciples. Peter and John, two of His disciples, ran to the tomb. It could not be true. Or could it? They found the linen cloths that had been used to wrap the dead body of Jesus. But where was Jesus?

.. [S]he turned around and saw Jesus standing there, and she did not know that it was Jesus. Jesus said to her, "Woman, why are you weeping? Whom are you seeking?" She, supposing Him to be the gardener, she said to Him, "Sir, if You have carried Him away, tell me where You have laid Him, and I will take Him away." Jesus said to her, "Mary!" –John 20:14b–16

Jesus Appears
New spread that Jesus appeared to many people after His Resurrection. Jesus appeared to Mary Magdalene (John 20:11–18). He walked along with two men on the road to Emmaus and explained to them how the Scriptures had pointed to His death and Resurrection (Luke 24:13–27). Jesus appeared to His disciples, but Thomas was not there (John 20:19–25), so He appeared again to the disciples including Thomas (John 20:26–29). He appeared to some of the disciples while they were fishing (John 21:1–13). He even appeared to over 500 disciples at once (1 Cor. 15:6)! He had risen from the dead!

Jesus' Post-Ressurection Appearances

	Location	To Whom He Appeared	Bible Reference
1	Near the tomb, Jerusalem	Mary Magdalene (alone at first)	John 20:11–18; Mark 16:9–11
2	Near the tomb, Jerusalem	Other women (including Mary the mother of James, Salome, and Joanna)	Matthew 28:1–10; Mark 16:1–8; Luke 24:1–12
3	On the road to Emmaus village (7 miles from Jerusalem)	Two disciples (Cleopas and another unnamed)	Luke 24:13–35; Mark 16:12–13
4	Jerusalem (upper room, evening)	The disciples (minus Thomas and Judas)	Luke 24:36–49; John 20:19–25; Mark 16:14
5	Jerusalem (upper room, 8 days later)	The eleven disciples (including Thomas)	John 20:26–29
6	Sea of Galilee (Tiberias)	Seven disciples (Peter, Thomas, Nathanael, James, John, and two others) – during a fishing miracle	John 21:1–14
7	Mountain in Galilee (appointed in advance)	The eleven disciples (and possibly others; over 500 mentioned in context)	Matthew 28:16–20; 1 Corinthians 15:6
8	Unspecified (likely Galilee or Judea)	Over 500 brethren at once	1 Corinthians 15:6
9	Unspecified (likely near Jerusalem)	James (the brother of Jesus), then all the apostles	1 Corinthians 15:7
10	Mount of Olives (near Bethany, east of Jerusalem)	The eleven disciples – during the Ascension	Luke 24:50–53; Acts 1:3–11; Mark 16:19

Faith Founded on Facts

The Bible records eyewitness accounts of the events about the death, Resurrection, and ascension of Jesus. Many people have made the decision to trust the Bible and believe what it says. This is called faith, and it is all we need to choose to become a follower of Christ. But our faith is also founded on facts. Ancient historians such as Thallus (A.D. 52), Mara Bar-Serapion (A.D. 70), Tacitus (A.D. 115), Lucian (around A.D. 115-200), and Josephus (A.D. 93-94) wrote about the historical Jesus, His death by the hands of Roman leaders, and the accounts of His Resurrection. These historians (along with many others) and their facts give us solid evidence to conclude that Jesus really did rise from the dead and lives today as the Savior of the world.

"About this time there lived Jesus, a wise man.... For he was one who wrought surprising feats and was a teacher of such people as accept the truth gladly. He won over many Jews and many of the Greeks. . . . When Pilate, upon hearing him accused by men of the highest standing amongst us, had condemned him to be crucified, those who had in the first place come to love him did not give up their affection for him.... the prophets of God had prophesied these and countless other marvelous things about him. And the tribe of the Christians, so called after him, has still to this day not disappeared."

Josephus, first-century historian

Antiquities of the Jews, section 18.3.3

Great Commission

After Jesus rose from the dead, He gave His disciples an important job to do. He told them to make disciples everywhere they went. This is known as the Great Commission (see Matt. 28:19–20). Jesus wants His followers to do the same. We can tell other people that they can enjoy a relationship with God through Jesus, and we can teach them how to follow Him.

Ascension of Jesus

After 40 days, the 11 disciples met with Jesus one final time at the Mount of Olives, where Jesus had been arrested. Then they watched as He rose up in the air until He disappeared in the clouds. Two men stood by them in white apparel. They said, "Men of Galilee, why do you stand gazing up into heaven? This same Jesus, who was taken up from you into heaven, will so come in like manner as you saw Him go into heaven" (Acts 1:11).

Jesus lived, died, and rose again during an era when Rome ruled the world. What was the Promised Land called at that time? God and the Jewish people called it Israel. When Jesus was young, He lived in Egypt with Mary and Joseph to escape persecution from Herod the Great. After Herod died, God told Joseph to take Jesus and Mary back "to the land of Israel" (Matthew 2:20).

Temple in Judea

Rome divided its empire into provinces (like a state or a county). Jerusalem was in the Roman province of Judea. Herod restored the Jews' holy temple in Jerusalem to unparalleled majesty. Jesus taught often at the temple. One day, the disciples pointed out the beauty of the temple buildings. Jesus told them, "Assuredly, I say to you, not one stone shall be left here upon another, that shall not be thrown down" (Matt. 24:2b). Because He is God, Jesus knew everything, even future events. Jesus knew the temple would soon be destroyed—very soon.

Jerusalem

After Jesus ascended into heaven, his half-brother James became the leader of the church in Jerusalem. Persecution against Christians in the city became so bad that James was killed (likely in A.D. 62) and the believers fled the city. A Jewish revolt against its Roman oppressors rose up, beginning in A.D. 66 and lasting for several years. Rome sent its armies to stop the revolt. Finally, the Roman general Titus and his legions broke through the fortified city walls.

Prophecy Fulfilled

In A.D. 70, Titus led his troops into Jerusalem. They looted the temple, carrying its gold and silver treasures to Rome. They set fire to the temple, knocking its stones to the ground. This fulfilled Jesus' prophecy of the destruction of the temple. Roman soldiers went on a rampage throughout the entire city until Jerusalem was destroyed.

The ruins of the Western Wall of the ancient Temple Mount in Jerusalem is a major Jewish sacred place and one of the most famous public domain places in the world.

Masada

Masada was the site of an ancient political fortress built on the flat top of a rocky cliff in the desert just west of the Dead Sea. Herod the Great built a formidable stronghold at Masada with palaces, forts, and towers. During the Jewish revolt against Rome, a group of Jewish zealots took over Masada. About 1,000 Jews lived there as a community of men, women, and children. After destroying Jerusalem in A.D. 70, Romans soldiers sought to squelch the Jewish rebellion completely, and they set about to conquer Masada. In A.D. 73, Masada fell to Rome. When soldiers broke through the city's walls, they discovered almost all the Jewish people were dead. Some historians believe the people had taken their own lives so they would not be forced to suffer as slaves of the Roman Empire. The site was left abandoned for nearly 2,000 years.

Judean Date Palm

The Judean date palm was famous for its sweet and delicious dates during Bible times—until it became extinct. Seeds from the date palm tree were found in the 1960s among the ruins of Masada. The seeds were around 2,000 years old! Dr. Sarah Sallon led a team of agriculture scientists in modern-day Jerusalem to plant some of the seeds—and one took root and became a tree! The tree is named Methusaleh after the oldest man in the Bible. More ancient seeds have since been planted with successful results, bringing the date palm tree back from extinction!

Aelia Capitolina

The Jews continued to revolt against Rome's harsh rule. Finally, Rome lost its patience. In A.D. 135, Emperor Hadrian rebuilt the city of Jerusalem, not as a holy site for the Jews, but as a pagan city for Rome. A temple for the false god Jupiter was built on the Temple Mount. The city was renamed Aelia Capitolina. The Roman province of Judea was renamed Palestina after the Philistines, ancient enemies of the Jews. All Jews were either executed or expelled from the city and the region, and many of their villages and towns were destroyed.

Nation of Israel

In A.D. 312, the Roman Emperor Constantine converted to Christianity. He changed the name of the city back to Jerusalem and built many Christian holy sites and churches. Rome was finally destroyed in A.D. 476, and the era of the Roman Empire came to an end. The land of Israel and its holy city of Jerusalem would change hands many times until 1948, when Israel became its own nation once again.

God is Creator of the whole world and everything in it. God is omnipotent (all-powerful). God is omnipresent (present everywhere at the same time). God is omniscient (all-knowing). He is holy and righteous. God is perfect. God is love. Everything He does is best because He does everything out of His wonderful love for us. God is our loving Father, and we are His beloved children. He wants to have a relationship with us because He loves us. He wants us to live with Him forever.

God's Holy Word

The Bible is trustworthy and true. It is the holy Word of God. It is the final authority on determining right and wrong. God is the Author of the Bible. The Holy Spirit inspired men to write down events of the past about the creation of the world, current events that they witnessed during their lifetime, and events that would happen in the future. Time and time again, archaeological finds support historic accounts in the Bible. Scientific discoveries support scientific truths found in the Bible long before science and technology could prove them. When people claim the Bible is wrong, they do not know the Scripture or understand the power of God.

Jesus, the Savior of the World

Jesus is God. Jesus is Creator. In Colossians, Paul wrote, "All things were created through Him and for Him. And He is before all things, and in Him all things consist" (Col. 1:16b–17). Jesus is God's Son. He is the "Lamb of God who takes away the sin of the world" (John 1:29b). Jesus died on the Cross, was buried in the tomb, and three days later rose from the grave. Now, He sits in heaven at the right hand of our Heavenly Father (Heb. 1:3). He is our living Savior. He loves each of us and wants to have a relationship with each of us. He wants to be our closest Friend. That is why He died for us.

Created to Choose

God did not create us as robots. They cannot love. Robots cannot choose to do what they want. They can only do what they have been programmed to do. God created us in His image and gave us the ability to choose. We can love or hate. We can choose right or wrong. We can choose to believe in Him or turn our backs on Him.

Eternal Plan

God created human beings, beginning with Adam and Eve. When they chose to listen to the serpent and disobeyed God, sin and death entered God's perfect world. God's relationship with human beings was broken. But God had a plan: He would send His Son, Jesus, to conquer the power of sin and death so we could have a right relationship with God. Jesus did this when He died on the Cross and rose again. God sent the Holy Spirit to live in us and guide us. One day, Jesus will come back as the conquering King. He will set up His Kingdom, and it will last forever. God wants everyone to live eternally with Him. How glorious and wonderful that will be!

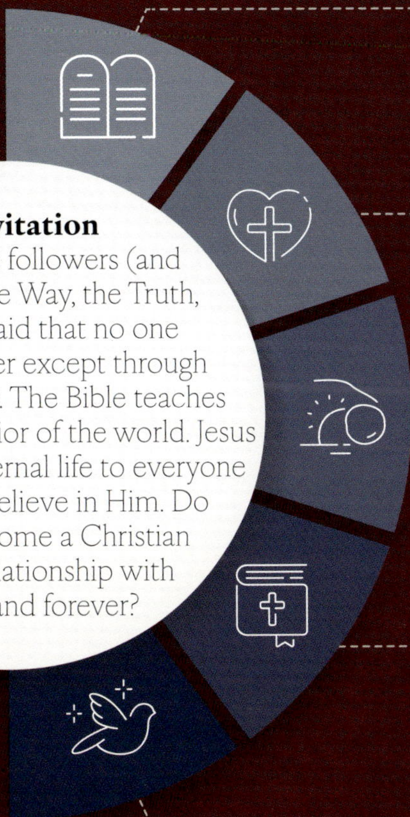

Your Invitation

Jesus told His followers (and us) that He is the Way, the Truth, and the Life. He said that no one comes to the Father except through Him (see John 14:6). The Bible teaches that Jesus is the Savior of the world. Jesus offers the gift of eternal life to everyone who chooses to believe in Him. Do you want to become a Christian and enjoy a relationship with God now and forever?

- Tell God you are sorry for your sins (the wrong things you have done).
- Ask God to forgive you and create a clean heart inside you.
- Tell Jesus you believe He died for your sin and rose again to give you eternal life.
- Ask Jesus to be your Savior and help you follow Him.
- Thank God for saving you and setting you free.

Now that you are a Christian, here are some important things that will help you grow:

- Read the Bible. It helps you know Jesus more. The Book of John (in the New Testament) is a good place to start.
- Find a church that believes in the authority of the Bible and will teach you how to grow as a Christian.
- Share with other Christian family members and friends that you have decided to follow Jesus! They can encourage you to grow closer to Him.

INDEX

A

Aaron: 92, 95, 97
Abednego: 147, 151
Aboriginal People: 37
Abraham: 9, 11, 65, 72-77, 84, 86-87, 88, 92, 96, 97, 108, 110, 180
Academy, The: 162
According to its Kind: 22-23, 26, 28-29, 40
Achievements of the Divine Augustus: 181
Aconcagua: 137 (map)
Acropolis: 80-81, 160-161
Actium: 149, 173 (map)
Adam and Eve: 8, 14, 24, 28, 31-35, 38, 39, 41, 58, 64, 114, 180, 207
Adams, Sebastian C.: 15
Adams Synchronological Chart: 15
Adaptations: 61
Adena: 135
Adonijah: 106
Aegean Sea: 78, 80, 100, 102, 152
Aelia Capitolina: 175, 203, 205
Africa: 6, 9, 43, 45, 58, 62-63 (map), 66, 102-103, 111, 112-113 (map), 114 (map)-115 (map), 166 (map), 168-170
- **Africa's Natural Wonders**: 112-113
- **African Savanna**: 112-113 (map)
- **Ancient Africa**: 102 (map), 112-113 (map), 114-115
- **Rock Art**: 115

Agora: 161
Ahab, King: 140, 142-143
Ahasuerus: 153
Ahaz, King: 91, 141, 143, 180
Ainu: 132
Akkad: 64 (map)
Akkadian Language: 82
Akrotiri: 79
Alaska: 62, 134 (map)
Aleut Unangan: 134
Aleutian Iislands: 134
Alexander Helios: 173
Alexander the Great: 101, 103, 119, 148, 164 (map)-165, 172, 176
Alexandria: 66 (map), 73 (map), 148, 164 (map), 165, 166 (map), 170 (map), 172-173, 174
Alexandrian War: 172
Allosaurus: 43
Almaty: 126
Alphabet: 67, 90-91, 103, 171
Alps: 63, 149, 166 (map)
Amazon: 37, 63, 120, 137 (map)-138
Ammonites: 158
Amos: 140-141, 180
Amun: 117
Ancient Africa: 114-115
Ancient Civilizations: 6, 38, 59, 68-60, 120, 135, 171
Ancient Flood Stories: 55
Ancient History: 15, 36-37, 52, 59, 64, 66, 82, 84, 86, 114 (map)-115
Ancient Man: 37, 114-115
Ancient Peru: 6, 138-139
Ancient Trade Route: 64 (map)
Andes Mountains: 63, 137 (map)-138
Andrew: 190
Andrews, Roy Chapman: 42
Ankylosaurus: 49-50
Anna: 149, 174, 182
Annals of the World, The: 15
Anno Domini: 174, 178, 180
Anointing at Bethany: 198
Answers in Genesis: 15, 27
Antarctica: 44, 57, 62-63 (map)
Antikythera Mechanism: 149
Antiochus: 149, 176
Antiquities of the Jews: 203
Antony, Mark: 149, 167, 170, 173
Apatosaurus: 44-45
Appian Way: 169
Aqua Virgo: 169
Aqueducts: 91, 139, 168-169
Arabia: 106, 110-111, 164 (map)
Arabian Peninsula: 110 (map)
Arabian Sea: 68, 110 (map), 164 (map)
Arabs: 101, 111, 140 (map), 158
Aramaic: 153
Ararat, Mount: 55, 58 (map), 145 (map)
Archaeological Finds: 10, 30, 36, 38-39, 54, 60-61, 63-64, 68-69, 70-71, 78-79, 81, 84-85, 100, 107, 115, 116-17, 121, 123-125, 129, 135-136, 139, 144-145, 146, 206
- **25th Dynasty of Egypt**: 116-117
- **Achievements of the Divine Augustus**: 181
- **Ancient Ur**: 59, 65, 72, 74
- **Assyrian Empire**: 9, 117, 144-145 (map), 146
- **Clare Gold Hoard**: 123
- **Cyrus Cylinder**: 152
- **Dead Sea Scrolls**: 10-11, 149, 177
- **Elephantine Island Documents**: 159
- **Gilgamesh Dream Tablet**: 145
- **Golden Cataphract**: 126
- **Jesus Boat**: 194
- **Law Code Stele of King Hammurabi**: 9, 82
- **Rosetta Stone**: 67, 149
- **Royal Library of the Hittites**: 84
- **Royal Library of Nineveh**: 144- 145
- **Scythian**: 127
- **Sennacherib Prism**: 146
- **Sumerian King List**: 63
- **Tel Dan Stele**: 105
- **Terra-Cotta Army**: 129, 149
- **Tomb Banner, China**: 130
- **Tunnel of Hezekiah**: 146
- **Tutankhamen, King (and Pharaoh)**: 77
- **Treaty of Kadesh**: 10, 84

Archimedes: 165
Arctic: 60-61, 134
Arctic and Subarctic Tribes of North America: 134

Arctic Ocean: 61 (map), 62-63 (map), 134 (map)
Aristotle: 18-19, 148, 162-165
Ark Encounter: 54
Ark, Noah's: 8, 47, 52-55, 60
Ark of the Covenant: 95, 104-105, 108-109, 184-185, 186-187
Artaxerxes, King: 157-158
Aryans: 9, 118
Asa, King: 141, 143
Ascension of Jesus: 174, 202-203
Ashdod: 100 (map)
Ashdodites: 158
Asherah: 142
Ashkelon: 100 (map)
Ashoka: 119, 148
Ashumasirpal II: 144
Ashurbanipal, King: 117, 145, 150
Asia: 58, 61 (map)-63 (map), 68, 102 (map), 110, 118, 126, 132, 135, 170 (map)
Asia Minor: 164 (map)
Assyrians: 9, 73, 91, 100 (map), 116-117, 127, 140-141, 144-145 (map), 146-147, 150, 164 (map)
Astronomy: 11, 89
Atacama Desert: 137 (map)
Atheists: 18, 27-28, 36, 178
Athens: 80 (map), 148, 160-164 (map), 166 (map)
Atlantic Ocean: 62-63 (map), 102 (map), 112, 122 (map), 166 (map)
Attributes of God: 12-13
Augustus, Caesar: 170-171, 173-174, 181
Austin, Steve :53
Australia: 37, 62 (map)
Austria: 91, 124
Author of Genesis: 14
Authority of the Bible: 6, 17, 30, 32-33, 36-37, 52, 55, 59, 64-67, 84, 105, 107, 114, 121, 159, 180-181, 189, 203, 204, 206-207
Avebury: 122
Aztecs: 167, 175

B

Baal: 86, 140, 142
Babel: 8, 58-64, 66, 68, 70, 78, 86, 114, 121-122, 134-135
Babylon: 8-9, 64 (map), 82-83, 91, 100 (map),101, 141, 145 (map)147, 150-151, 152 (map), 154-155, 164 (map)-165
Babylonia: 140, 144, 150, 164 (map)
Babylonian Empire: 9, 82-83, 91, 101, 141, 143, 145 (map), 147, 150-151, 154, 158, 182, 186
Bantu Language: 115 (map)
Bantu Migration: 9, 115 (map)
Baptism of Christians: 191, 196
Baptism of Jesus: 12, 174, 189
Barak: 90, 99
Bartholomew: 190
Bathsheba: 105-106
Batteries: 149
Battersea Bridge: 123
Bedouins: 110
Beehive Tombs: 81
Before the Flood: 38-39, 85
Belshazzar: 151
Ben-Hadad, King: 140
Benjamin, Tribe of: 76, 97, 140
Bering Land Bridge: 61 (map), 134 (map)
Beringia: 134 (map)
Bethany: 198, 202
Bethel: 86 (map), 140 (map)
Bethlehem: 11, 140 (map), 167, 170, 181-183 (map)
Bey, Theodore Makridi: 84
Bible: 6, 10-19, 22-25, 27-41, 45, 47, 51-53, 55, 57, 59-60, 63-67, 71, 73, 75, 77, 84, 86-87, 94, 100, 103-107, 111, 114, 116, 121, 125, 152, 159, 163, 165, 167, 178, 180-181, 189-192, 196-199, 202-203, 205-207
- **As #1 Bestseller**: 178
- **Authority of**: 6, 17, 30, 32-33, 36-37, 52, 55, 59, 64-67, 84, 105, 107, 114, 121, 159, 180-181, 189, 203, 204, 206-207
- **Bible in World History**: 10, 152
- **Dates New Testament Books Written**: 174-175
- **Jesus as God**: 196-197
- **Manuscript Reliability**: 11
- **Prophecies**: 11, 33, 154, 165, 176, 178, 182, 196-197, 204
- **Trust the Bible**: 6, 10-11, 17, 32-33, 36-37, 52, 59, 64, 67, 103, 105, 114, 159, 180, 203, 206

Biblical Worldview: 6, 17, 30, 36, 40-41
Big Al: 43
Big Bang Theory: 19, 24, 28
Biology: 11
Birds: 16, 20, 23, 26-28, 41, 52, 150, 163
Biremes: 102
Birth of Democracy: 148, 160-161
Birth of Jesus: 11, 167, 170, 173-174, 178, 180-181
Birthplace of Western Civilization: 63, 162
Black Pharaohs: 116-117
Black Sea: 58 (map), 91, 102 (map), 126-127, 145 (map), 152 (map), 164 (map), 166 (map)
Bluestones: 120
Boaz: 99, 180, 186
Book of the Law: 143, 159
Born Again: 191-192, 206-207
Brachiosaurus: 41, 45
Brachylophosaurus: 47
Brahmins: 118
Britain: 91, 125, 149, 167, 169-170, 175
Britain, Great: 63, 122-123
British Isles: 102, 120, 122-125, 169
Bronze Age: 39
Brontosaurus: 44, 51
Buddhism: 119, 131, 133, 148, 179
Building an Empire, Rome: 150, 168-169
Bull-jumping: 79
Burning Bush: 92, 197

C

Caesar Augustus: 170-171, 173-174, 181
Caesarion: 173
Cahokia Mounds: 59
Cainan: 14
Cairo: 66 (map)
Caleb: 96, 99
California, Tribes of North America: 135
Caligula, Emperor: 174
Canaan: 9, 73-75, 84, 86 (map)-88, 92, 96 (map), 98-100 (map), 101-102, 145 (map)
Canaanites: 58, 74, 86, 98-99, 102
Canada: 49, 134 (map)
Carbon Dating: 41, 67
Carbon-14: 41
Carnegie Museum of Natural History: 44

Carthage: 91, 102 (map), 103, 149, 166 (map)
Case for Christ for Kids: 178
Caste System: 118-119
Casting Lots: 98
Catapults: 141, 148
Caveman: 37, 39, 60, 61
Celts and Their Customs: 91, 123-125
Census: 170, 174, 181, 183 (map)
Central America: 59, 61, 136
Centrosaurus: 49
Cetaceans: 26
Chandragupta Maurya: 119
Chang'an: 130 (map)
Changsha: 130
Chavín Culture: 63, 91, 138
Chavín de Huántar: 138
Cherubim: 95, 109
Chichen Itza: 59, 136
China: 5, 48, 62, 64, 70-71, 90, 111, 126, 128 (map)-130 (map), 131-133, 149, 175
  Early Emperors: 70-71, 128-129
  River of Sorrow (China's Sorrow): 70, 131
  Yellow River Valley: 62, 70-71
Chi'in (Qin) Dynasty: 128-131, 149
Chogha Zanbil Ziggurat: 72
Chou (Zhou) Dynasty: 128 (map)
Christ Jesus: 12, 15, 32-33, 53, 74, 83, 87, 99, 103, 167, 170, 174, 178-179, 181-182, 189-190, 198-199
Christianity: 6, 10, 13,17, 20, 26, 33, 35, 53, 74-75, 125, 152, 174-175, 178-179, 182, 191-192, 195-197, 202-205, 206-207
  Among Celts: 125
  Baptism of Christians: 191, 196
  Born Again: 191-192, 206-207
  Christmas: 178
  Eternal Life: 13, 33, 35, 75, 191, 195, 197, 206-207
  Evidence for Jesus: 178, 196, 203
  Faith Founded on Facts: 10, 20, 26, 53, 152, 203
  Salvation: 13, 17, 33, 182, 195, 206-207
Christians: 17, 30, 33, 101, 174-175, 178, 192, 202-207
Christmas: 178
Chronicles of Narnia, The: 178
Chronological Chart of Ancient, Modern and Biblical History: 15
Church in Jerusalem: 196, 204
Circles, Calculating: 65, 120, 162
Circular Reasoning: 57
Circus Maximus: 168
Cities, Early: 8, 39, 59, 64-65, 68-69, 74
City-States: 65, 78, 80-81, 160-164, 166
Clare Gold Hoard: 123
Claudius: 125
Cleopatra: 149, 170, 172-173 (map)
Cleopatra Selene: 173
Code of Hammurabi: 9, 82-83, 150
Cold Case Christianity for Kids: 178
Colosseum: 168, 175
Columbus, Christopher: 102
Communion: 198
Confucius: 128, 130-131
Confucianism: 128, 130-131, 179
Congo Basin: 112 -113 (map)
Constantine, Emperor: 175, 205
Continents and Oceans: 62-63
Copper Mines: 107, 123
Corinth: 174
Corinthian Column: 161, 186
Covenant, God's: 52-53, 74-75, 83, 94
Cradle of Western Civilization: 162
Crater Glacier: 56-57
Crates of Mallus: 149
Created in God's Image: 28, 31-32, 37-39, 60, 114, 121, 207
Creation Account: 8, 14-31, 25, 47, 64, 94, 135
Creation Ministries International: 27
Creation Scientists: 15, 17, 25, 27, 30, 32, 39-41, 56-57, 61, 114, 135
Creation Week: 16-31
  Day One of Creation: 18-19
  Day Two of Creation: 20-21
  Day Three of Creation: 22-23
  Day Four of Creation: 24-25
  Day Five of Creation: 26-27
  Day Six of Creation: 28-29, 114
  Day Seven of Creation: 30-31
Creator God: 12-14, 16-32, 35, 37, 163, 179, 204-207
  Jesus as Creator: 16-17, 179, 204
Crete: 78-80 (map), 100 (map)
Crucifixion of Jesus: 11, 174, 185, 196, 199, 200, 203
Ctesibius: 149
Cuneiform: 10, 64, 67, 82, 145
Cush (Kush): 66 (map), 72, 73 (map), 91, 116-117
Cylinder Seals: 79
Cyprus: 86 (map), 102 (map), 145 (map)
Cyrus Cylinder: 152
Cyrus, King: 151-152, 154, 157

D

Dalits: 118
Damascus: 94, 140, 145 (map)
Dan, City of: 105, 140 (map)
Danger Cave: 135
Daniel: 14, 91, 141, 147, 151, 153, 165, 176
Darius: 151, 153-154, 157, 164
Darwin, Charles: 15, 18, 114
Dates New Testament Books Written: 174-175
David, King of Israel: 11, 37, 72, 74, 76, 90, 99, 101, 103-108, 141, 156, 180-181, 196, 198
Day One of Creation: 18-19
Day Two of Creation: 20-21
Day Three of Creation: 22-23
Day Four of Creation: 24-25
Day Five of Creation: 26-27
Day Six of Creation: 28-29, 114
Day Seven of Creation: 30-31
Dead Sea: 11, 62-63, 73 (map), 96 (map), 111, 140 (map), 145 (map), 177, 183 (map), 205
Dead Sea Scrolls: 10-11, 149, 177
Death Valley: 62
Deborah: 90, 99
Delphi: 124
Democracy: 148, 160-161
Demons: 195
Deportation: 141, 145, 147, 151, 154
Dido: 103
Dinosaur Park Formation: 49
Dinosaur Provincial Park: 49
Dinosauria: 51
Dinosaurs: 6, 8, 27, 29, 36, 40-51, 54, 61
  Allosaurus: 43
  Ankylosaurus: 49, 50
  Apatosaurus: 44-45
  Brachiosaurus: 41, 45

Brachylophosaurus: 47
Brontosaurus: 44, 51
Centrosaurus: 49
Diplodocus: 44
Edmontosaurus: 47
Giganotosaurus: 43
Gryposaurus: 46
Hadrosaurs: 46-47
Iguanodon: 40, 46
Lambeosaurinae: 46-47
Marginocephalia: 41, 48-49
Megalosaurus: 42
Ornithopods: 40, 46-47
Oviraptor: 42
Pachycephalosaurus: 48
Parasaurolophus: 47
Protoceratops: 48
Psittacosaurus: 48
Sauropods: 29, 41, 44-45, 54
Spinosaurus: 43
Stegosaurus: 41, 50
Styracosaurus: 49
Therapods: 40, 42-43
Thyreophora: 41, 50
Triceratops: 41, 45, 49
Tyrannosaurus rex: 43, 45, 47, 49
Velociraptor: 42
Dionysus, a Monk: 180
Dionysus, Theater of: 160
Diplodocus: 44
Dippy, the *Diplodocus:* 44
Disciples, Twelve: 190, 194-196, 198-199, 202-204
Divided Kingdoms of Israel: 90-91, 140 (map), 141-143, 145 (map), 146-147, 150-151
Divinity of Jesus: 12, 181-182, 194-203, 206-207
Djoser (Zoser), Pharaoh: 72
DNA: 14, 19, 23, 32-33
Dorians: 81
Doric Column: 161
Doubt and Deception: 37
Dromedaries: 111
Druids: 125

E

Early Years of Jesus: 174, 182-183
Eddie the *Edmontosaurus*: 47
Edict of Milan: 175
Edmontosaurus: 47
Edom: 96 (map), 97, 105, 107, 140 (map)
Edomites: 95, 107, 111
Effects of Atheism: 36
Egypt: 8-10, 58-59, 63-64, 66 (map)-67, 72-73, 76-77, 84-85, 86 (map), 88-89, 91-94, 96 (map), 97, 100 (map), 106, 110, 113 (map), 116-117, 120, 123, 135, 141, 144, 145 (map), 148-149, 152 (map), 159, 164 (map)-165, 167, 170, 172-173, 183 (map), 198, 204
Cleopatra, Last Pharoah of Egypt: 149, 170, 172-173 (map)
Egypt's 25th Dynasty: 116-117
Exodus, The: 90, 92-93, 96 (map), 109
Flight to Egypt: 183 (map), 204
Joseph in Egypt: 9, 76-77
Life Along the Nile: 66-67
Lower Egypt: 66 (map), 73 (map)
Mizraim Founds Egypt: 8, 66-67, 116
Moses in Egypt: 89, 92-93
New Kingdom, Egypt: 73
Old Kingdom, Egypt: 72
Upper Egypt: 66 (map), 72-73
Egyptian Demotic: 67
Egyptian-Hittite Treaty: 10, 84-85
Egypt's 25th Dynasty: 116-117
Einstein, the *Apatosaurus*: 44
Ekron: 100 (map), 140 (map)
El Castillo: 136
El-Kurru: 116
Eleazar: 98, 180
Elephantine Island: 159
Elephantine Island Documents: 159
Eli: 104
Elijah: 37, 140, 142
Elisha: 140, 142
Emerald Isle: 122
Emmaus: 202
England:42, 90, 120, 122 (map)-123, 184
Enoch: 8, 14, 39
Enos: 14
Ephron the Hittite: 77, 84
Epic of Gilgamesh: 55, 145
Equator: 63, 66, 112-113 (map)
Eratosthenes: 149, 165
Esau: 76, 97, 110-111, 184
Esther: 153, 158
Eternal King: 105, 178, 180-181, 207
Eternal Life: 13, 33, 35, 75, 191, 195, 197, 206-207
Eternal Plan: 6, 12, 19, 25, 35, 53, 206-207
Ethiopia: 32, 66 (map), 72, 116-117
Etruscans: 166
Euclid: 162-163, 165
Euphrates River: 58 (map), 62, 64 (map), 82, 97, 102 (map), 106, 145 (map) 150, 158 (map), 164 (map)
Eurasia: 63, 126-127
Eurasian Steppe: 126-127
Europe: 58, 78, 62-63 (map), 78, 102 (map), 122-127, 170
Evidence for Jesus: 178, 196, 203
Evolution: 15, 16-17, 18-19, 23, 25, 27-28, 32-41, 43, 47, 54, 57, 60-61, 64, 67, 73, 114, 121, 135
Exodus, The: 90, 92-93, 96 (map), 109
Expanding Universe: 19
Eyewitness Testimonies: 10, 53, 59, 89, 94, 178, 180, 190, 196, 203
Ezekiel: 91, 141, 147
Ezra: 148, 154-157, 159

F

Faith Founded on Facts: 10, 20, 26, 53, 152, 203
Fall, The: 8, 33-35, 38, 52
Fall of Roman Empire: 175, 205
Farmers, Early: 8, 38, 61, 64, 66, 68-69, 70, 114
Feast of Tabernacles: 155
Fertile Crescent: 64, 144, 145 (map)
Fibonacci Sequence: 24
First Dynasty of Egypt: 74
Flood, The: 4, 8, 22, 35, 38-39, 43, 45, 47, 49, 52-58, 60-61, 63-64, 85, 112, 114, 121, 122, 134-135
Evidence for the Flood: 35, 47, 52-54, 57, 63
Flood Stories, Ancient: 55
Pre-Flood World: 38-39, 85
Worldwide Flood: 8, 38, 52-54, 63, 121-122, 134

Forbidden Fruit: 34
Forests and Steppes: 91, 126-127, 129
Fossils: 17, 32, 35-36, 40-50, 54, 57, 60, 112
Transitional Fossils: 32, 41
France: 60, 82, 122 (map), 124, 167, 169-170
Frankincense: 182
Frescos: 78-79

G

Gabriel: 165, 174, 180-181
Galatia: 124-125
Galatians, Book of: 11, 125, 174
Galilee: 11, 188, 190, 194, 202-203
Gallic Wars: 149
Gaozu, Emperor: 130
Garden of Eden: 28, 33-34, 37, 58 (map), 64, 114
Garden of Gethsemane: 199
Garden Party Relief: 150
Gastroliths: 45, 48
Gath: 100 (map)-101, 140 (map)
Gatherers and Hunters: 38-39, 60-61, 64
Gaul: 166 (map), 167
Gauls: 124, 148, 171
Gaza: 73 (map), 100 (map), 164 (map)
Gebel Barkal: 117
Gender: 8, 31
Genealogy of Jesus: 58, 156, 180, 196
Genesis: 8, 11, 14-31, 33-35, 37-39, 52-53, 56, 58, 64, 74, 77, 87, 94, 110, 178
Gentiles: 182, 186-187
Gibeon: 98
Gideon: 90
Giganotosaurus: 43
Gilgal Refaim: 120
Gilgamesh Dream Tablet: 145
Giza Pyramids: 59, 66 (map), 72, 73 (map)
Glaciers: 56-57, 62, 68, 137
Glacier Girl: 56-57
God: 6, 8, 11-40, 45, 52-53, 55, 58-61, 64, 74-77, 83, 86-90, 92-99, 102-106, 108-109, 114, 117, 121, 140-143, 145-147, 149, 151-159, 163, 165-167, 170, 176, 178-182, 188-194, 196-197, 199, 203-207
Creator God: 12-14, 16-32, 35, 37, 163, 179, 204-207
Eternal Life with God: 13, 33, 35, 75, 191, 195, 197, 206-207
God as Omnipotent: 12, 206
God as Omnipresent: 12, 206
God as Omniscient: 12, 19, 206
God is Eternal: 13, 18-19, 75, 90, 92, 163, 206-207
God is Good: 12, 19, 156, 191, 197
God is Just and Merciful: 12
God is Love: 12, 206
God is Omnipotent: 12, 206
God is Omnipresent: 12, 206
God is Omniscient: 12, 19, 206
God is Perfect: 13, 59, 206
God the Father: 12, 16, 52, 59, 188-189, 196, 206-207
God the Holy Spirit: 12, 16, 181, 189, 196, 206-207
God the Son: 12, 16, 178, 189, 196, 199, 206-207
God's Covenant: 52-53, 75, 83, 94-95, 109
God's Eternal Plan: 6, 12, 19, 25, 35, 53, 206-207
God's Perfect Plan: 4 12-13, 25, 19, 25, 35, 75
Kingdom of God: 190-192, 197, 207
Trinity: 12, 16, 189, 196
Yahweh: 157
Gods, False: 18, 65, 67, 77, 83, 86, 98, 99, 106, 109, 118-119, 125, 132, 141-143, 145, 151, 153, 157, 161, 163, 167, 171
Golan Heights: 120
Gold, Gift of the Magi: 182
Golden Cataphract: 126
Golden Ratio: 163
Goliath: 101, 104
Gomorrah: 86 (map)-87
Goshen: 88-89, 92, 96 (map), 145 (map)
Grand Canyon: 36, 53
Great Barrier Reef: 62
Great Britain: 63, 122-123
Great Commission: 203
Great Dividing Range: 62
Great Fire of Rome: 175
Great Isaiah Scroll: 10-11, 149
Great Pyramid of Giza: 9, 72, 123
Great Sea: 86 (map), 96 (map)
Great Sphinx: 72
Great Wall of China: 129, 149
Greece: 8-9, 63, 78-79, 80 (map)-81, 91, 100 (map), 103, 124, 148-149, 152 (map), 160-165, 166 (map), 171
Alexander the Great: 103, 119, 148, 164 (map)-165, 172, 176
Birthplace of Democracy: 148, 160-161
Golden Age of Greece:162-163
Greek Architecture: 161
Greek Alphabet and Language: 64, 67, 91, 103, 171
Greek City-States: 160-161, 166
Greek (Macedonian) Empire: 148, 151
Greek Influence in Egypt: 148, 172-173
Javan Founds Greece: 8
Olympics: 91, 161
Greeks: 18, 67, 78-81, 91, 100, 102-103, 116, 119, 127, 160-166, 171-173, 176, 203
Greenland: 39, 56-57, 62, 134
Gregorian Calendar: 171, 178, 180
Grimspound Settlement: 90
Gryposaurus: 46
Gulf of America: 62, 136
Gulf of Aqaba: 96 (map)

H

Habakkuk: 141
Hadrian, Emperor: 101, 169, 175, 205
Hadrian's Wall: 169, 175
Hadrosaurs: 46-47
Hagar: 75
Haggai: 141, 157
Hall of Pillars: 107
Hall of Thrones: 107
Hallstatt: 91, 124
Ham, Ken: 54
Ham, Noah's son: 58, 66, 74
Haman: 153
Hammurabi, King: 82-83, 150
Hammurabi's Laws: 9, 82-83, 150
Han Dynasty: 130-131, 149
Hanging Gardens of Babylon: 91, 150
Hannah: 104
Hannah, the *Edmontosaurus*: 47
Hannibal: 149, 166 (map)
Haran: 9, 74-75, 100 (map)
Harappa: 68, 118

Hatshepsut, Queen: 73
Hattusha: 84-85, 100 (map)
Hattusili III: 10
Heaven: 6, 8, 12, 14, 16, 19-20, 23, 31, 34, 52, 56, 86, 88, 94, 114, 142, 154, 181, 189, 191, 196-197, 199-200, 203-204, 206
Hebrew, Language: 64, 66, 73
Hebrew People: 73, 77, 89, 92, 94, 141, 145, 151, 153, 165, 167
Hebrews, Book of: 11, 24, 175
Hebrides: 122
Hebron: 86 (map), 140 (map)
Hell: 191
Hellenism: 172
Hellenistic Age: 165
Hendrickson, Sue: 43
Henge: 120-123
Herders, Early: 8, 38, 64, 114-115, 135
Hero (Heron) of Alexandria: 175
Herod Agrippa I: 184
Herod Antipas: 184
Herod Archelaus: 184
Herod the Great: 149, 174, 176-177, 182-188, 204-205
Herodotus: 162
Herod's Temple and Temple Complex: 5, 174-176, 180, 182, 184-188, 198-199, 204
  Destruction: 175, 186
  Temple Complex Diagram: 186-187
  Temple Diagram: 185-187
  Temple Furniture: 184-185
Hezekiah, King: 91, 117, 141, 143, 145-146, 180
Hieroglyphs (Hieroglyphic): 67, 85, 117
Himalayas: 68
Hinduism: 118-119
Hippocrates: 148, 162
Hiram, King: 103, 107
Historical Jesus: 178, 180-181, 196, 203
Hittites: 9-10, 77, 83-86, 90, 100 (map)-101, 105
Hokkaido: 132
Holy of Holies: 95, 108-109, 184-187
Holy Spirit:12, 16, 181, 189, 196, 206-207
Homer: 80, 91
Honshu: 132
Hopewell: 135
Hosea: 140-141
House of the Forest of Lebanon: 107
Hsia (Xia) Dynasty: 128
Huang He (Yellow River): 9, 62, 70-71, 128 (map), 131
Huangdi, Emperor (Yellow Emperor): 71, 128-129
Humanism: 163
Huns: 127
Hunters, Early: 38-39, 60-61, 64, 115, 132, 134-135
Hyksos: 73 (map), 77

I

I AM Statements of Jesus: 197
I AM WHO I AM: 92
Ice Age: 36, 56-57, 60-62, 114, 134
Ichthyosaurus: 51
Idol Worship: 83, 109, 140-141, 142-143, 146-147
Iguanodon: 40, 46
Iliad, The: 80, 91
Imhotep: 72
Imperial Family of Japan: 132
In the Beginning: 14-15, 18-19
Incense Road, Arabia's: 111
India: 9, 62, 64, 68-69, 90, 111, 117-119, 131, 148, 152 (map), 164 (map)-165
Indian Ocean: 62-63 (map)
Indiana: 135
Indians (Indigenous Peoples) of North America: 55, 134-135
Indus Civilization: 8, 68-69, 118
Indus River and Valley: 8, 62, 65, 68-69, 78, 118, 152, 164 (map)
Institute for Creation Research: 15, 27, 47
Intelligent Creator: 14, 19, 24
Intelligent Design: 19, 24
Inuit: 39
Ionian Sea: 78, 173 (map)
Ionic Column: 161
Iran: 82, 150, 152, 154
Iraq: 55, 58-59, 63-64, 144
Ireland: 15, 122 (map)-123, 125
Iron: 8, 22, 29, 39, 85, 101, 105, 107, 115, 117, 124, 128, 132, 151
Iron Age: 39
Isaac: 58, 74-77, 96-97, 108, 110, 180
Isaiah:11, 14, 91, 117, 141, 143, 149, 154, 181, 196
Isaiah Scroll: 10-11, 149
Ishmael: 74-75, 110
Ishmaelites: 76, 110
Ishtar Gate: 150
Islam: 74, 179
Israel: 11, 30, 62-63 (map), 66 (map), 74, 76, 87, 90-91, 93, 95-96 (map), 97-99, 100 (map), 101-110, 120, 140-145 (map), 146, 154-157, 164, 170, 176, 180, 182, 184-189, 194, 204-205
  David, King of: 11, 37, 74, 76, 90, 99, 101, 103-108, 141, 156, 180-181, 196, 198
  Divided Kingdoms of Israel: 90-91, 140 (map), 141-143, 145 (map), 146-147, 150-151
  Golden Age of Israel: 106-107, 140
  Herod's Temple and Temple Complex: 174-176, 180, 182, 184-188, 198-199, 204
  Jacob (Israel), Isaac's Son: 9, 76-77, 84, 87-89, 96-97, 180, 184
  Kings and Prophets of Divided Kingdom of Israel: 140-143
  Second Temple: 148-149, 154-158, 176-177
  Solomon's Temple: 6, 90-91, 105, 107-109, 140-141, 143, 147, 151, 184, 186
  Ten Lost Tribes of Israel: 145
  Twelve Tribes of Israel: 97
Israelites: 30, 83, 89-90, 92-101, 103-104, 106, 108, 140
Issyk Burial Mound: 126
Italy: 1214, 166, 169

J

Jabin, King: 99
Jacob (Israel), Isaac's Son: 9, 76-77, 84, 87-89, 96-97, 180, 184
James, Book of: 174
James, Brother of Jesus: 196, 202, 204
James, Disciple: 184, 190, 202
Japan: 6, 62, 132-133, 148, 174
Japeth: 58 (map), 78, 122
Jared: 14
Javan: 8
Jehohanan: 159
Jehoiachin: 156
Jehoiakim: 141
Jehoshaphat, King: 141, 143, 180
Jéquier, Gustave: 82
Jeremiah: 91, 141, 143, 147, 154

Jericho: 86 (map), 90, 96 (map), 98-99, 140 (map)

Jeroboam, King: 140-141

Jerusalem: 11, 73 (map), 90, 98, 101, 102 (map), 103, 105, 107-109, 117, 140 (map)-141, 143, 145 (map)-149, 154-157, 158 (map)-159, 168, 170, 174-177, 182, 183 (map), 184-188, 196, 198-199, 202, 204-205

- **Assyrian Siege of**: 117, 145-146
- **Captives Return to Jerusalem**: 148, 154-155, 158-159
- **Church in Jerusalem**: 196, 204
- **Destroyed by Babylon**: 141, 143, 147, 154, 158
- **Destroyed by Rome**: 101, 168, 175, 204-205
- **Herod's Temple and Temple Complex**: 174-176, 180, 182, 184-188, 198-199, 204
- **Jesus in Jerusalem**: 11, 174, 182, 188, 198-199, 202
- **Nehemiah Rebuilds Jerusalem's Wall**: 148, 158-159
- **Political and Spiritual Capital of Israel**: 90, 105
- **Second Temple**:148-149, 154-158, 176-177
- **Solomon's Temple (First Temple)**: 6, 90-91, 105, 107-109, 140-141, 143, 147, 151, 184, 186
- **Western Wall**: 11, 184, 204

Jerwan Aqueduct: 91

Jeshua: 155-157

Jesse: 99, 180, 196

Jesus: 11-13, 16-17, 24, 28, 30-35, 53, 58, 74-75, 83, 87, 99, 103, 105, 125, 142, 156, 167, 170, 173-174, 176-183 (map), 184-185, 188-204, 206-207

- **Anointing at Bethany**: 198
- **Ascension**: 174, 202-203
- **Birth**: 11, 167, 170, 174, 178, 180-181
- **Baptism**: 12, 174, 189
- **Christmas**: 178
- **Crucifixion**: 11, 174, 185, 196, 199, 200-201, 203
- **Divinity**: 12, 181-182, 194-203, 206-207
- **Early Years**: 174, 182-183
- **Eternal King**: 105, 178, 180-181, 207
- **Evidence for**: 178, 196, 203
- **Flight to Egypt**: 183 (map), 204
- **Genealogy**: 58, 76, 99, 156, 180, 196
- **Historical Jesus**: 178, 180-181, 196, 203
- **I AM Statements of Jesus**: 197
- **Jesus as the Christ**: 12, 15, 32-33, 53, 74, 83, 87, 99, 103, 167, 170, 174, 178-179, 181-182, 189-190, 198-199
- **Jesus as Creator**: 16-17, 179, 204
- **Last Week of Jesus' Life**: 11, 198-199
- **Lineage of Jesus**: 58, 76, 99, 105, 156, 180, 156, 196
- **Lost at the Temple**: 188
- **Magi's Visit**: 182
- **Messiah, Jesus the**: 75, 143, 149, 174, 176-177, 180, 182, 189, 190, 196
- **Ministry of Jesus**: 146, 167, 190-191, 194-195
- **Miracles**: 12, 31, 190, 194-195, 196, 202
- **Parables**: 23, 192-193
- **Post-Resurrection Appearances**: 202-203
- **Preparation of Jesus**: 188-189
- **Prophecies, Fulfilled by Jesus**: 11, 105, 180-183, 190, 196, 198-199
- **Resurrection**: 11, 28, 74, 103, 174, 196, 200-202
- **Savior**: 8, 12-13, 33-35, 53, 75, 125, 177-179, 181, 190-192, 196-197, 203, 206-207
- **Temptation**: 189
- **Virgin Birth**: 11, 181

Jesus Boat: 194

Jethro: 92

Jewish Revolt: 175, 204-205

Jewish War, The: 175

Jews: 74, 99, 101, 148, 153-159, 165, 168, 175-177, 181-182, 188-189, 190, 193, 195, 198-199, 203-205

Jezebel: 140, 142

Jimmu, Emperor: 132

Joanna: 202

Job, Book of: 9, 29

Joel: 141

John the Baptist: 11, 174, 180, 184, 189

John, Book of: 10-12, 16-17, 87, 175, 190-191, 194-198, 202, 206-207

John, Disciple: 14, 175, 190, 202

Jomon: 132

Jonah: 91, 140, 145

Joppa: 140 (map), 156

Jordan, Country of: 96 (map), 107, 110-111, 148

Jordan River: 12, 74, 86 (map), 96 (map), 97-98, 100, 189

Joseph (Jacob's Son): 9, 73, 76-77, 84, 88-89, 97

Joseph, Jesus' Earthly Father: 170, 180-183 (map), 184, 188, 204

Joseph of Arimathea: 11, 199

Josephus, Flavius: 10, 175-176, 188, 203

Joshua: 90, 96, 98-101, 103

Josiah, King: 141, 143, 180

Jotham, King: 141, 143, 180

Judah: 11, 30, 76, 90-91, 97, 99, 105, 117, 140 (map)-143, 145 (map)-147, 151, 154-156, 176, 180

- **Kingdom of Judah**: 30, 90-91, 105, 117, 140 (map)-143, 145 (map)-147, 151, 154-156
- **Prophets of Judah**: 141
- **Return to Jerusalem**: 154-155, 158-159
- **Tribe of Judah**: 97, 104, 140, 151
- **Under Attack**: 117, 145-147

Judas, Disciple: 11, 190, 198-199, 202

Jude: 175, 196

Judea: 101, 149, 167, 170, 174, 176-177, 182, 184, 188, 199, 202, 204-205

Judean Date Palm: 205

Judge(s): 90, 99, 104

Julian Calendar: 149, 171, 180

Julius Caesar: 125, 149, 167-168, 170-173, 180

K

Kadesh: 10, 84-85, 100 (map)

Kashta, King: 116

Kazakhstan: 126

Kepler, Johannes: 15, 30

Khufu, Pharaoh: 72

Kind, According to its: 22-23, 26, 28-29, 40

King James Bible: 10, 15

Kingdom of God: 190-192, 197, 207

Kings and Prophets of Divided Kingdom of Israel: 140-143

King's Highway: 96 (map)-97

Knossos: 78, 80 (map), 81, 100 (map)

Kofun: 133

Korea: 130 (map), 132

Kshatriyas: 118

Kukulkan: 136

Kurgan: 126

Kush: See Cush

Kyushu: 132

L

La Venta: 136 (map)
Lachish: 140 (map)
Lake Biwa: 133
Lake Superior: 62
Lake Titicaca: 138
Lamassu: (Assyrian Winged Lion) 144
Lambeosaurinae: 46-47
Lamech: 14
Land of the Rising Sun: 6, 132
Last Supper: 198
Last Week of Jesus' Life: 11, 198-199
Latin: 171, 178
Law of Moses : 157, 159, 182, 190
Law of the Twelve Tables: 171
Lazarus: 195, 198
Lebanon: 102, 107, 156
Legalism, China: 128
Leonardo, the *Brachylophosaurus*: 47
Lepidus: 173
Levites: 95, 98, 108, 143, 155-156
Lewis, C.S.: 178
Library of Alexandria: 148, 165, 172, 174
Life After Babel: 60-61
Life Along the Nile: 66-67
Life in Sumer: 64-65, 74
Life, Value of: 8, 31-32
Lighthouse of Alexandria: 165
Lineage of Jesus: 58, 76, 99, 105, 156, 180, 156, 196
Linear A: 79
Linear B: 81
Lion's Gate: 81, 84
Literal: 15, 17, 23, 30, 37, 64
Little Grand Canyon: 53
Liu Bang: 130
London: 122 (map), 123, 174
Lost Tribes of Israel: 145
Lot, Abraham's Nephew: 34, 72, 87
Lots, Casting: 98
Louisiana: 9, 62, 135
Louvre, The: 82
Lower Egypt: 66 (map), 73 (map)
Lucian: 203
Lucy: 32
Luke, Book of: 11, 167, 170, 175, 180-182, 188, 192-195, 202
Luoyang: 131
Luxor, Egypt: 73, 77

M

Maccabeus, Judas (or Judah Maccabee): 149, 176
Macedonia: 119, 164 (map), 170 (map)
Madagascar: 113 (map)
Magi: 153, 182
Mahalael: 14
Malachi: 11, 141, 148
Manna: 94-95
Mara Bar-Serapion: 203
Marcus Aurelius, Emperor: 175
Marginocephalia: 41, 48-49
Mark Antony: 149, 167, 170, 173 (map)
Marriage. 8, 31, 83, 106, 142, 159
Mars, Roman god: 166
Mary Magdalene: 200, 202
Mary, Mother of James: 202
Mary, Mother of Jesus: 11, 170, 174, 180-183 (map), 188, 204
Mary, Sister of Lazarus: 198
Masada: 175, 205
Matthew, Book of: 10-11, 23, 170, 175, 180, 184, 190, 192, 194-196, 198, 200, 202
Matthew, Disciple: 10, 180, 190
Mature Universe: 24, 37
Maury, Matthew: 11
Mauryan Empire: 119, 148
Mawangdui Archaeological Site: 130
Maya: 67
Medes: 145, 150-152
Media, Kingdom of: 152 (map), 164 (map)
Mediterranean Sea: 58 (map), 62-63 (map), 64 (map), 65-66 (map), 73 (map), 74, 78-79, 80, 86 (map), 96 (map), 97, 100 (map)-102 (map), 103, 107, 111, 113 (map), 116-117, 122, 140 (map), 145 (map), 152 (map), 156, 158 (map), 164 (map), 165-166 (map), 169-170, 172, 183 (map)
Megalosaurus: 42
Memphis, Egypt: 64 (map), 66 (map), 72-73 (map), 100 (map), 102 (map), 117, 164 (map)
Menes, King: 72
Mercy Seat: 95, 109
Meroë: 117
Meshach: 147, 151
Mesoamerica: 136
Mesopotamia: 8-9, 55, 58-60, 62-64 (map), 68, 74, 82, 144-145 (map), 164 (map) 82, 144
Messiah, Jesus the: 75, 143, 149, 174, 176-177, 180, 182, 189, 190, 196
Messianic Prophet: 143
Methuselah: 14, 205
Mexico: 59, 90, 136, 175
Micah: 11, 141, 182
Middle East: 62-63 (map), 170, 173
Middle Kingdom, Egypt: 72
Midian: 92, 96 (map), 99
Migration of Humanity: 61, 134-135
Ministry of Jesus: 11, 146, 167, 189-191, 194-195
Minoans, The: 63, 78-81
Minos, King: 78
Miracles of Jesus: 12, 31, 190, 194-195, 196, 202
Mirian: 93, 97
"Missing link": 32
Mississippi River: 62, 135
Mississippian Culture: 59
Missouri River: 62
Mizpeh: 104
Mizraim: 8, 66-67, 116
Moab: 96 (map), 98-99, 140 (map)
Models and Theories of Science: 36, 41, 57
Mohenjo-Daro: 68-69, 117
Mongolia: 42, 48, 126, 129
Moral Right and Wrong: 33, 35-36, 83
Mordecai: 153
Morris, Henry: 15
Moses: 9-10, 14, 17, 73, 83, 89-90, 92-94, 96-98, 109, 142, 157, 159, 177, 182, 190, 197
Mound Builders: 59, 122-123, 126, 133, 135-136
Mount Everest: 62
Mount Horeb: 92, 96 (map)
Mount Kilimanjaro: 113 (map)
Mount McKinley: 62
Mount Moriah: 108, 186
Mount of Olives: 199, 202-203
Mount of Transfiguration: 142

Mount Sinai: 83, 94, 92, 96 (map)
Mount St. Helens: 53-54, 56
Mount Vesuvius: 169, 175
Mummies: 67, 77
Musical instruments: 8, 39, 60, 139
Muslims: 47, 74, 101, 139
Muwatalli II, King: 85
Mycenae: 80 (map), 81, 100 (map)
Mycenaeans, The: 63, 79, 80(map)-81, 100, 160
Myrrh: 110, 182

N

Naaman: 142
Nabataeans: 111
Nabonidus, King: 151
Nabopolassar: 150
Nagaoka-kyō: 133
Napata: 116-117
Nabta Playa, Egypt: 73 (map), 120
Nara: 133
Narmer, King: 72
Nathan: 180
Native Americans: 55, 134-135
Natural History: 175
Nazareth: 140 (map), 183 (map), 188, 190
Nazarite (Nazirite): 104, 180, 187, 189
Nazca Civilization: 139
Nazca Lines: 139
Neanderthals: 60
Nebuchadnezzar, King: 91, 101, 141, 143, 147, 150-151, 154, 158
Nehemiah: 148, 158-159
New Kingdom, Egypt: 73
New Orleans: 66, 135
New Testament: 10-11, 16, 35, 140, 177-178, 186, 196, 207
Newgrange Burial Mound: 123
Newton, Isaac: 15, 30
Nicodemus: 177, 191
Niger River: 115
Nile River: 58 (map), 63, 66 (map)-67, 77, 89, 92, 96 (map), 113 (map), 116, 145 (map), 159, 164 (map)
  - **Life Along the Nile**: 66-67
  - **Nile Delta**: 66 (map), 73 (map), 96 (map)

Nimrod: 8, 64
Nineveh: 64, 91, 100 (map), 144-145 (map)
Nippur Library: 63
Noah: 4, 8-9, 14, 22, 47, 49, 52-56, 58-61, 64, 66, 68, 70, 74, 78, 86, 112, 116, 122, 134
  - **Ham, Noah's Son**: 58 (map), 66, 74, 86
  - **Japheth**: 58 (map), 78, 122
  - **Mizraim**: 8, 66-67, 116
  - **Noah's Ark**: 8, 47, 52-55, 60
  - **Noah's Descendants**: 55, 58 (map)-61, 64, 66, 68, 70, 74, 78, 86, 116, 122
  - **Shem**: 58 (map)
  - **Worldwide Flood, See Flood**

North America: 45, 47, 59, 61 (map), 62 (map), 134-136
North American Indians (Indigenous Peoples): 55, 134-135
Northeast Tribes of North America: 135
Northern Ireland: 122 (map)
Nothing Is Nothing: 18
Nubia: 66 (map), 72, 116-117

O

Oard, Michael J.: 57, 61
Obadiah: 141
Obed: 99, 180
Observable Universe: 24
Octavian: 167, 170, 173 (map)-174, 181
Ohio: 135
Old Kingdom, Egypt: 72
Old or Young Earth?: 17, 35, 41, 53, 57
Old Testament:10-11, 16, 35, 64, 86, 106, 148, 159, 165, 177, 196, 198
Olives, Trees and Oil: 79, 104, 199
Olmecs: 90, 136 (map)
Olympia: 148, 161
Olympics: 91, 161
Omnipotent God: 12, 206
Omnipresent God: 12, 206
Omniscient God: 12, 19, 206
Omri, King: 90, 140
Ona: 137
Ophir: 107
Oracle Bones: 71
Orkney Islands: 122
Ornithopods: 40, 46-47
Othniel: 99
Outer Space: 16, 18-19, 20-22, 24-25, 37
Oviraptor: 42
Owen, Richard: 51

P

Pachycephalosaurus: 48
Pacific Northwest Tribes of North America: 134
Pacific Ocean: 62-63 (map), 132, 134 (map), 136 (map), 138
Palace of Zakros: 79
Paleontologists: 40, 42-43, 47
Palestina: 101
Palestinians: 101
Pangea: 45
Pantheon: 174
Papyrus: 9, 66, 89, 94
Parables of Jesus: 23, 192-193
Paracas Culture: 139
Paracas Peninsula: 139
Parasaurolophus: 47
Parchment: 149
Paris: 82, 122 (map)
Parthenon: 148, 160-161
Passover: 93, 143, 157, 188, 198-199
Patricians: 166
Patrick: 125
Paul the Apostle: 32, 125, 174
  - **Arrives in Rome**: 174
  - **Conversion**: 174
  - **First Missionary Journey**: 174
  - **Letters of**: 178

Peloponnesian War: 148, 160, 162, 164
Pentateuch: 94
Perfect Plan of God: 12-13, 19, 25, 35, 75
Pergamum: 149
Pericles: 160-162
Persepolis: 152 (map), 164 (map)
Persia: 149, 152-154, 158 (map)
Persian Empire: 151-152 (map), 153-154, 157, 159-160, 162, 164-165, 182
Persian Gulf: 58 (map), 64 (map), 65, 68, 145 (map), 152 (map), 164 (map)
Persian Wars: 148, 162
Peru: 6, 57, 63, 138-139
Peter, Books of 1st and 2nd: 25, 175, 190-191
Peter, Simon (Disciple): 184, 190, 194, 202
Petra: 110-111, 148

Pharaohs and Pyramids of Egypt: 10, 66 (map)-67, 72-73, 76-77, 84-85, 88-89, 92-94, 100, 106-107, 116-117, 135, 148-149, 172-173

Pharisees: 149, 176-177, 191-192

Pharos: 165

Phidias: 148

Philip, Disciple: 190

Philip II, King: 164

Philippians, Book of: 175

Philippines: 62

Philistia: 86 (map), 96 (map), 100, 102, 140 (map)

Philistines: 91, 99-102, 104-105, 107, 205

Phoenicia: 102 (map)-103, 140 (map), 144, 145 (map)

Phoenician(s): 90, 102-103, 107-108, 140, 142, 171, 186

Physics: 11

Pirates: 6, 102

Pithom: 89, 96 (map)

Piye (Piankhi): 116

Plagues of Egypt, Ten: 92-93

Planet: 18-19, 21-22, 24-25, 56, 61, 63, 110

Plate Tectonics: 22, 45

Plato: 148, 162

Plebians: 166

Plesiosaurus: 51

Pliny the Elder: 175

Pliny the Younger: 10

Poem of Pentaur: 84

Poetics: 163

Pompey: 149, 177

Pontius Pilate: 174, 199, 203

Porch, Herod's Temple: 185-187

Post-Resurrection Appearances of Jesus: 202-203

Potiphar: 76

Poverty Point: 9, 62, 135

Praetorian Guard: 168

Pre-Flood World: 38-39, 85

Prehistoric or Ancient History?: 36, 114

Preparation of Jesus: 188-189

Priest(s), God's Holy: 76, 98-99, 104, 108-109, 141, 143, 155-157, 159, 176-177, 180, 182, 184-187

Primary Sources: 10, 121

Promised Land: 88, 90, 92, 95-98, 100-103, 204

Prophecies: 11, 33, 103, 105, 117, 140-141, 151, 154, 165, 176-178, 180-183, 190, 196, 198-199, 203-204

- **Fulfilled Prophecies**: 11, 105, 117, 151, 154, 165, 180-183, 190, 196, 198-199, 203-204
- **Prophecies, Fulfilled by Jesus**: 11, 105, 180-183, 190, 196, 198-199, 203

Prophets, Biblical: 5, 11, 14, 94, 103-104, 140-142, 147, 154, 157, 177-178, 190, 196, 203

- **Amos**: 104-141
- **Anna (Prophetess)**: 182
- **Daniel**: 14, 151, 153
- **Elijah**: 140-142
- **Elisha**: 140-142
- **Ezekiel**: 140-141, 147
- **Habakkuk**: 140-141
- **Haggai**: 140-141, 157
- **Hosea**: 140-141
- **Isaiah**: 117, 181, 196
- **Jeremiah**: 140-141, 146, 154
- **Joel**: 140-141
- **John the Baptist**: 189
- **Jonah**: 140-141
- **Micah**: 140-141, 154, 182
- **Obadiah**: 140-141
- **Profiles of Prophets and Kings**: 142-143
- **Samuel**: 104
- **Zechariah**: 11, 140-141, 157, 180
- **Zephaniah**: 140-141

Prophets, Books of the: 177, 190

Prophets of Baal and Asherah: 142

Protoceratops: 48

Proverbs: 35, 106

Provinces: 101, 144, 153, 167, 168-170, 177, 204-205

Psalms: 11, 24-25, 76, 104, 177

Psittacosaurus: 48

Pterodactyl: 51

Ptolemaic Dynasty: 148, 172-173

Ptolemaic Period: 172-173

Ptolemy Philadelphus: 173

Ptolemy I: 148, 172

Ptolemy XIII: 172

Ptolemy XIV: 172-173

Punic Wars: 149, 166 (map)

Purim: 153

Pyramids: 6, 9, 59, 66 (map), 67, 72, 116-117, 123, 135-136, 167, 172

Pythagoras: 148, 162

Q

Qin (Chi'in) Dynasty: 128-129, 130-131, 149

Qin Shi Huangdi: 128-129, 149

Queen of Sheba: 106

Qumran, Israel: 11, 177

R

Raamses (Ramases): 89, 96 (map)

Rahab: 98-99

Rainbow: 53

Ramses II: 10, 84-85, 100

Ramses III: 100

Rebekah: 58, 76-77

Red Sea: 58 (map), 64 (map), 66 (map), 73 (map), 93, 96 (map), 110 (map), 113 (map), 152 (map), 164 (map)

Rehoboam, King: 140-141, 180

Remus: 166

Republic of Rome: 148, 166-167

Res Gestae Divi Augusti: 181

Resurrection of Jesus: 11, 28, 74, 103, 174, 196-197, 200-203

Return to Jerusalem: 154-155, 158 (map)-159

Rhind Papyrus: 9

Ring Forts: 123

River of Sorrow (China's Sorrow): 70, 131

Rock Art: 115

Roman Empire: 91, 99, 101, 125, 130, 146, 148-149, 151, 166-167, 168-170 (map), 171-175, 177, 181, 196, 199, 202-205

- **Alphabet**: 171
- **Building an Empire**: 168-169
- **Census**: 170, 174, 181, 183 (map)
- **Conquered Celtic Tribes**: 125
- **Conquered Israel**: 99, 101, 149, 204-205
- **Conquered Jerusalem**: 149, 204-205
- **Destroyed Carthage**: 103, 166
- **Destroyed Jerusalem**: 101, 168, 175, 104-105
- **Fall of Roman Empire**: 175, 205
- **Founding of Rome**: 91, 166
- **Great Fire of Rome**: 175
- **Law of the Twelve Tables**: 171
- **Occupation of British Isles**: 125

Provinces of Rome: 167-170, 177, 204-205
Republic of Rome: 148, 166-167
Rome, Attack of: 124, 148, 171
Roads: 169
Ruled the World: 167, 170-171, 204
Senate: 166-167, 173
Trade: 130, 166
War with Egypt: 173
Rome, City of: 91, 103, 124, 130 (map), 148-149, 166 (map)-169, 170 (map)-177, 184, 204-205
Romulus: 166
Rosetta, Egypt: 73 (map)
Rosetta Stone: 67, 149
Royal Library of the Hittites: 84
Royal Library of Nineveh: 144-145
Royal Road of Persia: 152 (map)
Russia: 48, 58, 132, 134 (map)
Ruth: 99

S

Saba: 111
Sadducees: 16, 149, 176-177
Sahara Desert: 63, 66, 112-113 (map), 115
Sallon, Sarah: 205
Salmon, Fish: 134
Salmon, Husband of Rahab: 99, 180
Samaria: 90, 140 (map), 145-146, 158-159
Samaritans: 140, 193
Samson: 99, 104
Samuel: 10-11, 90, 99, 104
San Lorenzo: 136 (map)
Sanballat: 158-159
Sanctity of Life: 8, 31-32
Sanhedrin: 199
Sanskrit: 90, 118
Santorini: 79
Sarah, Abraham's Wife: 74-77, 205
Sardis: 100 (map), 152 (map)
Sargon II, King: 140
Sarmatians: 127
Sarsen Stones: 120
Satan: 19, 33-35, 37, 189, 195, 198
Saul, King: 90, 101, 104-105
Saurolophinae: 46
Sauropods: 29, 41, 44-45, 54
Savanna, African: 112-113 (map)
Savior: 8, 12-13, 33-35, 53, 75, 125, 177-179, 181, 190-192, 196-197, 203, 206-207
Schweitzer, Mary: 47
Science: 10-11, 15, 17-19, 22, 25, 27, 29-33, 35-37, 39-43, 45, 47, 49, 53-55, 57, 60-61, 114, 119, 121, 135, 145, 160, 162, 206
Science and the Bible: 10, 15, 17-19, 29, 31, 36-37, 40-41, 54-55, 57, 60-61, 121, 206
Creation Scientists: 15, 17, 25, 27, 37, 39-41, 47, 57, 60-61, 114, 135
Laws of Science: 31
Scientific Discoveries: 11, 18-19, 33, 53, 121, 206
Scientific Methods: 17, 40-41, 57, 135
Scotland: 122 (map), 125
Scripture Confirms Scripture: 17
Scythia: 152 (map)
Scythian(s): 91, 127
Sea of Galilee: 140 (map), 145 (map), 194, 202
Sea Peoples: 81, 100 (map)-102
Second Temple: 148-149, 154-158, 176-177
Second Triumvirate: 173
Secular Worldview: 40-41, 57
Senate: 166-167, 173
Sennacherib Prism: 146
Sennacherib, King: 117, 145-146
Septuagint: 148, 165
Serengeti Plains: 112-113
Sermon on the Mount: 190
Seth: 14
Seven Wonders of the Ancient World: 150, 165
Shabako (Shabaqo), Pharaoh: 116
Shadrach: 147, 151
Shaft Graves: 81
Shang Dynasty: 9, 71, 128
Sheba: 106, 111
Shebitku, Pharaoh: 116
Shechem: 86 (map), 140 (map)
Shem: 58 (map)
Shepherds and flocks: 8, 38
Shetland Islands: 122
Shi Huangdi: 71, 128-129
Shikoku: 132
Shiloh: 96, 104, 140 (map)
Shinar: 58, 64
Shinto: 133
Shotoku, Prince: 133
Shudras: 118
Shuo Wen: 131
Siberia: 61, 134
Siddhartha Gautama: 119
Sidon: 102 (map), 103, 156
Silbury Hill: 122
Silk: 9, 71, 111, 130
Silk Road: 130 (map)
Siloam Tunnel: 146
Simeon: 76, 97, 145, 174, 180, 182
Simon, Disciple: 190
Simon Peter: 184, 190, 194, 202
Sinai Peninsula: 66 (map), 73 (map), 96 (map), 145 (map)
Sisera: 99
Sui Dynasty: 130
Six Dynasties Period: 130
Slavery: 73, 76, 82-83, 89, 92, 97, 166-168, 205
Smart from the Start: 39, 114, 121
Socrates: 148, 162
Sodom: 86 (map)-87
Solar System: 19, 22-25, 27
Solomon, King: 6, 90, 96, 103, 105-108, 140-142, 151, 180, 186
Solomon's Temple: 6, 90-91, 105, 107-109, 140-141, 143, 147, 151, 184, 186
Destruction of: 91, 147, 151
Diagram of: 108-109
Furniture: 108-109
Porch, Solomon's: 185
Rooms: 108-109
Song of Solomon: 106
South America: 59, 61-63 (map), 91, 102, 134, 136-137 (map), 138
Southeast Tribes of North America: 135
Southwest Tribes of North America: 135
Southern Ocean: 62-63 (map)
Spain: 166 (map), 169-170 (map)
Sparta: 90, 148, 160, 162, 164
Spartacus: 149
Spinosaurus: 43
Stegosaurus: 41, 50
Stele: 82-83, 105, 116
Step Pyramid: 72
Stephen: 174

Steppes: 91, 126-127, 129
Stone Age: 39
Stonehenge: 120-123
Strobel, Lee: 178
Stylus: 64
Styracosaurus: 49
Subarctic: 134
Sudan: 66 (map), 113 (map), 116-117
Sue, the Tyrannosaurus rex: 43
Sumer: 38, 63, 64 (map)-65, 67, 72, 74
Sumerian King List: 63
Susa: 82, 145 (map), 152 (map), 158 (map), 164 (map)
Syria: 164, 170 (map) 172

T

Ta Prohm: 50
Tabernacle: 94-95, 98, 104-105, 108-109
Tacitus: 203
Taharka, Pharaoh (Taharqa, Taharqo, or Tirhakah): 116-117
Tang (T'ang) Dynasty: 130, 133
Tang, Emperor: 9, 71
Tanutamani, Pharaoh (Tantamani): 116
Tarshish: 107
Tattenai: 157
Tel Dan: 105
Tel Dan Stele: 105
Temple for Jupiter: 205
Temple for Pagan Religions: 6, 50, 65, 67, 73-74, 80, 84, 100, 117, 133, 136, 138, 144-145, 150, 154, 160-161, 167-168, 176, 205
Temple for Zeus: 176
Temple in Jerusalem: 6, 90-91, 103, 105, 107-109, 140-143, 146-149, 151, 154-158, 174-177, 180, 182, 184-188, 198-199, 204-205
  Herod's Temple and Temple Complex: 174-176, 180, 182, 184-188, 198-199, 204
  Second Temple: 148-149, 154-158, 176-177
  Solomon's Temple: 6, 90-91, 105, 107-109, 140-141, 143, 147, 151, 184, 186
Temple Mount: 156, 184, 186, 202-205
Temptation of Jesus: 189
Ten Commandments: 4, 30, 83, 90, 94-95, 190
Ten Lost Tribes of Israel: 145
Ten Plagues:92-93
Tent of Meeting: 108
Teotihuacán: 175
Terah: 74
Terra-Cotta Army: 129, 149
Thaddaeus, Disciples: 190
Thagomizer: 50
Thales: 162
Thallus: 203
Theater of Dionysus: 160
Thebes: 64 (map), 66 (map), 73 (map)
Thera: 79
Therapods: 40, 42-43
Thomas, Disciple: 190, 202
Three-Act Structure: 163
Thucydides: 162
Thutmose III, Pharaoh: 73
Thyreophora: 41, 50
Tierra del Fuego: 137
Tigris River: 58 (map), 64 (map), 82, 144, 145 (map), 164 (map)
Tigris-Euphrates Valley: 62
Tirhakah, Pharaoh (Taharka, Taharqa, or Taharqo): 116-117
Titus, Book of: 175
Titus, Emperor: 101, 168, 175, 204
Tobiah: 158
Tomb Banner, China: 130
Tomb of Cyrus the Great: 154
Torah: 177, 191
Torii Gate: 133
Toutle River: 53
Tower of Babel: 8, 58-63, 66, 68, 70, 78, 86, 114 (map), 121-122, 134-135
Trade: 9, 62, 64 (map)-66, 68-69, 72, 74, 76, 79, 80-81, 83, 85, 89, 96 (map), 102-103, 106-107, 110-111, 117-118, 123, 125-128, 130 (map), 135-136, 141, 152 (map), 165-166, 188
Transitional Fossils: 32, 41
Treaty of Kadesh: 10, 84
Tree of Knowledge: 34
Tribes of North America, Indigenous: 134-135
Triceratops: 41, 45, 49
Trinity: 12, 16, 189, 196
  God the Father: 12, 16, 189, 196
  God the Holy Spirit: 12, 16, 181, 189, 196, 206, 207
  God the Son: 12, 16, 189, 196
Trojan Horse: 80
Tropic of Cancer: 120
Troy: 80 (map), 90, 100 (map), 164 (map)
Trust the Bible: 6, 10-11, 17, 32-33, 36-37, 52, 59, 64, 67, 103, 105, 114, 159, 180, 203, 206
Tunnel of Hezekiah: 146
Turkey: 74, 80, 84, 90, 124
Tutankhamen, King (and Pharaoh): 77
Twelve Tribes of Israel: 97
Tyrannosaurus rex: 43, 45, 47, 49
Tyre: 100 (map), 102 (map), 103, 107, 140, 156, 164 (map)

U

Uniformitarian Model: 57
United Kingdom: 122
United States: 134 (map)
United States Supreme Court Building: 83
Untouchables: 118
Upper Egypt: 66 (map), 72-73
Upper Room: 198, 202
Ur: 59, 64 (map)-65, 72, 74, 88, 145 (map)
Ural Mountains: 63
Uriah: 105
Ussher, James: 15, 30
Utah: 43, 54, 135
Uzziah, King: 141, 143, 180

V

Vaishyas: 118
Valley of the Kings: 66 (map), 73, 77
Value of Life: 8, 31-32
Vedas: 90, 118
Velociraptor: 42
Victoria Falls: 113 (map)
Victoria, Lake: 66 (map)
Vietnam: 130 (map)
Vikings: 39
Villages, Early: 39, 65-66, 68
Virgin Birth of Jesus: 11, 181

W

Waiting for the Messiah: 146, 176-177
Wales: 120, 122 (map)-123, 125
Wallace, J. Warner: 178
Wang Mang, Emperor: 131

Warring States Period, China: 128 (map)
West and Southwest Tribes of North America: 135
West Virginia Geological and Economic Survey Museum: 47
Western Civilization: 63, 130, 162
Western Han Period: 130
Western Wall: 11, 184, 204
Wheel, Invention of: 65
Wheel of the Giants: 120
Wilderness of Sinai: 96 (map)
Wilderness of Zin: 97
Winckler, Hugo: 84
Wise Men: 153, 174, 180, 182
Witchcraft: 143
Woolley, Leonard: 65
Worldview: 6, 17, 36, 40-41
Wu (Wudi), Emperor: 130-131

X

Xerxes (Ahaseurus), King: 153, 157
Xi Ling Ji, Empress: 71
Xia (Hsia) Dynasty: 71, 128
Xianyang: 128
Xin Dynasty: 131
Xi'an: 128

Y

Yahgan: 137
Yahweh: 157
Yamato: 132-133
Yangtze River: 70, 128 (map)
Yao, Emperor: 71
Yayoi: 132-133, 148
Yellow Emperor (Huangdi): 71, 128-129
Yellow River (Huang He): 4, 9, 62, 70-71, 128 (map), 131
Yellow River Valley: 9, 62, 70-71
Yemen: 111
Yo-Yos: 148
Young Earth: 17, 35, 41, 53, 57
Yu, Emperor: 71
Yucatán State, Mexico: 59

Z

Zakros, Palace of: 79
Zechariah: 11, 140-141, 157, 180, 198
Zephaniah: 141
Zerubbabel: 155-157, 180
Zeus: 148, 161, 176
Zhao Zheng: 128
Zhou (Chou) Dynasty: 128 (map)
Ziggurat of Ur: 59, 65
Ziggurats: 6, 59, 65, 72, 74, 150
Zipporah: 92
Zoroastrianism: 153
Zoser(Djoser), Pharaoh: 72

IMAGE CREDITS:

All images from Shutterstock.com and Adobe Stock are used under license with an active subscription. Wikimedia images are public domain (PD-US and PD-Art). Other credits are as follows:

Answers in Genesis / Creation Museum / Ark Encounter: p. 16 (Day 6); p. 32 (Lucy); p. 36 (Two Models); p. 54 (Ark Encounter); p. 114 (Dispersion of Humans by Early Ice Age)

iStock.com: p. 38 (Stone Kitchen Tool)

Design Pickle: p. 108–109 (Solomon's Temple); p. 184–185 (Herod's Temple)

Master Books — Bill Loney: p. 8; p. 29; p. 39 (Musical Instruments & Tower of Babel); p. 42 (Dinosaurs); p. 43 (Allosaurus & T-Rex); p. 44 (Diplodocus & Apatosaurus); p. 46 (Iguanodon); p. 47 (Parasaurolophus); p. 48 (Protoceratops); p. 49 (Triceratops; Styracosaurus); p. 51 (Pterodactyl; Plesiosaurus; Ichthyosaurus); p. 55 (Noah; Flood Legends); p. 58 (Noah's Sons; Tower of Babel); p. 59 (Leaving the Tower of Babel); p. 60 (Cavemen); p. 61 (Hunting; Ice Age); p. 96 (Joshua and Caleb); p. 98 (Battle of Jericho); p. 114 (Adam Farming); p. 199 (The Lamb of God)

Map Trek: p. 64 (Mesopotamia); p. 66 (Ancient Egypt)

Flickr.com: p. 123 (Shield / darkdwarf)

Superstock.com: p. 125 (Celtic Settlement)

NPS (National Park Service): p. 135 (Poverty Point Map and Artifacts)

NLPG Staff: p. 10; p. 15 (Adams Chart; Henry Morris); p. 178 (King James Bible); p. 186–187 (Herod's Temple Mount and Complex); p. 191 (God's Remedy)

Secrets of Ancient Man: p. 90; p. 136 (Olmec Culture)

Images from Wikimedia Commons are used under the CC0 1.0; CC BY-SA 2.0 DE; CC-BY-SA-3.0 license or the GNU Free Documentation License; Version 1.3.
Wiki/4.0 international/TomaszSwatowski: p 16 B.
Wiki/4.0/Geostationary Operational Environmental Satellite Program: pg 27 L
Wiki/4.0 International/Helioseismic and Magnetic Imagery (HMI): p 38

These images were AI-developed.

Cover images; p. 9 (Abraham; Jacob and Sons; Moses Born; Horse-Drawn Chariots; Joseph Sold); p. 14 (Adam to Noah); p. 16 (Day 1–Day 5); p. 34 (Robot or Human; Adam and Eve); p. 35 (Old or Young Earth); p. 37 (Caveman or Ancient Man); p. 52 (Noah; Water Covered Earth); p. 55 (Double-Hulled Canoe), p. 65 (Ancient Ur); p. 67 (Building Pyramids); p. 72 (The Middle Kingdom); p. 74 (Abram Leaving); p. 75 (Abraham and Sarah; Abraham and Son); p. 76 (all images); p. 77 (Horse-Drawn Chariots); p. 79 (Seafaring Traders); p. 80 (Trojan Horse); p 83 (Hammurab's Court); p. 87 (all images); p. 88 (all images); p. 89 (all images); p. 90 (Joshua Leads; David Becomes King; Israel Splits; Deborah; King David); p. 91 (Jonahand the whale); (Hanging Gardens; Jeremiah; Nebuchadnezzar); p. 92 (Ten Plagues of Egypt); p. 93 (all images); p. 94 (Mount Sinai; Moses Writing); p. 97 (Twelve Tribes); p. 98 (Rahab); p. 99 (all images); p. 101 (David and Goliath); p. 104 (Samuel; Broken Crown; Eli's Sons); p. 105 (Ark of the Covenant; David Leading); p. 114 (Scientist); p. 118 (Hinduism); p. 119 (Buddhism; Alexander the Great; Conqueror); p. 120–121 (Henge Construction); p. 123 (Celtic Life and Dress); p. 129 (Building China's Great Wall); p. 131 (Buddhism; River of Sorrow); p. 132 (Yayoi); p. 133 (Sacred Tomb); p. 140 (Solomon; Prophets); p. 141 (Peace and Prosperity); p. 142 (all images); p. 143 (all images); p. 145 (Jonah); p. 146 (Hezekiah Cried Out to God); p. 147 (all images); p. 148 (Hippocrates); p. 148 (Anna; Cleopatra); p. 150 (Hanging Gardens of Babylon); p. 151 (all images); p. 152 (Writing the Cyrus Cylinder); p. 153 (all images); p. 154 (Jeremiah; Cyrus Family); p. 155 (all images); p. 156 (Laying the Foundation); p. 157 (all images); p. 158 (Nehemiah; Building the Wall); p. 159 (Ezra Reading the Bible); p. 160 (Spartan Boys); p. 161 (Athens; Political Gathering in the Agora); p. 162 (all images); p. 163 (Literature; Art; Religion); p. 164 (Alexander Led His Troops); p. 165 (Daniel's Prophecy); p. 166 (Wolf and Twin Brothers; Social Structure); p. 167 (all images); p. 168 (Circus Maximus; Colosseum Cutaway); p. 170 (Mark Antony; Octavian; Cleopatra); p. 171 (Law of the Twelve Tables); p. 172 (Library; Cleopatra and Co-Rulers); p. 173 (Palace in Alexandria; Cleopatra's Family); p. 174 (Mary and the Angel; Birth of Jesus; Saul's Conversion; Paul in Rome); p. 175 (Colosseum in Rome); p. 176 (all images); p. 177 (all images); p. 180 (Zechariah and Elizabeth with Baby); p. 181 (Virgin Birth; Fit for a King; Heavenly Choir); p. 182 (The Magi; Magi Presenting Gifts); p. 183 (Decree From Herod; Flight to Egypt); p. 188 (Growing Up in Nazareth; Lost!); p. 189 (John Baptized Jesus; Jesus in the Desert); p. 190 (all images); p. 192 (all images); p. 193 (all images); p. 194 (Boy's Lunch; Healing the Paralytic); p. 195 (Casting Out Demons; Healing the Centurion's Servant; Raising Lazarus); p. 198 (all images); p. 199 (Garden of Gethsemane; Jesus in the Court; Death and Burial); p. 202 (all images); p. 203 (all images); p. 204 (Roman Soldiers); p. 206 (Jesus Teaching Children).Chat GPT: p 130 (The Silk Road map); p 158 (Map of Route from Susa to Jerusalem)

ChatGPT: p. 130 (The Silk Road Map); p. 158 (Map of Route From Susa to Jerusalem).

SELECTED BIBLIOGRAPHY

Bible Reference Books

- Silva, Moisé, J.D. Douglas, and Merrill C. Tenney. *Zondervan Illustrated Bible Dictionary.* Grand Rapids, MI: Zondervan, 2011.
- Tenney, Merrill C., ed. *The Zondervan Encyclopedia of the Bible, Volumes 1-5.* Grand Rapids, MI: Zondervan, 2009.
- Wigoder, Geoffrey, et al. *Illustrated Dictionary and Concordance of the Bible.* Jerusalem: G.G. The Jerusalem Publishing House Ltd, 1986.
- Youngblood, Ronald F. *Nelson's Illustrated Bible Dictionary.* Nashville, TN: Thomas Nelson Publishers, 2014.

Bibles

- Cabal, Ted, ed. *The Apologetics Study Bible.* Nashville, TN: Holman Bible Publishers, 2007.
- Morris, Henry. *The Henry Morris Study Bible: Apologetics Commentary and Explanatory Notes from the 'Father of Modern Creationism.'* Green Forest, AR: Master Books, 2022.
- Thomas Nelson. *The New Open Bible.* Nashville, TN: Thomas Nelson Publishers, 1990.

Books by the Author, Nancy I. Sanders

- Sanders, Nancy I. *Adventure Bible Guide.* Grand Rapids, MI: Zondervan, 2024.
- Sanders, Nancy I. *A Kid's Guide to African American History.* Chicago, IL: Review Press, 2007.
- Sanders, Nancy I. *Jesus (Get to Know Series).* Grand Rapids, MI: Zonderkidz, 2014.
- Sanders, Nancy I. *King David (Get to Know Series).* Grand Rapids, MI: Zonderkidz, 2014.
- Sanders, Nancy I. *Mary (Get to Know Series).* Grand Rapids, MI: Zonderkidz, 2014.
- Sanders, Nancy I. *Old Testament Days.* Chicago, IL: Review Press, 1999.
- Sanders, Nancy I. *The Bible Explorer's Guide.* Grand Rapids, MI: Zonderkidz, 2017.

Creation-Based Timelines

- Adams, Sebastian C. *A Chronological Chart of Ancient, Modern and Biblical History.* Green Forest, AR: Attic Books, 1871, 2021.
- Answers in Genesis. "Seven C's of History Timeline Poster." Published 2018. https://answersingenesis.org/store/product/seven-cs-timeline-poster/.
- Hannon, Katherine. *Big Book of Math: A Historical Timeline of Math,* Science, and Technology. Green Forest, AR: Master Books, 2024.
- Johnson, Terri. Wonders of Old: A Blank Timeline Book of World History. Green Forest, Arkansas: Master Books, 2007.
- Jones, Floyd Nolen. *The Chronology of the Old Testament.* Green Forest, AR: Master Books, 2009.
- Ussher, James. *The Annals of the World.* Green Forest, Arkansas: Master Books, 2006.
- Welch, Laura, and Ken Ham. *Big Book of History: A 15 foot fold-out time-line from Creation to Modern Computers.* Green Forest, AR: Master Books, 2011.

Creation-Based Websites

- Answers in Genesis at Answersingenesis.org/.
- Creation Ministries International at Creation.com/.
- Search Creation—Online search engine for Creation-based articles: Searchcreation.org/.
- The Institute for Creation Research at Icr.org/.

Encyclopedias in the General Market

- *World Book Encyclopedia.* 22 vols. Chicago, IL: World Book, 2013.
- Britannica. Accessed at https://www.britannica.com/.
- World History Encyclopedia. Accessed at https://www.worldhistory.org/.

History Books with a Christian Worldview

- Berry, Elizabeth, and Marion Hedquist. *New World History and Geography in Christian Perspective.* Pensacola, FL: Abeka, Books, 2001.
- Hicks, Laurel Elizabeth. *Old World History and*

Geography in Christian Perspective. Pensacola, FL: Beka Books, 1991.

- Hyma, Albert, and Mary Stanton. *Streams of Civilization Volume One.* Arlington Heights, IL: Christian Liberty Press, 2000.
- Moes, Garry J. *Streams of Civilization Volume Two.* Christian Liberty Press, 2008.
- O'Dell, Angela. *The World's Story 1: The Ancients. Creation to the Roman Empire.* Green Forest, AR: Master Books, 2018.
- O'Dell, Angela. *The World's Story 2: The Middle Ages.* Green Forest, AR: Master Books, 2020.

Life in Bible Times

- Gower, Ralph. *The New Manners and Customs of Bible Times.* Chicago, IL: Moody, 1987.
- Matthews, Victor H. *Manners and Customs in the Bible.* Peabody, MA: Hendrickson Publishers, 1991.
- Vos, Howard F. *Nelson's New Illustrated Bible Manners & Customs.* Nashville, TN: Thomas Nelson, 1999.

Miscellaneous

- Answers in Genesis. *Pocket Guides.* Hebron, KY: Answers in Genesis, 2022.
- Arnold, Clinton E. *How We Got the Bible: A Visual Journey.* Grand Rapids, MI: Zondervan, 2008.
- Bluedorn, Harvey and Laurie. *Ancient History from Primary Sources: A Literary Timeline.* Muscatine, IA: Trivium Pursuit, 2003.
- Campbell, Charlie H. *Archaeological Evidence for the Bible: Exciting Discoveries Verifying Persons, Places and Events in the Bible.* Carlsbad, CA: The Always Be Ready Apologetics Ministry, 2012.
- Campbell, Charlie H. *One Minute Answers to Skeptics' Top Forty Questions.* Vista, CA: Aquintas Publishing, 2005.
- Campbell, Charlie H. *Scrolls & Stones.* Carlsbad, CA: The Always Be Ready Apologetics Ministry, 2014.
- Campbell, Charlie H. *Teaching and Preaching God's Word.* Carlsbad, CA: The Always Be Ready Apologetics Ministry, 2013.
- Connelly, Douglas. *Amazing Discoveries that Unlock the Bible.* Grand Rapids, MI: Zondervan, 2008.
- House, H. Wayne. Zondervan Charts: *Chronological and Background Charts of the New Testament.* Grand Rapids, MI: Zondervan, 2009.
- Institute for Creation Research. *Guide to Creation Basics.* Eugene, OR.: Harvest House Publishers, 2021.
- Institute for Creation Research. *Guide to Dinosaurs.* Eugene, OR.: Harvest House Publishers, 2013.
- Institute for Creation Research. *Guide to God's Animals.* Eugene, OR.: Harvest House Publishers, 2015.
- Institute for Creation Research. *Guide to the Universe.* Eugene, OR.: Harvest House Publishers, 2016.
- Institute for Creation Research. *Science for Kids: Animals by Design.* Dallas, TX: Institute for Creation Research, 2023.
- Institute for Creation Research. *Science for Kids: Dinosaurs: God's Mysterious Creatures.* Dallas, TX: Institute for Creation Research, 2017.
- Institute for Creation Research. *Science for Kids: Earth: Our Created Home.* Dallas, TX: Institute for Creation Research, 2019.
- Institute for Creation Research. *Science for Kids: Space: God's Majestic Handiwork.* Dallas, TX: Institute for Creation Research, 2020.
- Landis, Don. *The Genius of Ancient Man.* Green Forest, AR: Master Books, 2012.
- Miller, Stephen M. *Incredible Mysteries of the Bible.* Grand Rapids, MI: Zondervan, 2008.
- Morris, John, and Steven A. Austin. *Footprints in the Ash.* Green Forest, AR: Master Books, 2009.
- Thomas, Brian, Timothy Clarey, et.al. *Parks Across America.* Dallas, TX: Institute for Creation Research, 2022.
- Vos, Howard F., and Joseph P. Free. *Archaeology and Bible History.* Grand Rapids, MI: Zondervan, 1992.

ABOUT THE AUTHOR

Bestselling & Award-Winning Children's Author
Nancy I. Sanders is a career children's book author of more than 100 books with publishers big and small. Her award-winning and bestselling books have been published by such houses as Focus on the Family, Tyndale, Zonderkidz, Sleeping Bear Press, Albert Whitman, and Scholastic Teaching Resources. First and foremost, she is a Christian who writes with a biblical worldview. Nancy believes in a literal interpretation of the Bible and supports James Ussher's chronology of creation and ancient history.

Nancy I. Sanders grew up on a dairy farm in the Appalachian Mountains of Pennsylvania, where she helped with the milking of her family's 100 Jersey cows and the care of one Texas longhorn named Tex. She fed the calves out of baby bottles so big a giant's baby could have used them. When she grew older, she drove a tractor back and forth across the fields while baling the hay. Winter was spent ice skating on their pond and sledding down the hills. In summer, she chased fireflies in the dark and collected them in glass jars before letting them go.

Nancy loved to read. She read *Little Women* perched high in the branches of an apple tree. *The Happy Hollisters, Beautiful Joe, Charlotte's Web, My Friend Flicka,* and *Freckles* were some of her childhood favorites.

Now Nancy loves to write. A bestselling and award-winning children's author of more than 100 books, she writes biographies, nonfiction books, and content for children's Bibles. Her books for younger children include retold Bible stories, baby board books, and nursery rhymes.

Nancy and her husband Jeff, a retired elementary teacher, live with their two cats in southern California near their two sons, beautiful wives, and grandchildren. They enjoy gardening, birdwatching, hiking, and singing in the 180-member choir at their church.